VOYAGER

Also by Russell Banks

FICTION

A Permanent Member of the Family

Lost Memory of Skin

The Reserve

The Darling

The Angel on the Roof

Cloudsplitter

Rule of the Bone

The Sweet Hereafter

Affliction

Success Stories

Continental Drift

The Relation of My Imprisonment

Trailerpark

The Book of Jamaica

The New World

Hamilton Stark

Family Life

Searching for Survivors

NONFICTION

Dreaming Up America

The Invisible Stranger (with Arturo Patten)

VOYAGER

Travel Writings

RUSSELL BANKS

An Imprint of HarperCollins*Publishers*

HarperCollins books may be purchased for educational, business, or sales promotional use. For information please e-mail the Special Markets Department at SPsales@harpercollins.com.

FIRST EDITION

Designed by Suet Chong

Library of Congress Cataloging-in-Publication Data has been applied for.

ISBN 978-0-06-185767-6

16 17 18 19 20   OV/RRD   10 9 8 7 6 5 4 3 2 1

To Chase, the beloved,
and in memory of Ann Hendrie, James Tate,
and C. K. Williams,
Fellow Travelers

As the voyager navigating among the isles of the Archipelago sees the luminous mist lift toward evening and slowly detects the outline of the shore, I begin to make out the profile of my death.

—Marguerite Yourcenar, *Memoirs of Hadrian*

CONTENTS

ACKNOWLEDGMENTS

Early versions of some of these writings were previously published in the following magazines and journals: *Brick, Condé Nast Traveler, Conjunctions, Esquire, Men's Journal, National Geographic,* and *Natural History.* The author is grateful to the editors of these publications, especially to Klara Glowczewska of *Condé Nast Traveler.*

PART ONE

VOYAGER

A man who's been married four times has a lot of explaining to do. Perhaps especially a man in his mid-seventies from northern New England who has longed since boyhood for escape, for rejuvenation, for wealth untold, for erotic and narcotic and sybaritic fresh starts, for high romance, mystery, and intrigue, and who so often has turned those longings toward the Caribbean.

Why the Caribbean? Who can reliably say? Whether arriving as conquistador or castaway, as fugitive financier or packaged tourist or backpacking lonely planeteer, whether costumed as Ponce de León or Robinson Crusoe or Errol Flynn or Robert Vesco or the little-known American writer bearing the name of Russell Banks, early on I got yanked by the bright green islands and turquoise seas of the Caribbean out of myself and home into high-definition dreams that I projected onto my larger world like a hologram. And while some of my dreams were innocent enough or merely naive, like Crusoe's, and some reckless, like Flynn's, all of them got broken and re-formed by the reality of the place and the people who lived there: Ponce got slain by the natives on a south Florida beach; Crusoe, meeting Friday, learned humanity and went home a better man; Flynn, sailing to Jamaica, stepped ashore as Captain Blood;

Vesco, conning Fidel, died in jail for it. And Russell Banks, that little-known writer from New England—it's still unclear what broke and re-formed him there.

It's certain that something about the Caribbean draws Europeans and, especially, North Americans out of their accustomed lives. One rarely goes there solely to satisfy one's curiosity. It's not the semitropical winter climate and the white sands, either—although that's the usual explanation. That's what's advertised. And it's not the myth of long-delayed, long-desired release from puritanical inhibitions. Also much promoted. One travels to the Antilles driven by vague desires, mostly unexamined, rarely named, never advertised. One goes like a bee to a blossom, as if drawn by some powerful image of prelapsarian beauty and innocence, where life as one has grown used to it at home—polluted and corrupt and cold and erotically constricted and dark—has somehow been kept from the garden. One likes to believe that in the Caribbean there are no snakes. The few found there surely came from elsewhere, *isolatos,* outliers from the north carried by tourists in their luggage.

I was no different. For years I, too, traveled to the Caribbean drawn by unexamined, unnamed desires, until in the late 1970s, still a young man, disillusioned by the poverty and corruption, and embarrassed and angered by what I viewed as my government's unwillingness to accept responsibility for both, and chagrined by my fellow American tourists, who were arriving in growing numbers in packaged and cruise-shipped hordes, and humbled by my inability to cross the racial and economic and cultural barriers that fenced me in and out, after a half-dozen island-hopping tours and eighteen months of living in rural Jamaica with my second wife, Christine, and our three daughters, I finally packed our bags, and we returned home to New England—for good, I believed—where I tried to stop dreaming up the Caribbean.

But it wasn't that easy. I thought when I got home that I had wakened, but in my dreams I kept remembering the sharp clarity

of the light, the overwhelming intensity of the landscape, the smell
of a wood cook-fire in a country village, the sense-surrounding passion and brilliance of Caribbean music and speech. I remembered
the excitement of learning to love a people and place not remotely
my own and the stupefying wonder of colliding with a cultural and
racial and geographic otherness so extreme that, no matter how
hard and honorably I tried to penetrate it, I was left exhausted and
confused and excluded. And alone. Especially that. As if I had finally
discovered there the meaning and permanence of solitude. Not just
my solitude, but everyone's.

One night in Jamaica I sat by a window in a Port Antonio
rooming house that overlooked the silver moonlit bay below, listening to the palm trees chatter in the evening breeze. Fifty miles
away, in a country village called Anchovy on the other side of
the island, Christine and our three daughters were asleep in our
rented house. I was studying scattered dots of light in the jungle-
covered hillside that danced their way from the bay up the silhouetted side of the volcanic mountain behind me. I wondered idly if
the yellow lights were fireflies—then suddenly realized that those
lights are *homes,* you idiot, homes, where real people live out their
real lives, hundreds of tiny, one-room, tin-roofed cinder-block and
daub-and-wattle cabins lit by candles and smoky kerosene lamps,
where men and women and children are living in a reality utterly
unlike my own, a world just as subjective as mine, but infinitely
more difficult and punishing, their lives and dreams putting the
ease and luxury of mine to shame. In the end their inner lives
and dreams were for me unknowable. Perhaps it had always been
so, but somehow at that moment my own inner life and my own
dreams became unknowable. As if they belonged to someone else.
As if they were a stranger's, and I myself had none of my own.

Afterward, back in the United States, my scattered, fragmented
memories slowly over the years began to attach to one another and
coalesce into a narrative. When Christine and I lived in Jamaica,
after years of unraveling and raveling, the sexual and political and

social and economic ties and our shared love for our daughters that for more than a decade had bound us in marriage somehow at last came completely and permanently undone. We did not intend or wish for it, at the time we barely noticed it, and for long afterward neither of us could say how or why it happened.

Narratives based solely on fading, vested memories, i.e., *memoirs,* are unreliable and tend to be self-serving projections anyhow. To bend, distort, and reshape those memories, hoping to make them into a coherent account I could trust, and expecting in that way both to learn and tell myself the truth of what had destroyed Christine's and my marriage, I wrote and published a book. It was called *The Book of Jamaica*—a novel, I insisted, not a memoir. Set in Jamaica, it was about a white American man, a university professor more than a little like the author, married to a woman more than a little like the author's wife.

Reliably narrated or not, in both the reader and the writer fictions engender desire. It's a paradox, counterintuitive, perhaps; but while an honorable, artistically ambitious, well-constructed work of fiction usually provides resolution, it doesn't necessarily satisfy or erase one's desire for a solution. When a novel or a story succeeds in penetrating a mystery, it proceeds at once to raise a further, deeper mystery. In answering one question, it asks a more difficult question that otherwise would never have been raised. For a long time I ignored or simply denied the existence of any mystery beyond the dissolution of my second marriage—as fictionalized in *The Book of Jamaica*—until a decade later, in the late 1980s, a third marriage and divorce later, when contemplating the commencement of a fourth marriage, I found myself drawn back to that further, deeper mystery.

I got invited by a glossy New York travel magazine to make and write about a winter-long, island-hopping journey through the Caribbean. Thirty islands in sixty days. No restrictions as to length. All expenses paid. Tempted by the thought of testing my constructed, decade-old, novelistic narrative against the mystery it had tried to penetrate, and hoping, if possible, to name the further mystery engendered there, I negotiated a sabbatical semester from my university and accepted the assignment. Chase, the woman I wished to make my fourth wife, was then teaching at the University of Alabama. She agreed to accompany me on my travels into my Caribbean past and the troubles that possibly resided there, troubles whose existence she was not yet aware of. She thought only that it was a posh writing assignment for me, one that happened also to offer her a few months away from Tuscaloosa, which was something she'd been trying to arrange since the day she first arrived from western Massachusetts three years earlier.

At the time, my divorce from my third wife, Becky, was working its slow way through the legal system, and though Chase was living in Tuscaloosa and I was commuting between a Manhattan sublet and my classes at Princeton, we had been lovers and all but husband and wife for nearly a year by then. Even so, I was still courting her—perhaps to a greater degree than at the beginning of our love affair the previous spring. Between the onset of the madness of falling in love and the sobering formalization of that state later through cohabitation and marriage, there usually unfolds a long period of mutual courtship. It's the period when lovers disinter their secrets and show them to each other, making it possible for both sets of secrets to be mingled into one. That's the usual need, anyhow; and the plan. Sometimes courtship continues well into the period of cohabitation and marriage. Courtship has even been known to extend beyond the end of one marriage and get paid forward into yet a new marriage—as if one were courting one's *ex*-wife or *ex*-husband as well, retroactively.

Unlike fantasies, secrets don't lie. They erupt from the depths of one's subconscious mind and harden like lava into the topography of one's character. Neither willed nor consciously shaped, secrets are epistemologically different from fantasies. They are not who we were or want to be; they are who we become. In revealing one's secrets first to oneself and then to one's lover, one makes a bond that is deeper and, one hopes, longer lasting than any tie established by merely falling in love.

The more difficult is the first part—dredging up and silently revealing one's secrets to oneself alone. It can be embarrassing. They will likely turn out to be those old longings for escape, for rejuvenation, for wealth untold; those erotic and narcotic and sybaritic dreams of fresh starts, high romance, mystery, and intrigue. Which can lead one, as I had learned by now, to commit acts of betrayal and abandonment, and thence to shame: one's secret character writes one's secret history. Thus embarrassment leads to shame. Then comes the second part, revealing one's secret history to one's beloved aloud, i.e., courtship, which runs the risk of casting a cold light on what's supposed to follow—cohabitation and marriage. Courtship is both self-revelation and public exposure and can be dangerous.

And so, for the first time, Chase and I became travelers together. Not tourists. Travelers. Most Americans and Europeans who fly or sail to the Caribbean islands are tourists. They go for a week or two and manage to visit and explore no more than a single island or, if they're lucky, a single cluster of islands. Sometimes they visit and explore no more than a single hotel. They rarely go like the starship *Enterprise* where no package tour has gone before, and consequently, no matter how many voyages they make, they remain tourists, satellites circling their home planet in low orbit.

Our voyage was designed to last most of the winter into the spring of 1988 and touch down for a brief stay on each of thirty-two of the Lesser Antilles, from the U.S. Virgins off Puerto Rico, east through the Leewards, and south along the Windwards, looping back toward the continent by way of Jamaica—the island that a decade earlier I had almost called home. We mapped out a spiral nebula of islands circling the blue-green Caribbean Sea. After a week of exploring the Florida Everglades and Keys, we would jump off the continent at Miami, travel by jumbo jet, by seaplane and tiny STOL (short takeoff and landing) aircraft, by freighter and ferry and fishing boat—island-hopping in the grand tradition.

One tries not to arrive anywhere at rush hour. Landing on St. Thomas at 5 P.M. was like arriving at JFK at 5 P.M., only worse, especially if you had to travel cross-island from the airport to the East End, where most of the hotels, beaches, and marinas were located. There was no way to get there except by crawling in line by car through the town of Charlotte Amalie, a maze of alleys and narrow one-way streets built by the Danes for donkeys and pedestrians before Denmark sold the Virgins to the Americans in 1917, clogged now with Japanese and German automobiles and American and British trucks and open-air sightseeing buses and hawkers of souvenirs for cruise-ship passengers.

In 1988 four or five cruise ships a day in season were putting in at Charlotte Amalie, and the entire town seemed to have organized itself around the cruisers' insatiable need for ceramic ashtrays and funny T-shirts, perfume, watches, jewelry, and liquor. It's a free port: $800 worth of duty-free goods allowed per person. They packed the streets—mostly Americans doing the buying and locals the selling, with barkers on sidewalks and in the doorways of shops pitching the goods inside as if working the crowd in front of topless bars on Rampart Street. As Chase and I crept along in our rented car I wondered why we hadn't stayed in Key West, where we'd spent the weekend before, where exhaust-emission controls were enforced and at least the chances of carbon monoxide poisoning were not so great. We shut the windows, sealing ourselves in, cranked the air conditioner to high, and scowled.

With fifty thousand people, St. Thomas is the most populous of the three U.S. Virgins (St. Croix and St. John are the others). It's small, barely thirty-two square miles, and therefore very crowded, especially from December to March. It was a tart of an island, hardly a virgin, with FOR SALE signs everywhere and headlong, heedless development. It had a "U.S. flavor," as the guidebooks say, which meant that Colonel Sanders and Ronald McDonald had set up shop. Triplex movie theaters and minimalls and, all over the East End, wherever there was a piece of land with a sea view, high-rising condominiums were breeding like bunnies.

But like every Caribbean island, especially the mountainous, volcanic isles where the land rises quickly from the sea, St. Thomas—once we got out of town—was still beautiful to look at. The prismatic Caribbean sky opened up exactly as I remembered it, lyrical and turbulent and erotic. West of the airport and north of Charlotte Amalie, the narrow road wound into the hills, giving spectacular views of glistening emerald-green slopes and long ridges and craggy peninsulas tumbling into an azure sea, dotted near the horizon with islets and cays. This was another reason I'd come back to the Caribbean: the sheer physical beauty of the place, the land and sea and sky, the Edenic firmaments above and below, and the bright green firmament between. I'd come back for the bone-clear light and the depth and power of color and the abundant, tumultuous play of forms. I was here, accompanied by my friend and lover, for the sake of my eyes. I said to her, I simply open my eyes and *look,* and I start to feel healed from a sickness I hadn't known I was afflicted with.

St. Thomas, because of its U.S. flavor, which meant decent roads and adequate up-to-date services as much as it did minimalls and Mr. Pizza, might be a nice place to live—and, indeed, a lot of affluent white Americans seemed to have retired here—but unless above all else one liked crowds and shopping, it was not the most enjoyable island merely to visit. Rising expectations combined with rigid racial and economic barriers had created the kind of racial and class antagonisms that in the 1980s one associated with inner-city life on the continent. Yes, there were lovely white sand beaches— Magens Bay, Sapphire Beach, and Coki Point—and many fine resort hotels where one never had to step outside the gated compound, especially at night. But package tours and cruise ships had come to control the economy, with the usual results—overbuilding and pervasive commercialism and abuse of the environment and a stunned, sullen, somewhat deracinated local population. We averted our gaze from the surly faces of the young black men hanging out on the streets of Charlotte Amalie and the edges of the Havensight shopping district: faces that seemed to say, *How can you who are so vulgar and rude to us be so fucking rich?* And: *Tell me again why I'm condemned to need you?*

Near Red Hook Bay, where there was a sprawling marina and ferry service to most of the nearby islands, we checked into a small hotel in the wooded hills, accurately named Pavilions and Pools. That's what it offered—suites, each with kitchen and small garden (the pavilion) and a private pool the size of our rented Toyota Corolla where we could skinny-dip. At night we lay in the darkness beneath a slow-turning fan and in bits and pieces told our stories to each other—our childhoods and love affairs and, in my case, marriages, three so far, and divorces, three so far, and who and what we had loved and the aspects of ourselves that scared us and those we admired: some of it we embellished and some we invented, more to meet the needs of narrative than merely to impress. Some we left out. And we made love together and with each passing night woke in the bright morning light increasingly entangled. I told her what I knew about the childhoods of my four daughters, and she told me what she knew about the childhoods and lives of her two adult sisters and her nieces and nephews. We described our parents' marriages and divorces. We exchanged stories and appraisals of our mutual and separate friends. All a part and consequence of courtship.

At the Red Hook Charter offices we dealt with a bearded man who said his name was Animal, who looked like a wolverine in cutoffs and booked for the dozens of fishing boats operating out of the marina. Animal sent us out for dolphin and yellowfin on the *Over Easy* with Captain Frank Griffin, a Florida Keys dropout. We swam at nearby Sapphire Beach and picked up the *New York Times* at the drugstore in Red Hook and in our pavilion watched the Cincinnati Bengals beat the Buffalo Bills in an NFL playoff game on cable TV. It was indeed like the Florida Keys. And this, you understand, was not bad—but it was also not what we came for. St. Thomas is where the United States ends; it's not where the Caribbean begins. For that, in the Lesser Antilles, we'd have to go to St. John and St. Croix and beyond.

And so we soon moved on. The ferry from Red Hook Bay on St. Thomas to Cruz Bay at the west end of St. John took twenty minutes, but it carried us to a very different world, thanks mainly to Laurence Rockefeller and his family, whose donated land and determined efforts to limit tourism on the island had turned two-thirds of St. John and many of the reefs that surround it into the Virgin Islands National Park. The whole island was meticulously clean and had been developed with overriding concern for the environment, both land and sea. There were hotels, even fairly large ones, led by the famed Caneel Bay and the new Virgin Grand, and guesthouse and camping accommodations, too. But without an airport or deepwater port, there was no way to accommodate package tours, no way to facilitate large-scale tourism, and no evident desire to do so.

With an enlightened, affluent population of only twenty-nine hundred and an area two-thirds that of St. Thomas, St. John, too, had a U.S. flavor, but one more like that of Aspen or rural Vermont than Key West. Instead of McDonald's, it was Ben & Jerry's. We took our breakfast at the Buccaneer Restaurant in Cruz Bay, where our slender waitress wore white-girl dreadlocks and Earth Shoes. A Windham Hill space music tape played in the background, and a rooster pecked in the dirt a few feet from our table—a strange mash-up of postmodern Mill Valley and prewar rural Caribbean. There were signs advertising foot massage and health food and acupuncture and low-impact aerobics on Monday, Wednesday, and Friday, and everyone looked healthier, younger, prettier than me and Chase. Tanned blond Americans and Nordic-looking Europeans with candy-colored nylon packs attached like marsupial pouches to their lean bodies strolled the narrow streets of Cruz Bay and hitchhiked the road to the Maho Bay campgrounds and trekked across the hills to ponder the mysterious Arawak Indian petroglyphs carved into and daubed onto the limestone rocks and walked on for a swim at Reef Bay. The slender, fit, tanned blond ones were here for the hiking and camping, snorkeling and scuba diving, and of course for each other—here to view and be viewed and to move freely as perhaps nowhere else in the Caribbean through the extraordinary natural beauty of the mountains and the sea, as if visiting a theme park.

On St. John, that ten-thousand-acre theme park was the work of aggressive private philanthropy and the U.S. National Park Service, a collaboration between a Rockefeller and a Roosevelt. Elsewhere in the Lesser Antilles, where national parks existed at all, as in Dominica, Guadeloupe, Tortola, and Martinique, they seemed to have been established merely because there was nothing more immediately profitable to do with the land—they had come into existence by default, usually on hinterland tracts of wooded mountainside where escaped slaves once hid out and where no tourism, agriculture, industry, or housing seemed possible. Nobody wanted the land, so why not make a national park out of it?

Why not, indeed? One was grateful for the preserves and public set-asides, no matter where they appeared or what the motive, no matter how casually or poorly run. The parks were, after all, protecting the remnants of an extremely fragile ecosystem in the midst of uncontrolled exploitation and pollution. One suspected, however, that on most of the islands—but not, of course, here on St. John—if a new source of bauxite were discovered beneath the rain forest, making the land commercially valuable, or an international consortium wanted to put up a three-hundred-room beachside resort hotel, the national parklands would quickly shrink or disappear altogether. And, given the dire need of foreign currency in many of these tiny, severely indebted, overpopulated island nations, who could argue with a decision to let their parkland shrink or disappear?

In the context of Caribbean economics, St. John's Virgin Islands National Park was a luxury, like a private club in the Adirondacks. Unfortunately, it was also a necessity. The island was essentially defined by the park, and given St. John's easy access to the international airport over on St. Thomas and to North American investment capital, with spectacular beaches and deepwater bays and lovely forested hills that clambered to the sea as if to drink, its hundreds of species of birds, tropical flowers, trees, butterflies, and other insects, its miles of rich underwater reefs and dozens of tiny, beach-rimmed cays and matchless views of the sea, St. John without the Virgin Islands National Park in a decade would be overwhelmed by day-tripping visitors from the mainland and the other, larger Virgins.

But for all its natural beauty, the island felt like a *tableau vivant*. Chase and I looked, at least to ourselves, like mannequins, props, fashion models dressed up like white middle-aged parents in a high-end ad for Abercrombie and Fitch resort wear. After half a day, we canceled our hotel reservations and caught the late ferry back to St. Thomas, where we didn't feel as much a part of the picture as its ironically detached observers.

The following morning we were at St. Thomas Harbor at Charlotte Amalie boarding *The Goose,* the seaplane shuttle to St. Croix. The flight took twenty minutes. Taking off and landing was a little like high-speed waterskiing, but the rest of the flight was a low-altitude scenic cruise above sailboats and tiny cays and islets. The sea glistened below us in the morning sun like hammered tin. As we approached St. Croix, we saw the east end of the island first, low and pale green, almost arid looking. The west was higher and more lush, and the rolling hills were dotted with Senepol and Brahman cattle, and here and there we spotted the ruins of sugar mills. In the late eighteenth century, thanks to these same low, fertile hills and the labor of more than thirty thousand slaves, St. Croix was one of the richest sugar islands in the Caribbean. Having by now grown used to my compulsion to explain the history of nearly everything and still finding it faintly amusing, Chase, my beloved, rolled her eyes and smiled.

Even from three thousand feet we could see that the island was halfway to losing its tranquillity. But St. Croix, unlike St. Thomas— despite the cruise ships disgorging tourists in Frederiksted and the usual feeding frenzy and condo developments on the north coast in and around Christiansted, the larger of the island's two towns— might still be saved by its more diversified economy, also visible from the air: cattle, oil refining, bauxite processing, rum, and even a cluster of small cinder-block manufacturing plants, industries that can save an island from total dependence on tourism. Though there were nonetheless a number of new or expanded four-star hotels and resorts, like the Carambola Beach and the Buccaneer, the place didn't seem to have the same obsessive, needy fix on tourism as St. Thomas. Besides, St. Croix is more than twice as large as its sister island, with approximately the same number of inhabitants, so there was still room—and air—to breathe.

Later, tooling across the island in a rental car, I felt, for better and then for worse, a much stronger sense of the rich and bloody Caribbean past on St. Croix than on the other U.S. Virgins, especially in the towns of Christiansted and Frederiksted, where rows of eighteenth- and nineteenth-century homes and public buildings had been carefully preserved, many of them under the protection of the American National Park Service. And when we drove into the countryside, we saw the sugar plantations, almost all of them in ruins now, like overgrown, tumbledown, remnant fortresses from an all-but-forgotten colonial war, photogenically recaptured in one, the Estate Whim Plantation Museum, which had been meticulously restored by the St. Croix Landmarks Society.

In some ways, the more nearly perfect the restoration and the more informative the tour through a complex of buildings and machinery for growing and refining sugar, the more depressing I found the whole thing. Where are the slaves? I wanted to ask the kindly white docent lady. Where, madam, is the grief, the horror, the shame? These restored plantations in the Caribbean are almost always designed to provide aesthetic pleasure and value-neutral historical and economic information, but I wanted them to be offered up instead as somber shrines, as dark memorials to man's incredible, shameful inhumanity to man. They should be preserved the way Auschwitz-Birkenau and Ground Zero at Hiroshima have been preserved. Instead, they're laid out to educate the mainland visitor about the manufacture of sugar, with slavery treated, if at all, as a slightly embarrassing by-product. These tasteful, expensive restorations dishonor the dead and humiliate the living. Their lies about the past disguise the present.

In the evening we flew *The Goose* back to St. Thomas, splashing down in the harbor at the edge of Frenchtown, where we had plans for dinner. I decided first to check on the car, the rented silver Toyota Corolla that we'd left parked all day in the unattended lot next to the terminal. As I approached the car, it looked fine, untouched. I reached for the driver's-side door, the key extended to unlock it, but, strangely, the door was not locked and swung open at my touch. The vehicle had been vandalized. Worse, it had been attacked. It was ripped to shreds inside. Someone had broken into the car and had gone mad or simply, as if desperate and enraged beyond all capacity to say why, had reacted to this piece of machinery like a Luddite, smashing the steering wheel and shift lever, kicking in the padded dash, leaving the radio dangling from its wires, the seat backs broken, the upholstery slashed and gouged. The shiny new sedan, from the outside still intact, seemingly untouched, had been violently destroyed inside. Nothing had been stolen: the radio and speakers, yanked from their moorings, were there; the ignition hadn't been jimmied or jammed; Chase's forgotten rain jacket lay crumpled on the floor in back. The attack seemed purposeful—a warning to the owners of the vehicle, specifically to me and Chase, and what we represented. We saw ourselves as we were seen, and we were suddenly eager to leave these American Virgins.

We'd try the British Virgins instead. We'd start with Tortola. Only fifty-nine square miles and about ten thousand people, it's the largest and most populous of the more than fifty tiny islands and cays that make up the group. The main islands, other than Tortola, are Virgin Gorda (the "fat virgin") and Anegada, with fewer than three thousand people between them. The waters that surround and connect this cluster are among the best yachting waters in the world, with hundreds of short crescent-shaped beaches and shallow bays nestled between volcanic cliffs that, if you can get there, make you feel indeed like a latter-day Robinson Crusoe.

On the palm-lined northwest coast of Tortola, when I parked our replacement rental car at the edge of the otherwise deserted beach and stood in the shade of a casuarina tree and watched the waves break on the trackless sand, I indulged in clichéd suburbanite fantasies of dropping out of the rat race. *Indulged* isn't the right word. It's a compulsion, it's what I do, make up narratives and narrators, stories and storytellers with voices that sound like mine, but mine as heard on the radio or a recording. The voices in my head never shut up. *What the hell, I could sell the house in Morristown, quit the job on Madison Avenue, wave good-bye to the bewildered spouse and kids, and split*—the kind of get your ya-yas back fantasies that harried American men and women were induced to conjure fifteen or twenty years earlier by the long, white, deserted beaches of Jamaica's Negril, by the abundance of local fish and produce, by the sexy interracial ease, and, yes, by the easily accessed mind-busting ganja. Before cocaine and crack and guns and AIDS. Before the economic collapse of the seventies and the desperation and rage of the eighties. Before the names *Negril* and *Jamaica* got linked to easy drugs and exotic interracial erotics and armies of local hustlers. Before I grew weary and wary of white Americans bewitched by Jamaican patois and reggae and cigar-sized spliffs and chillum pipes and Rastafarian logic and ital cooking—that is, before I grew suspicious of people like me. And, okay, yes, before my second ex-wife, Christine, married a handsome, dreadlocked Jamaican man and made her permanent winter home there.

A breathtaking drive—over the mountains from the bustling old-time port village of Road Town, through the primeval rain forest of Mount Sage National Park, down narrow, precipitously winding roads to the coast, past banana groves and small country villages—led us finally to Apple Bay, where an enterprising Rasta-man named Bomba had built a driftwood-and-thatch shack on the beach, stuffed a cooler with ice and beer, collected a bunch of reggae tapes and a boom box, and hung out his roughly lettered shingle, BOMBA'S SURF SHACK. Another sign said, SUNDAY REGGAE PARTY, and a third, SURF UP BEWARE UNDERTOAD [*sic*].

Offshore, long rollers coiled in rows near the horizon and grew in height and volume as they neared the beach, where, bobbing in the water, a half-dozen suntanned surfer dudes caught an alpha wave at its crest and rode their boards gracefully in. We cracked open a pair of Bomba's cold Red Stripes, listened to Peter Tosh and Ziggy Marley on his boom box, plus a lot of reggae musicians we'd never heard of, and admired Bomba's eclectic collection of flotsam, animal bones, Rasta carvings, hubcaps, and American street signs dangling from the walls and ceiling and the thicket of sea grapes outside. In a sweetly humorous way, it was blissful and calm and outside of time.

But even on sunny, funky, laid-back Tortola it can cloud over and rain, and it did, and soon a chilling wind blew in from the south, and the surfer dudes paddled to shore and turned out to be mostly stoned or from habit talked like they were, while Chase and I stood shivering under the dripping thatch and wished we were someplace

else, someplace clean and dry where the sun was shining and there
was somebody intelligent or at least sober to talk to. In the Caribbean there is not much distance between the height of ecstasy and
the slough of despond. It's the constant contrast between the over-
abundant physical beauty of sea and land and sky and the grinding
poverty of most of the people who live out their lives here. One is
either too high to think straight or one is suicidally low. Finding an
emotional middle ground is as difficult in the Caribbean as finding
the middle class.

The cold wind-driven rain persisted, until even Bomba gave
up. He locked his cooler, tossed his boom box and tapes into the bed
of his rusted-out pickup, and rumbled off. The surfer dudes cradled
their boards and, staring opaquely out to sea as if all the way to
Malibu, waited for the rain to stop, and Chase and I got into our
car and moved on to the yacht basin at West End, had lunch at a
sailors' café, and arranged an afternoon's fishing. Later we checked
into Fort Recovery Estates, a sand-in-your-shoes complex of cabanas
built around the ruins of a seventeenth-century Dutch fort. Evenings, we walked the narrow streets of Road Town, a busy old-time
Caribbean port; days, we combed the beaches, fished, or drove the
ridge road for unending mountain views. Driving and walking and
lying in bed in our cabana at Fort Recovery Estates, in my day-and-
night courtship of Chase I had come to the chapter that described
my first marriage, a subject and a period in my youth that I usually
tried to skip over, as if my late adolescence and early adult years had
been pretty much the same as everyone else's.

But, of course, they hadn't. No one's adolescence and early
adult years are like anyone else's. And mine had been unruly and
turbulent and reckless, even for a troubled adolescent and young
adult, and in long-lasting ways they had proved harmful—to myself
and to a young woman and a baby girl, my first wife and daughter,
who were much less deserving of harm, certainly, than I. To Chase,
my newly betrothed, here is what I revealed. The young woman's
name was Darlene; years later, after attending many annual gather-

ings of the Rainbow Family, she would call herself Morning Star. In the spring of 1959, when we first met in St. Petersburg, Florida, she was an eighteen-year-old girl, and I was a boy about to turn nineteen who had washed ashore in Miami that winter on a politically romantic pilgrimage to join Fidel Castro and his bearded band of revolutionaries, who were holed up in the Sierra Maestra mountains of Cuba—a partly fictional story I've told many times many ways elsewhere. In January 1959, Castro and his men marched in triumph into Havana and no longer needed the services of a beatnik dropout from New England who spoke no Spanish and had no idea how to get from Miami to Cuba anyhow. Thanks to a modest artistic talent and a sketchbook of schoolboy drawings and pastels, I landed a job as an apprentice window trimmer at a Burdines department store in Miami, then quickly got myself transferred to a slightly better window-trimming job at the new St. Petersburg branch on the Gulf coast and bought a battered bottle-green 1948 Studebaker sedan and moved into a rooming house there.

Darlene, less than a year out of high school, worked as a salesgirl in women's sportswear on the second floor of the store. She was strikingly beautiful in the way of gingery blond, blue-eyed, peaches-and-cream southern girls of the 1950s. She modeled one-piece bathing suits in the weekly Burdines shoppers' fashion show and if she had been a few inches taller could easily have been a beauty contest winner, a Miss Florida or Miss Georgia. She lived with her parents and two younger sisters and brother in a cinder-block ranch house in a new housing development in Pinellas Park, and like them she was kind and gentle and sad and Christian. In her large, innocent, naive eyes, I was the dark, dangerous, unattached stranger from an exotic place far away, like Hal, the William Holden character in the 1956 movie *Picnic*. Darlene, played by Kim Novak, was Madge, the cloistered small-town girl who secretly writes poetry and longs to escape her destiny before it becomes her fate and believes that only a dark, dangerous, unattached stranger like me or Hal can make that escape possible.

She had a warm, open heart back then and appeared to understand how alone and lonely and lost I was, despite my reckless, self-confident, swashbuckling affect, and seemed to love me for who I really was. I knew that I was alone, yes, but did not think I was in the slightest lonely or lost. No, merely adventurous and artistically intense and literary was all. I believed that I could rescue her from her fate and that I in no way needed rescuing from mine.

But I had a cold, stupid heart. Without knowing it, instead of loving her for her lovable self, I was deliberately, if unconsciously, casting her in the story of my life solely for the purpose of reenacting my parents' catastrophically broken marriage, my father's rampaging violence and alcoholism, his relentless womanizing, and his abandonment of his four children. I was the eldest of the abandoned four, and like so many eldest children of violence, alcoholism, sexual promiscuity, and divorce, I was trying to turn my as-yet-unwritten adult domestic life into a rewrite of the story of my parents' disastrous marriage and make it into a story with a happy ending. To that cloudy, dubious end, I was a teenaged boy searching for a teenaged girl who seemed in no way to resemble his mother—just as he in no way resembled his father. When he found her he would make her fall in love with him, and he would marry her for it, and they would live happily ever after. He found her standing on a low, carpeted platform like a goddess on a pedestal modeling bathing suits on Friday afternoons on the second floor of the Burdines department store in St. Petersburg, Florida.

And, Reader, I married her.

But I could not see her for who she was, or I might have spared her the ordeal of becoming my wife and the mother of my first child. I could not see that in every underlying way Darlene fit my mother's template exactly: physically beautiful, with perfect pale skin and large blue eyes that opened wide—eyebrows raised—the second that someone, particularly a man, or a camera lens glanced in her direction. She was cunningly intelligent and knew how to light up a room, as they say, but did not possess the physical and emotional energy to pass herself off as charismatic, which kept her from being fearsome, especially to men, which in turn only made her all the more attractive to men, including me, who was little more than a boy.

At eighteen, my mother must have been a lot like Darlene—the bottomless depth of her insecurity and need for attention not yet hardened into full-blown narcissism; her capacity for love not yet disassembled by rejection; her sexual desires not yet turned strategic. But even then, when still a girl, Darlene was two people, as my mother must have been, one person watching the other, an angry, impossible-to-please ghost keeping track of a wayward chimera. Which made her a sucker for a good-looking charmer like my father.

Who, your mother? Or Darlene? Were you, at nineteen, like your father? Chase wanted to know.

Probably. Well, yes. A lot like he was at that same age, I confessed. Thanks to a phony ID I'd purchased the previous fall in Boston's Scollay Square, I was already, like my father before me, a heavy drinker. There were nights when, driving my green Studebaker at a wobbly drunken crawl from the bars on Boca Ciega back to my rooming house in downtown St. Petersburg, I had to pull over halfway across the bridge and stagger from the car and vomit into the gutter. My nineteen-year-old father and I were barroom brawlers. He was angry for his reasons, I for mine, which weren't all that different from his, although neither of us knew what those reasons were. Which is why we brawled. Oh, and we were both smooth talkers, good dancers, sharp dressers. We were clever autodidacts and could successfully pass ourselves off as budding intellectuals. We played chess. We read difficult books and could quote from them. We both had good flash-card memories. We made friends and gained the trust of strangers easily. And we were compulsive serial seducers of girls and women, not that we deserved or even wanted their love, so much as we believed that we ourselves were unlovable and needed constantly to test and disprove that belief.

Which was, of course, impossible. Thus the seriality of our seductions. And thus the violence of our eventual, inevitable rejection of any girl or woman who turned out to be foolish enough to love us. Like Groucho Marx, we kept applying for membership but refused to join any club that would admit us.

Darlene was foolish enough not only to love me but to want to marry me, and her parents did not object. In 1959 in the South—and all of Florida was then the Deep South, mired in the Jim Crow apartheid that, once the shock of it had worn off, bewildered and sickened me—it was not uncommon for white working-class boys and girls to marry within a year of graduating high school. Especially if the boy were gainfully employed. From the point of view of her good Christian parents, Darlene was at an optimal marriageable age, ready for connubial sex and motherhood, and I was a good prospect.

Though by then most of my mind had been swallowed whole by literature and on the basis of no reliable evidence or encouragement I had begun to imagine myself as a writer, I was about to take a position as the display director of a Montgomery Ward store in Lakeland, fifty miles east of St. Petersburg in the cattle-raising, citrus-growing, phosphate-mining center of the state. I would be the youngest Montgomery Ward department head in Florida—hired to oversee only two employees, however, an alcoholic carpenter who showed up drunk every morning and left even drunker at the end of the day and a seventy-five-year-old semiretired sign painter. Nonetheless, Darlene's parents and Darlene and, for a few months, I myself saw the position as a significant, promising step up the corporate ladder. We all knew that if I left St. Petersburg for Lakeland without first marrying Darlene, she and her parents were likely to lose me, and I them.

And so in August 1959, there was a wedding. My mother somehow managed to raise the money for plane tickets for her and my seventeen-year-old brother, Steve, who stood nervously, protectively, beside me as my best man, surely more aware than I of what was coming. Darlene was never again as beautiful to me or as happy as she was that day. We gave ourselves a weekend honeymoon in a motel in Sarasota, got crisped by the summer sun lying by the pool, visited the Ringling Circus Museum, and the following Monday moved into our newly rented, freshly painted garage apartment in Lakeland.

Three months later, I climbed back down the corporate ladder to the ground and quit my job at Montgomery Ward. Darlene was three months pregnant, and we were driving north to Boston in winter with all our worldly goods stuffed into a 1953 Packard the size of a Conestoga that I had bought with my old Studebaker plus five hundred dollars. I was nineteen years old and married and soon to be a twenty-year-old father. I had decided that I was a poet or perhaps a novelist and had typed up a sheaf of manuscripts to carry with me to Boston to prove it. With no idea of how to combine all those warring facts peacefully in one young man's life—the only life I had—in Lakeland, Florida, I thought that maybe they could somehow be made to blend in Boston, where I knew I'd find other young, impoverished poets, writers, and artists, some of whom were likely also to be married and parents. I could learn from them how to invent my life, the way the young Hemingway learned from Gertrude Stein and Ezra Pound. I had no intentions of abandoning my teenaged bride and unborn child, however. I was not my father, after all. Nor was I Ernest Hemingway. But late those last nights in Lakeland and during that long drive north, I sometimes caught myself silently moaning, Oh, Lord, what have I done to my life? What am I doing to it now? What will I do with it when the future becomes the present?

Happily, the moment arrived quickly when Chase and I had to return from Tortola to St. Thomas and catch our scheduled STOL flight to Sint Maarten and resume our Caribbean hegira, and I was able to put a halt to the story of my first marriage. Though Chase was neither interrogator nor priest, but like a reader of fiction was merely a listener, my courtship narrative felt more like a confession than a story. I was glad, therefore, and relieved whenever reality intruded and I was able to switch my attention over to the logistics and exigencies of travel. Which is how I have lived much of my life. My writing life as well. It has allowed me to keep on telling the truth, while avoiding anything that resembled a confession.

As Tortola was to the British Virgins and St. Thomas to the U.S. Virgins, the Dutch half-island of Sint Maarten was to a third small constellation of islands. It was where you had to go in order to go someplace else: in this case, we had to fly from St. Thomas to Sint Maarten in order to get to St. Martin, the French half of the island; or to Anguilla, which is a British dependent territory; or to tiny conical Saba, another Dutch island; or over to St. Barthélemy, which is a *subpréfecture* of Guadeloupe, which in turn is an overseas *région* of France.

Like St. Thomas, Sint Maarten was the most populous of its sibling isles and the one most given over to sating the desires of package tourists and cruise-ship passengers. In those strictly commercial terms, it was a success story, a happy hooker. Philipsburg, the capital of Sint Maarten, reminded me of Charlotte Amalie: it was like being caught in a swarm of locusts. Only worse—perhaps especially for me, who had been here fifteen years earlier with my wife Christine and our three daughters and had loved strolling the quiet, clean streets of this sweet little Dutch port. All that had changed. Now huge crowds of confused and suspicious and racially anxious white American tourists just off the boat or tour bus packed the narrow, littered sidewalks and streets, being pecked at by souvenir hawkers and hustlers and barkers perched outside duty-free shops and casinos and bad restaurants. The din of automobile horns and exhaust beat against our heads and made us gasp for breath. Neon and garishly painted signs covered every inch of wall space and shrieked, *Buy me! Buy me! Buy me now!*

A single afternoon in Philipsburg sent us fleeing to the French half of the island. In moments, we had passed out of the Dutch side and had made our way to St. Martin, and it was as if we had been transported to another island altogether, one much more to our liking. We put up at a slightly down-at-the-heels hotel that seemed half-occupied, Le Galéon Beach on the Baie de l'Embouchure, ten miles from the airport and Philipsburg and an easy drive to the towns of Grand Case and Marigot, where we planned to eat good creole food and hunt for Haitian paintings, both of which, the food and the paintings, I remembered with nostalgic affection from that familial visit fifteen years earlier. But who was that mustachioed, sideburned man in his early thirties back then? I wondered. The man leading his family down the narrow street. And that dark, long-haired woman striding intently along beside him. Those three little suntanned girls running to keep up. In memory, the man and woman, their breakup and divorce still years away, seem unconsciously estranged from each other, residents of their own private islands, and the three little girls seem to know it better than their parents and are afraid of what they know.

Despite the blocks of condo construction in and around Marigot and Grand Case and the spanking new resort hotels spreading along the north coast, St. Martin in the intervening years had not changed significantly. Outside the towns, cattle grazed in the wide, pale green valleys, and every farmyard kept its fattened geese, hens, ducks, and a well-fed pig loosely fenced, looking more like family pets than livestock. There was some spillage from the package-tour crowd and the mania for development on the Sint Maarten side, but the French half was still relatively sleepy and laid-back and, except in downtown Marigot, uncrowded, rural.

And still very French, which meant that when we struggled to speak French, the locals switched to bad English, and if we spoke English, they stuck to French and seemed not to understand us. This would turn out to be true on all the French islands—St. Martin, St. Barthélemy, Guadeloupe, and Martinique—but I was in a good mood, glad to be exactly where I happened to be, if a little agitated by the troubling overlay of freshly unlocked memories of my earlier visit with Christine and the girls—and I found the natives' perverse condescension somehow amusing, even endearing, as if it were a measure of their provincialism, rather than mine.

There were many traditional French restaurants in Grand Case and Marigot, and the guidebooks listed them all, and in the interests of the magazine article I was supposed to be writing, we tried a few. But after one meal at a tiny, unlisted bistro called Bistro Nu, we instantly became regulars. It was tucked into a dark alley in Marigot, off rue de Hollande, between rue de la République and rue de Galisbay. We stumbled onto it one night by accident and returned again and again—for the creole food, of course, that syncretic mingle of French and African and Arawak/Carib cuisine with local produce, meat, and fish; and for the nonvintage Rhone wine, which was cheap, more than adequate, what we used to mean by "decent house red." We returned for the friendly company of our fellow diners, who were local folks, mostly black, enjoying a family night out, and for the nervous, earnest, young white Frenchman named Raoul who acted as headwaiter, waiter, and busboy, with a different posture and patter for each role. We went back for the blaff, the West Indian lime-marinated bouillabaisse, and the black boudins and tiny octopuses called chatrous and the lambi colombo, callaloo, and accras. And to wait for a glimpse of the Haitian chef and owner, also named Raoul, a sweating black behemoth who rose from the kitchen in back every half hour or so and came and stood at the swinging door and glared out at the diners as if we did not deserve his cooking.

But something more kept drawing us back to Bistro Nu. It wasn't just the dim light and the ten small, square, cloth-covered tables that reminded us of the perfect French neighborhood bistro, nor the old-style Caribbean building that housed the restaurant, a hundred-year-old daub-and-wattle cabin with a steeply pitched tin roof and an unpainted door on the street and window shutters thrown open to the tropical night and the seaport darkness of the alley and the sounds of young couples talking in low voices as they strolled past. In some crucial way, this generous, intelligent, humorous blend of the best of Europe, Africa, and Mesoamerica, this process called creolization, which we heard in the language and music and saw in the art and architecture and tasted in the food, was embodied in this tiny restaurant itself. Sometimes two people in midlife come together and against all odds their pasts suddenly mingle and blend, as if they had once been young together, almost as if they had shared a childhood, like cousins or even siblings, and though they remember them differently, they remember the same things, especially the moods and atmospheres, the tone and coloration of the past.

Bistro Nu was Chase's and my first shared, unspoken, romantic vision of the Caribbean. Bomba's Surf Shack back on Tortola, despite our initial attraction, was its opposite. For both of us the little St. Martin bistro was based in a private, fondly remembered, literary vision of a Paris we had each visited separately long ago, when she was a teenaged schoolgirl traveling with her schoolmates and twenty years later when I in my mid-thirties arrived in Paris accompanied by my third wife, Becky, for the first publication of a book of mine in France. And now those private images were Chase's and mine together, regathered, blended, remade—creolized. We wanted only to linger here for as long as we could.

But one morning, our St. Martin mission accomplished—Haitian paintings bought and shipped home, guidebook-recommended restaurants sampled and evaluated, magazine article notes for the St. Martin paragraphs finished and typed—we boarded a skiff called *Big Bird,* captained by an Anguillan named Tall Boy, at the pier in Marigot and headed for Anguilla, eight miles north of St. Martin.

Seen from the bow of *Big Bird,* Anguilla, a pale pink and light green hummock lying low in the water, resembled not at all the eel that Columbus on his first sail-by thought it resembled and named it after. Like Anegada in the British Virgins, it is a coral island, not volcanic, surrounded by shallow reefs and long beaches with sand as white and soft as talc. The island is windblown and dry, and the economy is defined by the sea—commercial fishing, sailing, and, of course, beaching. There were a half-dozen small hotels and even a few new resorts, like the chic and luxurious Mal-liouhana, most of them clustered near the settlements of West End and Sandy Ground. In the late 1980s, large-scale tourism had not yet taken root here, and the local population sounded ambivalent about its coming. They needed the income that tourism and new construction would bring—every Anguillan male, besides being a fisherman, seemed to be an unemployed stonemason and car-penter as well. But the Anguillans had seen what had happened to Dutch Sint Maarten and were not eager to follow suit.

The island is, after all, very small—thirty-five square miles, less than the land area of a New England township—with barely seven thousand people back then, many of whom lived off-island, working illegally and sending money back to family in Anguilla, where they fully expected to return in a few years to fish or drive a taxi to the beaches and the hotels from the landing at Blowing Point. All over Anguilla, neat cinder-block bungalows under slow one-man construction attested to young couples' long-range family plans.

In the 1980s Anguilla was essentially a country village that happened to be an island with four or five spectacular beaches. But my mood had changed. I was not happy here. If all one wanted out of the Caribbean was a week or two lying in powdery sand and bathing in water clear enough to read through, this was the place to be. But if, like me, one was not a sun worshiper and found Carib-bean country villages boring or impenetrable, as they usually are to outsiders, and if an arid landscape with little more than sea grapes, prickly pears, and other types of cacti clinging to it was tedious to one's eye, then one might want to limit his stay to a day or two before moving on down the archipelago.

The truth is, while on Anguilla I became inexplicably restless and dissatisfied. When I remembered that I had not finished my account of my first marriage, my mood was no longer inexplicable. Unfinished business: it always makes me restless and dissatisfied. I had not told Chase how my marriage to Darlene had ended and had not acknowledged to myself that I did not want to tell her that story. I was courting Chase, remember? It's not a good idea when courting a woman to reveal how selfish and hard-hearted one was when young. She might suspect that possibly, even well into deep middle age, one is still selfish and hard-hearted. I did not know if she believed that a man's character was capable of change. I was not even sure I believed it myself. So I kept silent on the subject and tried to hide my anxiety as much from myself as from Chase, and instead focused on the logistics of the transition from Anguilla back to Sint Maarten and on to Saba.

In the distance, we saw Saba, a green cone surrounded by a turquoise sea, looking like a volcanic island rising out of the South Pacific. From the air, Mount Scenery (aptly named), three thousand feet high, made the island look as tall as it was wide and long. A lower ring of mountains plummeted straight into the sea below, where we could make out huge black rocks and crashing waves. Not a beach in sight. And then we saw the landing strip, no bigger than a basketball court, stuck out on a promontory with sheer cliffs at both ends and a long drop to the sea.

Scary, especially in a rattling old STOL. I was seated just behind the pilot and over his shoulder had his view of the approach, which I'd rather not have had: we were headed straight for a rock wall when suddenly he cut the engine back almost to a stall, and we dropped and then skidded to a stop a few feet from the precipice.

It's a Dutch island, a five-square-mile circle with just over a thousand residents, mostly fishermen and subsistence farmers, and four tiny villages. The population was approximately half black and half white, and there appeared to be no racial tension between them. Whites and blacks alike tipped their hats and smiled and greeted one another equally. Everything about Saba was miniaturized, squeaky clean, and green. The half-dozen tourists we passed appeared to be day-trippers from Sint Maarten. Like us, they gawked at the scenery, which was enchanting, climbed the thousand steps to the top of Mount Scenery for an otherworldly view of the entire island, and descended for a simple lunch at one of the two or three pleasant outdoor restaurants. You could see it all in a half day, which is what most visitors chose to do, and return to the discos and gaming tables in Sint Maarten.

But you wouldn't have penetrated the quaint surface of the place to the interesting microsociety that existed beneath it. For 250 years, fewer than a thousand white and black Sabans have lived on this tiny island side by side without the presence of tourism and the tortured history of the slave-powered plantation system to dehumanize the residents and their descendants and threaten the island's fragile ecology. It was idyllic, a pocket-sized tropical province made possible because the inhabitants could grow enough to feed themselves year-round and thus needed to import very little, with nothing left over to sell to foreigners— no sugarcane, no white sandy beaches, no drugs, no bauxite, no oil. There was, therefore, no crime and no overweening wealth and no apparent poverty. The soil was fertile, the climate perfectly suited to the natural bodily needs and physical comfort of *Homo sapiens*. Most Sabans lived in small, neat white hillside cottages with gingerbread eaves and red tile roofs and a kitchen garden in back. The Sabans we met were shy, but hospitable and curious once they knew that we had more than a day-tripper's interest in their island. There was a single narrow road paved with hand-cut stones that wound across the island from the airfield and passed through the four settlements (one can't call them towns or even villages) of Upper Hell's Gate, Windwardside, St. John's, and the Bottom. Until the late 1940s, when the road was built, everyone walked everywhere. Most people, despite the recent availability of ten rental cars, still walked everywhere.

We set up at Scout's Place, one of the four or five small bed-and-breakfast guesthouses, run by Scout Thirkield, an expatriate American who had left Sint Maarten twenty-five years earlier because it was too crowded, whose cook, Diana, served wholesome, spicy West Indian food in an open-air dining room with grand views of the hills and the sea fifteen hundred feet below. This was the late-twentieth-century expatriate's fantasy of the Caribbean, where the last few centuries seem almost not to have happened. Saba looked and felt outside time, at least modern time, like a Benedictine monastery in Tuscany or a Shaker settlement in rural New Hampshire.

Later that first evening, as we walked beneath wide swaths of stars from Scout's Place downhill to the settlement of Windwardside, I silently mused that if I ever wished to escape my past or, indeed, my present, I could slip away to the Dutch island of Saba. Yes, I could rent a little house on the side of a hill just beyond one of the villages. Perhaps the very hill we are now descending. I might plant a vegetable garden behind my house—maybe that whitewashed stucco cottage over there in the moonlight beside the road. To pay for my few living expenses I can learn from Scout's chef, Diana, how to cook creole style and open a four-table restaurant in the shaded terrace. Once a month the packet boat or plane from Sint Maarten will bring me a replacement batch of books from the lending library in Philipsburg and batteries and tubes for my Hallicrafters two-way shortwave radio and a stack of English-language newspapers. I might begin a benign, low-key love affair with a Saban widow who has taken over her late husband's position as the island postmaster. Our love affair will gradually intensify, until either the widow moves in with me or I move into her whitewashed cottage down in the settlement. Then the question of marriage will arise . . .

My past and my present will have caught up with me again. My longing for escape will have begun again.

If one is an escape artist, and one has finally managed successfully to escape—to the island of Saba, for instance—where does one run to then? Is it an infinite egress? I was surprised that even here, in the company of the woman I hoped would become my fourth wife, I had seduced myself for the hundredth time, if only briefly, into inventing a story about the possibility and pleasure of running away from my interlocked past and present and the future they portended.

My compulsion, if that's what it was, momentarily embarrassed me. Perhaps that's why I was able to summon the courage to resume telling Chase the true story of the end of my first marriage. Or maybe I sincerely believed that, despite my past and slowly fading escapist fantasy of the present, this time my future really would be different, and thus I could risk revealing my past. Maybe, now that I had fallen in love with Chase, I was at last no longer an escape artist.

There was no way in this for me to make myself look good— or even mildly sympathetic—and still tell what happened. Or what I thought happened. Or, on the island of Saba some twenty-eight years later, what I remembered as having happened. Or now, more than a half century later, what I imagine happened. But these were the indisputable facts. In May 1960, Darlene gave birth to our daughter, whom we named Leona. In September 1960, Darlene and Leona left Boston by Greyhound for Darlene's parents' home in Pinellas Park, Florida. Or was it November 1960? Or December? I don't remember. I do know that I was still twenty years old and Darlene was still nineteen. I tried, and am trying again now, fifty-five years later, to recall how I made this take place, how, without my leaving our small, one-bedroom, third-floor apartment on Peterborough Street in Boston's Back Bay, I managed to abandon my teenaged wife and infant daughter.

But except for that deep knowledge—that it's I who was responsible for it, that Darlene did not want to leave me or the city of Boston and the hardscrabble, bohemian life we had made for ourselves there, and did not want to raise our child without me beside her—I have almost no sequential, linked memories of the events of that summer and fall. I know only that somehow I managed to convince her to return to her parents in Florida and raise our daughter there alone. I did not abandon my wife and daughter; I drove them away.

Over the years I have retained only isolated, disconnected scenes and images. If I tried to connect them now it would create a false narrative. I told Chase that I remembered packing and shipping Darlene's and the baby's clothing and bedding and photograph albums and the other personal possessions that she had asked for. We owned very little else: furniture mostly found on the street, a mattress on the floor, some Sears and Roebuck pots and pans, minimal kitchenware, a record player, books and records, many of them stolen. I remembered weeping guilty tears as, alone in the apartment, I sealed the boxes and wrote Darlene's married name and her parents' Florida address on the labels, and on the return labels my name and our Peterborough Street address.

It was as if I had leaped from a cliff and was now in free fall, my life controlled solely by the force of gravity. Memories and desires and fears flashed past as I plummeted—not falling to earth, but out into deep space, as if drawn neither up nor down but away by the irresistible gravitational pull of an uncharted black hole located light-years beyond my personal planet. It was the first time, and by no means the last, that I had deliberately rejected the forces that had taken control of my life.

No, that's not quite true. I had done it at least twice before. Trial runs, as it were. Practice launches. In fact, my mother liked telling friends and strangers alike that even as a baby I was a runaway: in San Diego during the war, when my father was attached to the naval base there and I was three years old, I managed to untie the rope that she'd used to leash me to the back porch banister while she tended to my baby brother Steve inside, and rode my tiny tricycle across a four-lane highway into a cemetery where the police finally found me dipping VFW flags in a puddle. It was a story she enjoyed telling. And I have a clear memory of bicycling at the age of nine from our tenement apartment in downtown Concord, New Hampshire, five miles to the airport, where I planned to stow away on an outgoing flight to . . . where? I remember only the impulse and what it drove me to, not the plan, and the Concord police catching up with me at the airport. Perhaps I had no plan, no chart or map, only an impulse, liftoff, aimed at no destination other than the whole wide endless sky.

In April 1956, my mother and her four abandoned children were living in Wakefield, Massachusetts. Two weeks after I turned sixteen and got my driver's license, my high school pal Dario Morelli and I stole his father's 1953 Oldsmobile 88 and lit out for the territory, heading west by southwest on Route 66. Eight weeks later, after a lengthy stop to raise gas money by working the night shift flipping burgers at a White Tower in Amarillo, Texas, we pulled up at the Pacific Ocean in Pasadena, where we got a room at the YMCA and jobs selling shoes at a Thom McAns. This time I had a plan. Morelli and I were planning to escape to Australia, but it wasn't clear what or whom we were trying to escape from—our recently glimpsed fates, I suppose. Then one Sunday Morelli, who was Catholic, went to Mass and confessed to the priest what we had done, and the priest turned us in to the Pasadena police. Morelli's father did not press charges, and we had enough gas money to drive the Olds back to him. Morelli got sent to military school, and I managed to make up three months' lost high school homework in the remaining few weeks of the semester. The escapade became a line item in my academic record, however, and kept me from being offered a scholarship at Yale. But at Colgate University, where the administration was trying to broaden the student demographic without admitting too many blacks or Jews, my white, Presbyterian, fatherless family's extreme poverty embellished my SAT scores and athletic achievements sufficiently that I was given a free ride—room and board and full tuition and a grant for books.

In the fall of 1958, ten weeks into my first semester at Colgate, came the second—or fifth, or tenth—time I deliberately can-

celed control of my life. Confused and intimidated by my role as
grateful beneficiary of the college's attempt at affirmative action, I
walked away from the scholarship, stole off-campus in the middle of
a snowy autumn night, and to make sense of what I had done, hoping to avoid being called a dropout, which would have shamed my
mother, who had finally recovered from my runaway with Morelli,
and angered the high school teachers who had worked so hard to
get me the scholarship, I declared that I had left college in order to
join Fidel Castro and his men, who were holed up in Cuba's Sierra
Maestra mountains, which I had read about in a long, glorifying
article by Herbert Matthews in the *New York Times*. Which is how I
washed up in Miami, on the north shore of the Caribbean Sea, a few
months too late for the revolution, and moved to St. Petersburg, on
the Gulf Coast, where I met and married Darlene.

I told Chase that I remembered Darlene sobbing inconsolably
facedown on the cold tiles of the bathroom floor. I was sure this had
happened early in our marriage, and it may as easily have been the
bathroom floor of our garage apartment back in Lakeland as our
third-floor flat on Peterborough Street. It happened early and often,
however; I knew that much. It was always in the gray predawn light
at the end of a night that had seemed interminable. Her nightgown
was tangled around her body like a flimsy shroud. I saw the pink
bottoms of her bare feet, her freckled shoulders and arms, her swol-
len wet face turned away from my gaze, half hidden beneath her
long, blond, matted hair. More than weeping, she was keening, crying out from deep inside her chest for . . . for what? For something I
could neither imagine nor give. My mother had always sobbed like
that, as if panic-stricken, gasping for breath, flailing her limbs like a
grieving widow, all but rending her clothes.

I had learned early on to harden my heart to her cries. Even
before I was twelve—before my father informed me that I was now
the man of the house and walked out the door, leaving my mother
and his four children behind—I had learned to stand just outside
the bathroom or her bedroom or wherever my mother was having

her weeping fit and silently wait for the storm to pass. I had learned that if I entered the room and threw my arms around her shuddering shoulders and wept alongside her or tried in vain to comfort her, which as a small child I had done many times, it would only extend her seizure long into the night. But if I did nothing more than stand by the open door and watch, while my two younger brothers and my little sister huddled together in the background like scared puppies, she would soon regain her composure, wipe her face, and smile bravely up at me, like an actress who knew that her performance hadn't quite come off. It was the same with Darlene. So I watched and waited in silence, like a bodyguard, instead of a husband. Or son.

I remembered telling Darlene—just before she agreed to leave me and return to her parents—that I no longer loved her, even though it was a lie. It would have been easier for both of us and for our daughter if it had been the truth, however. Because I loved Darlene then and for the rest of her life. Which would not have comforted her then or ever. But I think she knew it anyhow, because our daughter, Leona, must have believed it and could only have acquired that belief somehow from her mother, or she would not have had the courage as a fourteen-year-old girl to seek me out and eventually come to trust me enough to live with me and let me take care of her until she could take care of herself.

"Each man kills the thing he loves," wrote Wilde. I did not understand then how that was necessary or even possible, and certainly it was not desirable. The sentence didn't make sense to me. But it was what I was doing. Or rather, what I tried and failed to do, kill the thing I loved, which was my love for Darlene and our baby girl. And so I not only permanently wounded Darlene's heart and Leona's, I wounded my own as well.

I remembered staying out all night, playing chess for hours with my fellow beatniks at the Zazen Coffee House on Hemenway Street and later telling my troubles to sympathetic women in their apartments—not sleeping with them, at least at first, just talking and drinking cheap wine and smoking cigarettes and sometimes pot. One of the women was from Colombia, an artist, petite and pretty, who taught at the School of the Museum of Fine Arts, Boston, and beat me regularly at chess. To my surprise she revealed to me late one night, probably to keep me from coming on to her, that she was a lesbian, and while she thought Darlene was beautiful and sexy, she was not intelligent enough for me. Feeling somehow wronged, I left her apartment and never returned or played chess with her again.

Another was an older, tall, blade-faced woman in her mid-twenties who had a long, thick, roan-colored braid that hung to her waist. She was rumored to be the mistress of Gerry Mulligan, a famous jazzman in his mid-forties, which is why, when she invited me into her bed, I said I couldn't because I was married.

Then there was an actual consummated love affair with the daughter of a black photographer, who I learned many years later was as famous as Gerry Mulligan, but whom I had not heard of then. She was a gifted pianist studying at the New England Conservatory of Music, and I remembered and told Chase that she had a Steinway baby grand piano in her apartment and played Chopin for me. I had never seen a Steinway or heard Chopin before. It was a sexually fierce affair that briefly overlapped with the weeks before Darlene left with Leona for Florida. The affair continued for months afterward, until the woman abruptly quit school and ran off to Paris with a French art critic who was writing a biography of her father and with whom she had been sleeping whenever she went home to Manhattan on school holidays.

I could not understand why, or quite believe, such women were attracted to me and found me interesting. This was shortly before I met Christine, who was then a theater student at Emerson College. She, too, seemed exotic and rarified, a type of female human being altogether new to me, unlike any woman I had known or loved, or so I then believed. She was from Richmond, Virginia, and, despite her Christian name, Jewish, and with her reckless and carefree ways—leaving her sumptuous Lord & Taylor winter coat in a taxi and showing up the next day with another, skipping her final exams for a road trip to Vermont, springing for meals for her impoverished beatnik friends and fellow students, living in an apartment on Beacon Street instead of a college dorm room—she let me know that her family was rich and she was spoiled. I didn't care. I may even have been attracted to her *because* she was rich and spoiled. She wore her long chestnut-brown hair like Joan Baez and played the guitar and sang folk songs from the Weavers' and Pete Seeger's songbook. She was not melancholy in the way of folksingers, however. She was loud and had a raucous laugh. With her oval-shaped face held close to her listener's face, dark brown eyes open wide, eyebrows raised, she spoke in a strangely affected Virginia Tidewater accent colored by long drawn-out vowels and swallowed consonants. She was verbally surprising and vulgar and funny, especially when describing her eccentric southern Jewish family, a mash-up of Aeschylus and Tennessee Williams, *Electra* meets *The Glass Menagerie*.

I could not believe that a woman like Christine could be attracted to a man like me. I was poor and by comparison uptight and boring. A very bad bet by anyone's standards, I was a twenty-year-old divorced dropout and father of an abandoned child, a man who had made a mess of his and several other lives already. I had moved by then from Peterborough Street to a cheaper, smaller flat on Symphony Road, and to pay the $36 monthly rent washed dishes part-time at the Rathskeller in Harvard Square. I wrote terrible Whitmanesque poems and neo-Faulknerian stories and spent the rest of my waking hours reading all the books listed on the syllabi of a friendly Boston University English major.

Nonetheless, Christine was attracted to me. Obsessively so. Which astonished and pleased me. But that is another story, I said to Chase. I did acknowledge that my fourteen-year-long marriage to Christine and divorce were linked in important ways to the story of my prior marriage to Darlene and its brutal end, but they were complicated links, not simple cause and effect—even though my second marriage and divorce would never have happened if not for my first—and could not be quickly described. It was late at night at Scout's on the island of Saba; it was time to pack our bags so we could depart early the next morning for St. Barthélemy. The present and future beckoned; the past could wait.

But it can't wait for long. Whether teller or listener, to get a story straight—which is, after all, one of the things I'm trying to accomplish here—one has to go back to its beginnings. Last April, my Miami friend, the poet Tom Healy, and I were biking the Overseas Highway from Key Largo to Key West and return—two and a half days, about two hundred miles of pedaling—when the past, or a crucial part of the past, came unexpectedly back to me. It was a tough ride. The Seven Mile Bridge between Knight's Key and Little Duck Key was the worst of it, our bikes squeezed on the right by a low guardrail, while eighteen inches off our left shoulders, semis and RVs and tourist-laden cars blew by. Fifty feet beneath the bridge, the ultramarine waters of Florida Bay merged with the turquoise-blue Gulf of Mexico. It was very humid, in the mid-eighties, with a fifteen-mile-an-hour headwind and only occasional cloud cover.

At least once a year, especially since moving to Miami four years ago, I've driven down the Overseas Highway by car to visit friends or participate in the annual Key West Literary Seminar. So I was surprised to find myself deeply and oddly stirred by traveling the same route on a bike, at ground level. Then I remembered. Fifty-three years ago, a wheezing, round-shouldered 1950s Greyhound bus from Miami dropped me off at a single-pump gas station in the fishing village of Islamorada. The bus lumbered back onto the Overseas Highway, old Route 1, and headed for Key West eighty miles beyond. I was lugging all my worldly possessions in an olive-green army-surplus duffel. I hefted the duffel to my shoulder and crossed the now empty road to a two-story, Bahamas-style rooming house with a wide porch that faced the highway.

I was certain of that much; those images were clear. But the rest of my memories of those early months in Islamorada and then later in Key West were vague and uncertain, even as to when I was there exactly, and for how long. I know that I was very young at the time, in my early twenties. I tried telling the story to Tom but couldn't get it right. I must not have been paying attention back then. Or else paying attention to everything that wasn't worth remembering now, more than a half century later.

I used to tell people that it happened in 1962 or '63, when I was twenty-two or twenty-three. But a few years ago I gave a reading from a recently published novel at the Booksmith, a bookshop in Brookline, Massachusetts, just outside Boston. It was one of the several stores and restaurants and contractors that had given me part-time employment in the early 1960s. It was a nostalgic event for me and a kind of triumphant homecoming, and I told the audience that many years ago I had quit my job at the bookstore and hitchhiked alone down to Miami and ridden a bus out to the Florida Keys, where I rented a tiny Airstream trailer in Islamorada, pumped gas part-time to pay the rent, and began to write my first short stories in the cool shadow of Ernest Hemingway, whom I associated with the Keys, although he had long since moved on to Cuba. It was a story I had told many times, whenever asked how I began my life as a writer. Although unsure of the exact date, I usually added that later that year Hemingway shot himself—as if to imply a slightly melodramatic connection between me, the apprentice writer, and Ernest Hemingway, the doomed master.

Later, while I was signing copies of my book at a table, a man appeared in line—a bony guy in his late seventies, slouch cap, thick mustache, Irish face. He leaned in and whispered, "That ain't how it happened, Russ. That bit about you and the Keys." Anyone who called me Russ was someone from my distant past, from before I divorced Christine and became Russell. I recognized him at once, Joe Kerr, a.k.a. Joker, who back in the early 1960s rounded up young Boston artists and beatniks like me and my friends to work as carpenters and stagehands in amphetamine-fueled thirty-day bursts for the Opera Company of Boston. Joker was a likable guy who we all knew was a small-time, but well-connected, mobster. We were his non-union scabs. "I'll be across the street at the Tam," he said. "C'mon over when you're done signing. I'll tell you what really happened."

Joker told me, over drinks at the Tam, that back then I was having a nervous breakdown, he called it, over a dame named Christine who'd left me for another guy. I couldn't get out of bed and come in to work, he said, so the bookstore manager fired me. "You was crying like a fucking baby, man." It was the winter of 1961, he said. "Same year Hemingway stuck his shotgun in his mouth. Not '62 or '63, like you said." Joker had taken pity on me and sent me down to the Florida Keys to work with some associates of his who were helping train Cuban exiles to invade Cuba. He said he had helped get Rose La Rose, the famous stripper, out of Havana when Castro closed down the nightclubs in '59, and he was still tight with the Miami mob. "You were a smart kid, Russ. You woulda made a pretty good gangster," he said and laughed. "I made some calls and set you up at that rooming house in Islamorada where the Miami and CIA guys were staying. But I guess you got scared or something and moved the fuck out. They told me you disappeared. That's probably when you started being a writer," he said. "But it didn't have nothing to do with Hemingway."

There are three interwoven, underlying contexts to the story, the personal, the social, and the historical—as there are to all stories, true or not. The personal context, that weepy, disabling end of a love affair with a girl named Christine, was deeply embarrassing to me, somehow weirdly shameful, and I had forgotten it, so that later I could develop and elaborate the social context and make it into myth, the old story of a young artist's solitary, dedicated apprenticeship in the shadow of a doomed living master. The historical context, Miami mobsters working with the CIA to arm and train Cuban exiles for the infamous Bay of Pigs invasion—looking back now, surely the most interesting part of the story—I left out alto-gether. It would have diminished the romantic, self-embellishing myth of how, in following Hemingway's suicidal footsteps in the sands of the Florida Keys, I became a writer. Because I was mainly interested in shaping how I was perceived by others, by that audi-ence in the Booksmith in Brookline, for instance, I literally forgot what really happened. Personalized myth displaced personalized historical reality. Until the night in the bookshop and at the Tam, when Joker made me want to get my story straight.

Were Joker's Miami mob guys really rooming at the four-square, wooden, two-story building with the long porch while they and a CIA cohort trained the Cuban exiles? Or was Joker, a story-teller himself, making it up? I have no memory of the men individu-ally, but I do have a clear visual memory of the building and of some Americans living there, images recently freshened by my bike ride down the Keys with my pal Tom. The images, however, seem to have been drawn, not from lived experience, but from my memo-ries of a movie or a play in which a group of people, mostly men, are trapped in a hotel bar by a hurricane.

At first I thought the images might have come from *To Have and Have Not,* with Bogart and Bacall, the film version of the 1937 Hemingway novel set in Havana and Key West. Then, as Tom and I rode our bikes past the old, remarkably unchanged rooming house in Islamorada, I realized that I was remembering images from a different movie, *Key Largo.* Did it really happen to me—the hurricane, being trapped in the hotel with a bunch of gangsters—or did I merely see it in the movie? Or did I imagine it? Or dream it? And if it did happen, why after a month or so did I leave the hotel and the gangsters and the CIA agents and rent a little trailer across the road?

Tom is gay and was convinced that Joker had been a gay gang-ster with a crush. No house, no wife, in Boston in the late fifties, early sixties, providing non-union workers for the Opera Company of Boston by hiring handsome young artists and writers to make sets and be stagehands. "It was an *opera* company," Tom pointed out. "Not a waste disposal company. Give me a break, Russell."

A gay Irish mobster? Well, yes, it was possible. And if so, I was too oblivious to have guessed it. But why else would Joker want to help a brokenhearted kid having a nervous breakdown over a busted romance by sending him off to train Cuban exiles in the Keys with his mobster friends so the kid could maybe become a mobster himself? Joker's little mobster.

And could it really have been that early, the winter of 1961, in time for the Bay of Pigs, an event that at the time seemed to have escaped my notice? Or had no memory of, anyhow. As Tom and I pedaled on, I did the numbers. I needed to establish when, exactly, this happened. I'd fallen in love with Christine when she was a student at Emerson College and I was living on Symphony Road in Boston, working part-time at the bookstore and the Rathskeller restaurant and in binges at the Opera Company of Boston. She left me for another boy, ran off with him to finish college in Richmond, Virginia. I remembered pumping gas at the filling station in Isla-morada next to my Airstream on old Route 1. Then at some point I left Islamorada and rented a room by the week at a whorehouse in Key West that took me two weeks or more to figure out actually was a whorehouse. Key West was a navy town then, and I was very naive and, as I said, oblivious. I was writing my neo-Hemingway short stories and paying more attention to my sentences than to my surroundings.

I remembered that a few months later I delivered a drive-away Opel picked up in Miami to its owner in San Diego by way of northern Mexico, with an extended stopover in New Orleans, accompanied by two guys who ran a card game at the Key West whorehouse, Frank, a strip show barker recently released from jail in New Jersey, and an AWOL sailor from Oklahoma whose name I can't remember. I stayed for a few weeks in San Diego, where my mother had recently moved, then hitched back east to New Hamp-shire. Temporarily reconciled with my father, I moved in with him and his new wife where he was living in his parents' home in Barnstead and began working alongside him as a union plumber, the Banks family trade for three generations. Returning to Boston the following summer, I renewed my relationship with Christine. And on October 29, 1962, married her. The marriage did not last as long as we hoped, of course—they never do; that is, mine never do—but the date is indelible, part of the record.

So the numbers confirmed it: yes, I was in Islamorada in April 1961, which is when the Bay of Pigs invasion occurred, and I must have been frightened by whatever was happening before my eyes, which I could not have understood, so I fled the rooming house and the men living there, abandoning the life of a gangster for the life of a writer in an Airstream trailer just across the road. And the rest became my more sharply remembered life: Key West, New Orleans, Mexico, San Diego, New Hampshire, a second early marriage, college in North Carolina, Jamaica, and on.

Still chasing down the imagery, at home in Miami a few nights after my bike ride with Tom, I rented and watched the movie *Key Largo*. The film is adapted from the play by Maxwell Anderson. Richard Brooks and John Huston wrote the screenplay, Huston directed. Released in 1948, it starred Bogart, Bacall, Edward G. Robinson, Lionel Barrymore, and Claire Trevor. I'd forgotten the weirdly racist Seminole Indian aspect—it opens with a local sheriff looking for "two young bucks" who'd busted out of jail. Me and Morelli on the lam in a '53 Olds? The real action begins when Major McLeod (Bogart) arrives by bus at the Hotel Largo, a Bahamas-style wood-frame rooming house and bar with a long porch facing the road. He's come to keep a vow made to a guy in his outfit who was killed in Italy in the war. He's promised to visit the guy's wheelchair-bound dad (Barrymore) and gorgeous sister (Bacall) and report that their beloved son and brother died heroically in battle.

Bogart finds the hotel taken over by a posse of American gangsters up from Cuba led by Johnny Rocco (Robinson), a short, round, cigar-chomping Capone type, there to meet some Miami mobsters and exchange a suitcase of phony money printed in Cuba for a bag of real cash—when the hurricane hits. The wind rises to a roar. And then comes a strangely ominous scene in the hotel bar where Robinson leans in to Bacall and whispers something in her ear that the audience can't hear, something that frightens and repels her. She recoils, and he does it again. This time she spits at him and claws his face with her nails. Bleeding, he backs off. Throughout the scene Bogart stands and watches from the bar, but does nothing.

The scene is ugly and realistic in a way that the rest of the movie is not; the rest is operatic and stagy. But for me that exchange between Robinson and Bacall carries the emotional and moral meaning of the film. Everything seems to hinge on whispered words that we never hear. We're invited to imagine the filthiest, most degrading words possible. It was shocking and frightening and deeply felt by me in a way that nothing else in the film was.

When did I first see *Key Largo*? Not when it was released in 1948—I was only eight years old. It is possible, of course, that I saw it a year later at the Star Theater in Concord, New Hampshire; I went to the movies at least once a week starting when I was nine, regardless of what was showing. But at that age what, if anything, would I have made of Edward G. Robinson's whispering into Lauren Bacall's lovely ear? The scene might have frightened me, but only a little. Bacall's response would have frightened me more—a beautiful young woman reacts violently to an ugly man's unheard words by spitting at him and scratching his face with her nails. The sexual element would not have occurred to me. Not consciously.

It's more likely that I watched the film for the first time many years later, after I had actually lived in the Keys, in the 1980s, late at night on the Turner Classic Movies channel. And just recently, prompted by my bike ride down the Keys with my friend Tom, when I watched it again, this time via Netflix, and it became clear that the scene with Robinson and Bacall was the emotional and moral center, not just of the movie, but of my all-but-forgotten, long-ago months in Key Largo.

But I couldn't be sure of the differences between what I remembered experiencing in 1961 and what I saw decades later in the movie. They flowed together like Florida Bay and the Gulf of Mexico under the Seven Mile Bridge and elaborated and extended each other. This time the movie stirred up a wave of impacted and disturbing and mysteriously mingled memories, all brought on by Joker's revelations at the Tam and the bike trip with Tom years later: lived experience first, then a long half century of forgetting, then a willed return to the location and to the film—followed, as I write, by these overflowing memories, making it possible for my early lived experience to be relived now, in my mid-seventies.

Almost relived. For at the very center there floats a small, opaque gray circle, an absence, behind which something shameful lies hidden. It's what no one hears Robinson whisper in Bacall's perfect ear. It's what I imagine he said to her. Something I myself must have said to a beautiful young woman. To Christine, driving her into the arms of another, a man standing at the bar, watching, like Bogart. She evidently forgave me, or she would not have married me. But I cannot remember what I said to her and can neither imagine nor acknowledge it, and thus cannot be truly forgiven. All I can call up today is the emotional residue: which is shame. Guilt dissipates over time; shame, like a man's character, stays.

When Tom and I biked our way back from Key West to where we had left the car in Key Largo, we pulled off at the old place in Islamorada. Freshly painted, it looked the same outside as it did fifty-four years earlier, except for a resort-wear boutique and a real estate office on the first floor and what appeared to be a rack of studio apartments upstairs. I stepped into the real estate office and spoke to the Realtor, a pretty, very pregnant, young Hispanic woman with frizzy dark hair seated in front of an electric fan. I asked her if the building used to be a bar and rooming house. She said that was before her time. But yes, she'd heard it was once a roadhouse. Where a lot of bad things happened, she added, smiling. Except for her office and the boutique next door, it was condos now. There's one available, she told me. An end unit. Just came on the market. A view of the Gulf on one side and Florida Bay on the other. Would I be interested in seeing it?

I hesitated a few seconds, then said no, and Tom and I mounted our bikes and rode on.

Meanwhile, in harmonious, if asymmetrical, late 1980s counter-point, my courtship tour of the Caribbean continued. Chase and I returned to Sint Maarten from our sojourn in Saba and imme-diately departed for St. Bart's. Though not as terrifying as its counterpart on Saba, the single scariest thing about St. Bart's was the approach to the landing strip. The rickety old STOL passed through a cut in the steep hills west of the town of Gustavia, a defile, actually, not much wider than the wingtips. When the pilot suddenly cut the engine, the plane literally dropped toward a run-way that ended precisely at the edge of Baie de St. Jean, where several half-submerged planes that had missed the stop lay mold-ering below. After that, touring the tiny eight-square-mile island was mainly a matter of restaurant-hopping. St. Bart's may have the most restaurants per capita of any place in the world—at last count when we were there in 1988, sixty restaurants for thirty-five hundred residents. And I'm talking French restaurants, from the elegant high-end hilltop Les Castelets to Chez Joe's on a Gustavia backstreet.

After visiting the American and British Virgins, Sint Maarten and St. Martin and Anguilla and Saba, it was a visual surprise to arrive at St. Bart's and realize that almost everyone was white—the tourists, of course, and the large number of island entrepreneurs, but also the natives, who were mostly descendants of the original Norman and Breton settlers and had traditionally been small farmers instead of plantation owners. Plantation culture and its painful residue were as foreign to St. Bart's as to St. Moritz, and the place felt a little like St. Moritz, though more laid-back, if that's possible, and more expensive. In a sense, the entire island was a huge, chic French gated resort. There were many private villas in the hills, luxury hotels and bungalows along the coves and beaches of the north coast, and a picture-perfect yacht basin in the one town, Gustavia, a regular stop for the Lesser Antilles sailing crowd.

Popular with entertainers hiding from their fans, models working on their tans, and a large number of balding businessmen in their sixties and seventies strolling the beaches alongside very attractive, much younger women in string bikinis, St. Bart's provided little of interest for travelers like me and Chase, voyagers interested in the five-hundred-year clash-and-blend of diverse cultures, races, and classes that makes the Caribbean so exciting and so threatening. St. Bart's was lotusland. But even the most intrepid of travelers can use a break now and then, so we settled into a cabana at Baie de St. Jean for a few days and tried not to be too distracted by the perfect beaches, the cuisine, the designer boutiques, and the discos. And—no surprise—we slumbered our days and nights away as if on holiday in St. Moritz, thousands of miles from the Caribbean, and I spoke almost not at all about my marriages and divorces. And it was painful to leave.

Our itinerary and booked flights, however, obliged us to head next for Antigua. After reading native daughter Jamaica Kincaid's book *A Small Place,* one might think, as one approached Antigua for the first time, that one was entering the third circle of hell. And, indeed, there was much about the island to offend the sensitive visitor and perhaps even more to offend a native Antiguan like Kincaid, who left her idyllic island home and returned twenty years later to find a country on the make and the local politicians on the take. Antigua is the largest of the Leewards, 108 square miles, seventy-six thousand people. It is also the most entangled in the history of British imperial ambitions. The economics and culture of sugar and

slavery shaped its destiny to a degree matched only in Barbados
and Jamaica. As a general rule, these are the islands most tragically
caught in the subtly interwoven conflicts between hatred and slav-
ish adoration of the mother country, between third-world national-
ism and hopeless dependence on foreign loans, between profound
affection for their island's natural resources and relentless determination to develop, at all costs, the tourist industry. Antigua was an
island at war with itself, and it showed.

But if all we saw of the island were the congested, filthy streets
of St. John's, the capital, and its deepwater port, where the cruise
ships touched down, and the recklessly developed north coast
along Dickinson Bay to the airport, where the jumbo jets disgorged
troops of tourists from the mainland, we would have concluded
that, just as on St. Thomas and Sint Maarten, the island's war with
itself had been won by the darker forces. A drive across the island
to Nelson's Dockyard and the famed English Harbour would have
only reinforced that view, for the elaborate restorations and recon-
structions painted the history of colonialism and slavery in what
can only be called a sanitized, benign, almost nostalgic light. And
if we had followed the handsome art deco signs posted all over the
island pointing proudly to something called Carlisle Bay, all the way
through the Shekerley Mountains to the southeast coast, until we
finally came to Old Road—where a two-hundred-year-old village
of local farmers and fishermen was in the process of being removed
and a vast mud hole was surrounded by a high chain-link fence with
a rusting bulldozer in the middle—we would have smelled arro-
gance, greed, foreign capital, greased palms.

Yet inland, away from St. John's and over on the east coast,
where large-scale tourism hadn't yet taken over, the country was
beautiful and clean, and the residents, mostly small farmers, were
both proud and friendly. We could still find the Antigua mourned
by Jamaica Kincaid, but we had to work at it, and it would not, could
not, last much longer. Small guesthouses and owner-operated hotels,
like the Long Bay on the east coast, where there were no social direc-

tors and no free drinks with cute names and paper parasols and we were free to talk and read, were rapidly being shouldered aside by the huge resorts, casinos, and condo complexes. All the good roads on the island now led only to where the air-conditioned tour buses wished to go.

We made a day trip to Antigua's country cousin, Barbuda, which had recently received its first attention from U.S. tourist publications, but the dry, low-lying platter of an island, located a few miles northeast of Antigua and part of the same political unit, offered little that had not been more interestingly, and prettily, offered by Saba. There were coral beaches here, however, and one (expensive) resort hotel, Coco Point Lodge. Barbuda was essentially a fishing and salt-producing island, isolated, sparsely populated, poor, with no scenic attractions, almost no tourist services, and a somewhat irritated local populace—irritated that Antigua, like a glamorous, gifted older sister, got all the attention and money and political power in what is supposed to be a two-island nation.

We left Barbuda the following day and returned to Antigua, the transportation hub for the region, where we were to switch planes for St. Kitts–Nevis. Antigua's huge V. C. Bird International Airport is named after Prime Minister Vere Bird, who had run Antigua and Barbuda like a fiefdom for the previous forty years. Built by the U.S. military in World War II, the airport was as large as the one the Cubans had built on Grenada, the airport that so famously alarmed President Reagan's national security advisers. Steel bands played "Island in the Sun," and grinning hostesses in Aunt Jemima costumes offered us free rum punch in plastic cups.

The difference between Bird International on Antigua and the single short landing strip and rough one-room open-air terminal that greeted us on Nevis was extreme and captured the difference between the two islands. It wasn't just size. It was character. Kincaid was right to be pissed off. We climbed out of the Winnair single-engine STOL plane that had carried us and three other passengers from Antigua, stretched our cramped legs, and instantly, because there wasn't much else to do, admired the scenery—the glittering Caribbean Sea with emerald-green St. Kitts five miles in the distance, the palm-lined beach, the forested slopes leading quickly to the volcanic cone of Nevis Peak, 3,232 feet high, set smack in the center of the thirty-six-square-mile, circle-shaped island. A soft breeze blew, and except for the gentle clatter of palms at the edge of the field, all was quiet. This, we thought, might be the perfect Caribbean island. This is a North American's idea of paradise.

We were not alone in thinking that. A pair of white American teenaged boys in cutoff jeans, barefoot and shirtless, were hanging out at the airfield building—latter-day Huck Finns gone way south of south. They could have been me and Morelli in Amarillo thirty-some years earlier. One of them was explaining what a skateboard was to a puzzled local kid who was not sure what a skate was, while the other, red-haired and taller and seemingly in charge, tried in vain to make the pay phone on the wall work by every now and then giving it a slow whack with his open hand. "Dis t'ing vex me, mon!" the redheaded boy said in a sad, lame version of West Indian Rasta talk. "I-an'-I cyan' mek de dam t'ing wok fe I-an'-I!" They couldn't have been older than fifteen or sixteen, and in spite of their long hair, which had been forcibly knotted into pathetic imitations of Rastafarian dreadlocks, and their wispy blond mustaches and thin chin whiskers, they were still children. Their glazed, red-rimmed eyes and slow-motion gestures suggested more than occasional recreational use of cannabis.

The half-dozen black taxi drivers in the terminal waited like pelicans on a pier for us to check our bags through the one-man customs dock and politely ignored the American boys. We understood why. The boys were painful to look at. They had covered their skinny, sunburnt arms and legs and hairless chests and bellies with brightly colored tattoos of lions, portraits of Haile Selassie, Jamaican flags, dreadlocked Rastaman heads, marijuana leaves, and mottoes like JAH LIVES and ONE LOVE. They'd turned their slender pink bodies permanently into reggae record jackets. We winced and, like the taxi drivers, averted our eyes.

Throughout our brief stay on Nevis and long after, the image of the tattooed, dreadlocked American boys stayed with me. We took a room in one of the many small guesthouses for which the island is famous, snorkeled off Pinney's Beach, strolled the six or eight narrow streets of Charlestown, and visited the birthplace of Alexander Hamilton and the church where Lord Nelson and Frances Nisbet's 1787 marriage certificate is kept. We did what you can do on Nevis—but I was unable to stop grieving over the boys and their absurd Rastafarian fantasy. I wondered if the occasional adult who saw me and my pal Morelli when we made our runaway drive across the continent in 1956 had averted his eyes and felt as sad and sorry for us as Chase and I felt for those lost boys on Nevis. The mythology that turned me and Morelli into teenaged car thieves chased by a nationwide all-points bulletin was the same one fictionalized the next year by Jack Kerouac in *On the Road*—the male romance of the West and the open road and the promise of ecstatic freedom from the conformist, repressive, suburban 1950s. Not to mention our deep unacknowledged desire, like Kerouac's, to escape from our respective dysfunctional families—*dysfunctional,* a social condition that in the 1950s had no name. Like Kerouac, my and Morelli's sacramental drug had been alcohol, not cannabis— rotgut jug wine we convinced drunks off the street to buy for us that we guzzled until we were throwing-up sick behind the stolen Olds 88 parked beside open-all-night roadside diners in Kansas City and Denver and in our grim, bare YMCA rooms in Amarillo and Pasadena.

I wondered what myths had plucked the boys on Nevis from their suburban homes in the late 1980s and led them to fry their brains on ganja and cultivate their white-boy dreadlocks and tattoo their bodies, before finally dropping them off here in Nevis. In those days, all over the Caribbean, especially on the English-speaking

islands, one encountered the occasional white Rasta, but it was usually an American woman, not a man or teenaged boy, in her twenties or early thirties wearing an ankle-length Ghanaian kente cloth
wraparound skirt, her straight hair wrought into a matted version
of the leonine dreadlocks worn by the handsome black Rastaman
walking a short, but discernible, few steps in front of her. One naturally tended to view the woman's relation to the man's apparent Pan-
African mysticism with a bit of skepticism, since her racial, political,
and cultural experience was not only radically different from his,
but was profoundly antagonistic to it. Rastafarianism is rooted in
the black oppressed victim's experience of the history of slavery
and colonialism, in the African diaspora and Marcus Garvey's Pan-
Africanism, in the abject hopelessness of Caribbean ghetto poverty,
and in the prophetic power of the "sufferers in Babylon" evoked by
the image of the late emperor Haile Selassie of Ethiopia, the Lion of
Judah in full military regalia astride a white horse, and the music of
Bob Marley.

It is hard to understand how this autochthonous, mainly
Caribbean mix of black suffering and imagery can make religious
or historical sense of the world as experienced by middle-class white
Americans. One tends to attribute the conversion of the Americans,
if indeed they are converted, less to religion and history and sympathetic identification with the oppressed than to the Rastafarian use
of cannabis as a sacrament and the seductive social rhetoric associated with reggae music—pacifistic, communal, and apocalyptic—
and sex. And, of course, there is the fact that since the late 1960s all
young white middle-class American men and women have known
that nothing is more threatening to their parents than joining a
black, ghetto-based, dope-smoking religious cult whose heroes are
powerful, sexy black men with beards and weird hairdos who speak
and sing an English patois no white American parent can understand. It's the forbidden, eroticized.

But the Rastafarian fantasy, and perhaps the permanent fog-inducing effects of ganja on still-unformed adolescent male brains, had taken the tattooed boys on Nevis beyond escape or rebellion. They could twist and roll their long blond and red Caucasian hair into rough, ropelike approximations of an African's dreadlocks, but since they couldn't turn their pink skin black, they had covered it instead with non-erasable graffiti, making it useful only as signage. Perhaps that was why they disturbed me so. The unconscious racial self-loathing and rage expressed by those tattooed young white bodies was my culture's racism turned violently against itself. And possibly it was something closer to home, as it were, something more personal. Something to do with me and Christine and our time living in Jamaica in the 1970s and afterward, when our marriage came apart and she took a dreadlocked Jamaican lover and a few years later moved back to Jamaica and eventually married a different dreadlocked Jamaican man.

When Chase and I visited the country, the government of St. Kitts–Nevis, led since 1984 by the People's Action Movement and Prime Minister Kennedy Simmonds, was one of the most enlightened and stable governments in the Caribbean. The total population of the two-island nation was barely forty-five thousand, and the capital, Basseterre, on St. Kitts, had but fifteen thousand inhabitants. Tourism had been controlled, developed slowly and with careful regard for the environment, the cultural integrity of the populace, and the larger economic picture, which was mostly agricultural, with some small manufacturing and assembly plants developed by off-island companies. The largest employer was the government itself, which, in St. Kitts especially, was in the sugarcane business; but the laborers and farmers were organized, and although they were not exactly partners in the vast operation, they were protected to a degree unknown in the rest of the Caribbean.

On the map, if Nevis, because of its shape, was a ball, then

St. Kitts was a cricket bat. At least Kittians—cricket fanatics, like most West Indians—enjoyed thinking of it that way. The island is mountainous in the center, rising to 3,792 feet in the north at Mount Misery, dropping nearly to sea level along the bat handle, and rising again at the end. The coastal plains were given over mainly to growing sugar, and the only roads on the island looped along the coast around the fat part of the bat, passing through farming and fishing villages that seemed not to have changed in a hundred years. There were beaches at either end of the bat, and that is where you found most of the larger hotels—Frigate Bay, Jack Tar Village, Banana Bay Beach—where they could do the least damage to island life. This was rational tourist development, the kind of development that did not in the process destroy the product itself. In Basseterre and scattered throughout the island, there were numerous smaller hotels and inns, most notably the Ocean Terrace, and Rawlins Plantation, a tastefully renovated (not restored) old plantation house with eight guest rooms, set in a cane field at the foot of Mount Misery with expansive views of the sea.

Here we settled for a few days, exploring the forested, mountainous backcountry by horseback, playing tennis on a grass court and croquet on the meticulously kept lawns, walking through spectacular gardens of hibiscus and bougainvillea, and sitting up late over cognac on the veranda, watching bats dart above the lawns while we talked of times past and times to come.

This is the sort of experience that gave Caribbean tourism a good name in the first place and still generates most people's fantasies of island travel. It's what the tourist boards, airlines, hotels, and cruise lines advertise. But it's a fantasy that has been too often clipped and cheated by reality, which is why so many visitors to the islands come home vaguely disappointed, feeling both gulled and gullible. Even so, the following winter the fantasists buy into it again. Because the reality that created and feeds the fantasy can still be found—at least in a few places out there it can—as we were discovering on St. Kitts, with variants available in some of the less-developed islands, like Saba and, as we later learned, Dominica, St. Vincent, and Tobago—so people sign on for the trip again and again. To connect the reality to the fantasy, however, one has to be willing to invent one's own private itinerary and avoid the crowds, as we were doing, and, of course, be able to finance it—since the only way to travel cheaply in the Caribbean then and now is in a packaged crowd, or else to count on the kindness of strangers and rough it. And risk having to make collect calls home for money on a pay phone that doesn't work, like the tattooed boys on Nevis.

The second day on St. Kitts we rented equipment for scuba at the Fisherman's Wharf in Basseterre and learned basic diving in Banana Bay. Another day, we chartered a sailboat and crossed the seven-mile channel to St. Eustatius, one of the most lovely and least developed of the Dutch Antilles, for a day and a night. There we climbed through orchids to the Quill, an eighteen-hundred-foot-high extinct volcano, and later visited Fort Oranje, where the American flag got its first foreign salute in 1776. The following morning, we sailed back to St. Kitts and strolled along the narrow streets in and around Independence Square in Basseterre, where eighteenth-century Georgian houses had been renovated and turned into artists' studios and boutiques. Later, we were back at Rawlins Plantation, sitting on the veranda, dressed for dinner, aperitifs in hand, for all the world looking and acting like Chase's elegant globe-trotting grandparents in the 1920s and not at all like who we were, a middle-aged, middle-class pair of professors gone a-courting in the 1980s. Actually, Chase was only thirty-eight then; at forty-eight, I was middle-aged. We listened to the chortle of ground doves and the quiet click of sugarcane in the evening breeze as the sun set at the edge of a sky gone to gray velvet streaked with plum, the sea a flattened pink-and-cobalt plain. For a few hours we believed that we had never been this contented in our lives.

Maybe it was Chase, maybe it was me, I can't recall now, but one of us popped our blissful Caribbean bubble and brought me back around to the subject of my second marriage and its turbulent end. I know it sounds absurd, I told her, but on some level I truly believed that by marrying Christine I could somehow shuck the guilty weight of having married Darlene. I thought it would nullify the first marriage in a way that a divorce couldn't. I hoped it would nullify the divorce, too—although I had no idea at the time that it was merely the first of what would eventually be three. And the abandonment of my child. That, too. It all—marriage, divorce, abandonment—felt like a serial crime to me. And marrying again was supposed to expunge my criminal record—just as my marriage to Darlene had been unconsciously designed to expunge my parents' record. The sad truth is that I would not have married Christine at twenty-two if I had not married Darlene at nineteen and divorced her and abandoned our child at twenty. So, yes, although I didn't know it at the time, or was only vaguely aware of it, my two early marriages were profoundly, if not causally, connected.

Otherwise, there was too much against me and Christine to marry. Our youth, for starters. Even though in the early 1960s men and women married at a much younger age than now, Christine and I each had a lot of unfinished business that would be harder for us to finish as a married couple—like college in her case and some sort of profession (back then she said she wanted to be an actress), and everything else in mine. I had no college degree and was barely employed, after all, with no imaginable way to provide for Christine in the style to which she was not only accustomed but was sure she deserved as well. Her father and uncle owned and ran a large pharmaceutical business, and the family on her father's side by any standard was rich and had been for generations; my family had been working-class poor even longer, and, after my father's departure, poverty stricken. Also, well before meeting me in person, having only heard about me from Christine, her parents, especially her father, hated and mistrusted me. Her mother less so, maybe, but enough to say that she'd be relieved if Christine left me for another boy, and she had a few suggestions.

They had learned of my first marriage and fatherhood and divorce by hiring a private detective who dug it out for them and then sprang their discovery on Christine, home from college during spring break. She quickly disappointed them by telling them that they'd wasted their money, because she had known about it from the start. Which was true. I had told Christine the whole sad story, at least as much of it as I knew and understood at the time, the first night we were together, making out passionately in the backseat of her roommate's boyfriend's Thunderbird on an after-party, alcohol-fueled, overnight trip from Boston to Vermont. To my surprise, my confession seemed to give me, in her eyes, a certain mystery and gravitas. Christine whispered that she'd never been fucked by a divorced man before. I assumed that meant that as soon as we got back from Vermont and went to her apartment or mine, she would want me to fuck her. And she did, and I did. So I was glad I had told her the truth about Darlene and Leona.

Her parents not only distrusted me, they were also afraid of me, especially her father—rightly, perhaps, but not for the reasons they gave. This is Christine's imitation in bed in Boston of her father speaking on the phone from the brick Colonial family home in Richmond in his long-voweled Tidewater drawl: *Christine, the young man is not Jewish. Doesn't have to be Jewish, you understand. But it'd help a whole lot if you and he had a similar background. A college dropout who claims to be a writer, but he hasn't published anything yet, has he? Maybe never will. Not that I hold it against a young fellow who wants to become a successful writer, you understand. But it might help the boy's prospects some if he got himself a college degree or two. And a reliable source of income. How do you know the boy isn't some kind of gold digger, anyhow? His father is a plumber or something like that in New Hampshire. An alcoholic. Abandoned the family years ago, you said. I feel sorry for the boy, naturally. And the mother, too. The mother, she's a kind of clerk or something out in California? And the boy, all he does for a living is wash dishes part-time in a restaurant? Or house-paint? Wasn't that in the private investigator's report? Honey, it just sounds like he sees*

you as an opportunity, his golden calf. Don't laugh. If he were Jewish I
wouldn't think it. But a poor Gentile wouldn't likely be all that attracted
to a Jewish girl in the first place if it wasn't for her family's money . . .

Except for the business about my early marriage, fatherhood, and divorce, which she was still trying to process into a bawdy narrative, Christine had told him all of it herself, volunteering the information as a way to make her new Yankee boyfriend's family background, literary ambitions, even his poverty, exotic and scary to her parents and her older sister and brother and her ten-years-younger sister. It worked on her siblings all right, but so far was wasted on her parents. It was part of the process of turning her new boyfriend gradually into a story, as she did with her family members themselves, as she did with practically everyone she knew, first by objectifying them, then by appropriating their personal, sometimes private and secret stories and taking possession of them, finally telling and retelling the stories with increasing elaboration and verve and clever impersonations, exaggerating and embellishing the stories until they were inimitable, so that only Christine herself could tell them. For example, only she could reveal to her new boyfriend the length, girth, and other distinguishing characteristics of her previous boyfriends' penises and do it in a way that was so broadly comical that the details did not seem quite believable and thus cause her new boyfriend to laugh and not fear that soon she would be regaling strangers with accounts of the length, girth, and distinguishing characteristics of his penis, too.

Her parents' opposition was unyielding. Unfortunately, most of their worst fears were validated by my behavior, especially after they pulled her out of Emerson College and brought her back to Richmond and got her enrolled for the coming fall at Virginia Commonwealth University. A few weeks later, like a lost dog, I showed up on their doorstep. Within twenty-four hours I had totaled her mother's brand-new Volvo and got myself tossed into jail for driving without a driver's license, having loaned it to my underage brother, Steve, so he could buy booze for his air force buddies. Christine's father had to bail me out of jail. By the time I went before a judge, Steve had mailed my license back, but I got hit with a two-hundred-dollar fine, most of which I had to borrow from Christine's father. I talked my way into a job as assistant buyer of fabrics and draperies at Thalheimer's Department Store downtown, despite knowing nothing about fabrics, draperies, or buying wholesale, by claiming to have attended Harvard for three years; rented an apartment on Monument Avenue; and tried to convince Christine's parents of my worth and promise, mainly by way of attending with great sincere sensitivity to her mother, who was in psychoanalysis then and, against her better judgment, believed that I was a decent person and was intelligent and possibly talented.

My memory is a little vague on the next sequence of events, but I believe it was around this time that Christine's parents decided that the best way to get rid of me was to take Christine and her younger sister on a two-month Grand Tour to Paris, London, and Edinburgh, where I couldn't follow. By the time they returned to Richmond, I had quit my job at Thalheimer's, decamped for Boston, rented an apartment on Symphony Road again, and got a part-time job as a basement stockboy in the bookstore in Brookline that half a century later would become the Booksmith, where Joker showed up at my reading. Christine talked her parents into letting her return to Emerson for her senior year, and we soon resumed our love affair there, although by then we had both given up trying to convince her parents to do more than merely tolerate my existence on the same planet with them and their middle daughter.

A year later, I was working in New Hampshire as a plumber, Christine was back in Richmond at Virginia Commonwealth and sleeping with at least two young men that I knew of, and at the same time exchanging passionate, sexually explicit love letters with me and making long, painful, weeping telephone calls in which we declared our desperate, undying love for each other. Until I couldn't take the intensity and unsettledness anymore and said what I thought was my last and permanent good-bye. Within a day of my having said good-bye, she came knocking at the door of my third-floor flat in Concord, New Hampshire.

So we eloped. Well, not really—Christine eloped. I stayed put. I was a plumber who had to go to work the next day.

From St. Kitts, Chase and I moved south and slowly curled back toward the west. The link between the Leewards and the Windwards—either the last of one or the first of the other—was Montserrat, a two-flight Leeward Islands Air Transport hop from St. Kitts by way of Antigua. Back then, before the 1995 and 1997 volcanic eruptions in the Soufrière Hills destroyed the capital, Plymouth, and made more than half the island uninhabitable and caused widespread evacuations, Montserrat was a tiny, seldom-visited British crown colony located halfway between St. Kitts–Nevis and Guadeloupe. Settled in 1632 by Irish Catholics fleeing persecution over on neighboring St. Kitts, it was a lonely forty-square-mile dot, mountainous, verdant, and winsome.

With only a few brown-gray beaches, and those practically inaccessible, and but a handful of small hotels, the island had remained free to pursue matters other than tourism—mainly agriculture (limes, vegetables, and sea island cotton) and, surprisingly, recording studios, such as the George Martin–run Montserrat AIR Studios, which had brought to the island a relatively large number of international recording stars, who, when there, were all business. Montserrat was not a secret waiting to be told. It was simply unable to support tourism and, wisely, had long refused to try. We duly noted this and respectfully moved on down the archipelago.

From the air, the large French island of Guadeloupe looks like a bright green butterfly. In fact, it is two very dissimilar, geologically distinct, wing-shaped islands, Grande-Terre and Basse-Terre, separated by a narrow seawater channel and connected by a mere drawbridge. Grande-Terre, to the east, is formed of coral and is flat and ringed by pink and white beaches; Basse-Terre, the western half, is volcanic and mountainous, covered with rain forest, and capped by its own La Soufrière, a forty-eight-hundred-foot smoldering volcano.

Guadeloupe is the spot in the Lesser Antilles where two long geological arcs intersect. One arc, that of the Late Cretaceous coral shelf, starts way to the southeast at Barbados, emerging from the sea at nearby Marie-Galante and again here in Guadeloupe at Grande-Terre and in the north at Barbuda, Anguilla, and Anegada. This type of island is low, windswept, usually dry, and surrounded by white beaches, reefs, and old shipwrecks. The second arc, that of the Miocene volcanic islands, is slightly to the west of the first and runs from Grenada northward to Dominica and on to the Basse-Terre wing of the Guadeloupan butterfly, where it curves slowly, passes through St. Kitts–Nevis and Antigua, and goes on to Tortola, Virgin Gorda, and the U.S. Virgins. This type of island is mountainous, moist, and heavily forested, with fewer, sometimes brown or even black sand beaches and many deepwater ports. This second arc of islands lies over a subduction zone—where the American Plate, situated beneath the Atlantic Ocean, grinds against and is shoved downward by the Caribbean Plate—and is one of the most geologically active parts of the earth's crust. Thus the frequency of those devastating earthquakes and constantly smoldering volcanoes.

Most visitors to Guadeloupe see only the Grande-Terre half of the island, where the airport, the congested city of Pointe-à-Pitre, the long white beaches, and the resort hotels are located. But the most remarkable thing about Guadeloupe was to be found on the other side of the drawbridge, on Basse-Terre, and that was the 74,100-acre Parc Naturel, which is where we headed. Guadeloupe is large, 530 square miles, but even so, the Parc Naturel constitutes a significant set-aside of public lands. The island's population, however, was growing rapidly and spreading out from Pointe-à-Pitre into the lush foothills of Basse-Terre, and one could foresee a coming shift in priorities, when this enormous rain forest preserve would seem a luxury. An island can support only so many people, and then it begins to eat itself.

But if one wanted to get away from it all (and was not interested in mountain climbing in Basse-Terre), there were several tiny island dependencies off Guadeloupe that could be reached by ferry from Pointe-à-Pitre and the village of Trois-Rivières, where we found nearly empty beaches, fishing villages, a guesthouse or two, and better food than one might expect. Closest were the Îles des Saintes, eight islets settled by Breton and Norman fishermen and boatbuilders. A little farther on was Marie-Galante, which was larger and had a population of nearly eight thousand and a town, Grand-Bourg, with several seaside cafés and bistros and a handful of small hotels. It was a miniature, countrified version of St. Bart's. Services were minimal and it was difficult to get to, but this is where the most seasoned travelers to Guadeloupe holed up, especially those who, like us, were seeking privacy and calm.

By now, in my courtship of the woman who would become my fourth wife, I had managed to account for events leading up to my second marriage. After I endured six weekly sessions in the history and beliefs of Reform Judaism—Christine's failed attempt at reconciliation with her parents—on a cold, wet afternoon in late October, the nuptials were performed in a synagogue office in Concord, New Hampshire, by a liberal rabbi, with only my father and his second wife in attendance to witness the event. I was neither obliged formally to convert to Judaism nor, to my relief, was I required by Christine or the rabbi to be circumcised. I sensed a sadness in the rabbi as he went about his task of marrying us, as if he knew it wasn't going to take, and a similar sadness in my father, who, like me, had taken the afternoon off work. Even his wife had a long, sad face that day. I didn't know it then, but their marriage was cracked and about to collapse beneath the weight of my father's alcoholism and violence and his philandering ways. Eventually, he, too, would be married four times and divorced three.

It was October 29, 1962, one day after the happy ending of the Cuban Missile Crisis, when the world backed away from certain nuclear suicide. Everyone should have been filled with light and joy and relief and optimism. But in Concord, New Hampshire, in the rabbi's back office at Temple Beth Jacob, only Christine seemed happy that day.

Usually, betrayal in a marriage precedes abandonment, but in Christine's and my case, abandonment long preceded betrayal. And it was mutual. That is, after nearly fourteen years of marriage, after conceiving three daughters and raising them together, after my return to college in North Carolina on Christine's mother's kindly dime and desire to save her daughter from being married to an artistic plumber, after making a big Victorian farmhouse in New Hampshire the center of an elaborately staged, decade-long, ongoing gala that Christine called our social life and I called my woeful burden, after our rambunctious travels in the Caribbean and living in Jamaica, we both saw that we were alone. Each abandoned by the other. Probably we had been alone from the beginning and just hadn't known it—not until, by betraying each other, we tricked ourselves into separating and getting divorced from each other and then came to the slow realization that in our secret inner lives nothing had changed. Not since that autumn day in 1962 in the sad young rabbi's office, when we both came to be alone. In marrying each other we were, for different reasons, abandoning each other, both of us sentenced to unexpected solitude, she by virtue of the end of the long, ongoing drama of our romance, which until then had kept her such good company, and I by virtue of her relentless need to appropriate and objectify my subjective life, a direct consequence of her inability to perceive the autonomous existence, never mind the essence, of another person's inner reality. It was as if I had been born and raised to cultivate this strange form of solitude and had deliberately sought out the one woman who could accommodate it in this unique and peculiar way.

It was all too familiar to me, I said to Chase.

She said, So you courted, married, betrayed, and abandoned your mother again. And Darlene again. What about your third marriage? she asked. What about Becky?

She was different, I said. Or maybe she wasn't. I had a life-long habit of falling in love with women who needed me to solve their insoluble problems more than I needed them to solve mine. I needed to be seen as the fixer. Mr. Fixit.

And now? With me?

You're the first woman I've loved who doesn't need me more than I need you, I said.

Thanks . . . I *think,* she added and smiled.

Despite the pleasure we took from the calm and privacy of the Îsles des Saintes, our more persistent interests lay not with small, homogenous, figuratively gated communities like Marie Galante, but with the larger islands, where there were lively and unpredictable native populations, where the land could not be surveyed by a single glance from the air or a half-hour drive in a rented car, where classes, races, cultures, and languages mingled and strove against one another. Thus from Guadeloupe, moving on down the Windwards, we flew to Dominica, which was large, mountainous, crowded, and complex.

On our approach to Dominica's Canefield Airport, the pilot suddenly got waved off and told to land at Melville Hall Airport, way across the island to the north. The single Canefield Airport fire engine had thrown a rod, which meant the airfield had to shut down until it was fixed. From Melville Hall we were obliged to hitch a long ride back over the mountains down to Springfield Plantation, where we had reservations.

Not to worry, I reassured Chase. In the Caribbean, when things screw up, as they always do, they usually get better.

And indeed, our bumpy ride in a van loaded with shy but cheerful Dominicans on their way to the capital, Roseau, took us along the sparsely populated northeast coast, where the wind-driven surf crashed against volcanic rock, past the Carib Reserve, where the only surviving Carib Indians in the world resided, and through the wondrous Northern Forest Preserve, wild and impenetrable, the home of the endangered Sisserou and red-necked Amazon parrots, found now only here on Dominica. We wound through groves of ferns fifteen feet high, through rain forest climbing up to cloud forest and over the top, curling down the western side of the nearly five-thousand-foot-high cordillera, until finally, amazed, dazzled, we were let off at a roughly restored eighteenth-century country mansion called Springfield Plantation, within sight of the port of Roseau far below and the glittering sea.

Springfield Plantation, a rambling hillside guesthouse with several adjacent cut-stone outbuildings, was owned and operated by an American, John Archbold (Princeton '34), who had sailed from New Jersey to Dominica in June 1934 in his graduation present, a fifty-foot two-masted schooner, and had fallen in love with the island and never left. Eventually he became a cocoa, citrus, and coffee planter. And now a semiretired innkeeper.

Evidently, we were the only guests at Springfield Plantation. Archbold had observed from the registry that I was employed at his alma mater, and later, when he invited us to join him at his table, we accepted. Chase and I had already quietly noticed that the coffee-and-milk-colored waiters and waitresses, the cook, and even the several maids and gardeners seemed to have the same bright blue eyes as old John Archbold. Chase remembers his eyes as green; my memory says blue. We both remember the strong familial resemblance. A blunt-speaking, presently unmarried septuagenarian—I later learned that he'd been married four times (what is it about *four*?)—he was one of the last of his particular kind in the islands, the unapologetic neocolonial who believes he earned his place in the sun the old-fashioned way and not by dint of race and birthright and can't understand why others, especially the "natives," cannot or will not do the same. He was not the sort of man with whom one argued the virtues of democratic socialism or reparations. He was a curiosity, an antediluvian relic from another age whose dream of the Caribbean—suggested by the portraits of the British monarchs from Victoria to Elizabeth on the dining room walls—was the dream of empire, an empire in the tropics inhabited by people he had come to know and, in his perverse way, to love more passionately, perhaps, than he knew and loved the cold northern people and land he had left behind. Or, judging from the biracial appearance of his staff, maybe it was the slaveholder's dream. It's sometimes hard to distinguish between the two desires, empire and slavery, and the racial fantasies and projections they engender.

Our dinner with our garrulous, opinionated host lasted long into the night over port and Cuban cigars. Although one could call it interesting, it was a bit like dining with a public executioner who loves his job. Archbold's assumptions of racial and class solidarity with his two white American guests led him early on to share his low opinions of Dominicans, people like the caramel-colored waiter with half-closed blue eyes expertly refilling our wineglasses, and of Afro-Caribbean people and culture in general. I listened in silence and wondered if he would feel the same racial and class solidarity with the sunburnt, tattooed white boys on Nevis, or with the American real estate developers whose signs on Antigua pointed the way to Carlisle Bay and led nowhere, or with the throngs of white cruise-shippers with funny T-shirts at every port of call, or with the dudes at Bomba's Surf Shack on Tortola, or with the white women with clumped dreadlocks strolling the beach at Negril with their rent-a-Rastas—all those Caucasian appropriators of the Caribbean. Would Archbold see a connection to his own atavistic neocolonial racist fantasy? Or was it the nature of the fantasy itself—and the reason it so often ends up thwarted, doomed to disappointment, frustration, and bitterness—to recognize no other?

And what was our white people's Caribbean fantasy, Chase's and mine? Was ours an unexamined, equally privileged version of Archbold's, too?

I thought I could recognize Chase's. It was almost scientific—
tentative and exploratory and cautious and curious—with a modest, open-minded acceptance of my role in our mutual courtship
as guide and narrator of her journey. She would not have made
this voyage without my having initiated it. The Caribbean held no
romance for her, except by way of my attachment to it. My own
fantasy, however, was turbulent and moody, alternating between
painful personal memories and nostalgia. Subjective in all ways. For
me, this was both a compulsion and a willed return trip entered
upon with a certain ill-defined reluctance, and I was confused by
the conflicted emotions it evoked.

The third night at Springfield Plantation, our last before departing Dominica for Martinique, we met a new addition to our catalog
of versions of Archbold's vision of the Caribbean. We decided that
we'd had more than enough of the old man's cranky racist company
and would dine alone. We entered the dining room and saw at his
table a strange-looking white man in his late forties wearing a seer-
sucker suit, polka-dotted bow tie, white buck shoes, and owl-eyed
tortoiseshell eyeglasses. His straight flaxen hair was parted in the
middle, combed to matching partial bangs on his temples. Archbold
waved us over and introduced us by first and last names to the man,
whose name was Clive Cravensbrooke, which suited him almost
too perfectly. His accent was an American version of British English,
early *Masterpiece Theatre*. For a few seconds I wondered if he might be
a clever downtown Manhattan performance artist having us all on.

It turned out that he was an adjunct professor of the history of
landscape at Colgate University and was leading a group of students
on a winter-term field-study trip, his costs underwritten by the parents of his students, much as ours was underwritten by that slick
New York travel magazine. The students were all staying in a youth
hostel down in Roseau, he said and chuckled, while he bunked up
here at Springfield Plantation with his dear old friend John Archbold.

I did not mention my brief enrollment as a student at Colgate.
Probably before his time, anyway. A mildly unsettling coincidence

was all. It's hard to escape one's past, even this far south of it. When
we turned to leave for our corner table, Clive Cravensbrooke asked
Chase if her birth name was Penelope.

Startled, she said yes. Chase was actually her middle name,
she said.

Cravensbrooke said he knew her father long ago. And how
was her dear mother, Ann? Was she still living in Little Compton?
And was her father enjoying his retirement from Choate? Still living
alone in his cabin hideaway in the Adirondacks?

Cravensbrooke had at hand an astonishing amount of both
new and old detailed information about Chase's entire family, as
if for a lifetime he'd been compiling a dossier on them. Her uncle
Dave and his wife, was he still headmaster and teaching middle
school biology at Browne & Nichols? He even asked after her pater-
nal grandmother by name. Was she still living at 436 Saint Ronan
Street in New Haven?

Chase stammered, No, not now. My grandmother, she died
some years ago.

Cravensbrooke seemed momentarily saddened, but not surprised, as if he'd already known of the woman's death.

Chase asked him how he knew so much about her family.

He flashed the smile of a lizard, implying that actually he
knew much, much more than she suspected, and dodged her question by asking her another batch of questions, as if showing off. Is
your cousin Joe still making his beautiful furniture? And your sister
Eliza, is she happy living in Standfordville? Still divorced? Her oldest
must be about twelve by now.

Cravensbrooke would admit only that many long years ago,
too many to admit, he said with a wink, Chase's father had been his
Latin teacher at Choate. Which did not explain much. He remembered him, he said, with great affection.

Clearly, he was obsessed with Chase's entire family and had
been tracking their lives for decades. But why? Over the years she
had run into dozens of her father's ex-students, none of whom had

much interest in or information about her family members or about her father himself, for that matter. There was something sinister about this man, and something pathetic and creepy. Meeting him in Dominica in the dining room of an old plantation house two thousand miles south of New England made her feel she was being stalked. Without her knowledge, it had been going on for many years. Too many, as he said, to admit.

Months later, back in the Adirondacks, Chase and I recounted to her father our strange meeting in Dominica with the man named Clive Cravensbrooke. It took a while, but then he vaguely recalled a boy with that name, a student at Choate in the late 1950s. Chase's father had caught the boy cheating on his final exam in Latin class, he recalled. He'd seen to it that the boy was expelled from the school. What was he doing way down there? In the Caribbean?

He might as well have asked what we were doing way down there, in the Caribbean. Chase would have had a plausible answer, but I'm not sure I would have, or that it would have been any more legitimate than Archbold's or Cravensbrooke's or the tattooed boys of Nevis's or any of the others'. I was beginning to think that all of us, in our own weird ways, were vampires.

And that fellow who owned the hotel, Chase's father said. What was his name?

Archbold. John Archbold, I said.

Oh, him I actually know! Longtime member of the Choate board. Class of 1918, I read somewhere. Small world!

By the time we were ready to leave Dominica for Martinique, the airport fire engine had been repaired and we were able to fly out of Canefield Airport, a small strip on the coast near the town of Roseau where, happily, jumbo jets could not land. Where we were headed, however, they could land, and with them the disgorged hordes—package tours, the bane and, as some persist in thinking, the salvation of tourism in the Caribbean.

After landing, we drove north from Martinique's Pointe du Bout and the south coast, where most of the larger, better-known hotels and topless beaches were located. We skipped a visit to the Musée de la Pagerie, birthplace of Napoleon's Empress Josephine, for lunch at a waterfront café in bustling, cosmopolitan Fort-de-France. Then it was up the scenic coast to Le Carbet, where Gauguin had briefly lived and painted. At the Musée Volcanologique in the town of St-Pierre, we turned inland and uphill, and once again we were in a mountainous rain forest, the Parc Naturel Régional, with deep gorges, waterfalls, and, in the distant mist, the green cone of Mount Pelée, which had erupted as recently as 1902, destroying St-Pierre and killing thirty thousand people. Thus the Musée Volcanologique.

By late afternoon we had reached the northern tip of the island, a rolling coastal plain covered with banana trees that slowly rose to a long wooded ridge. We checked in at the Leyritz Plantation Hotel, which, instead of the restored sugar plantation described in the guidebooks, was a half-renovated ruin with a few new cabanas and a low-roofed kitchen, dining room, bar, and gift shop freshly constructed on top of and inside the shells of the original cut-stone plantation outbuildings.

On registering, we learned that the main building, called the Great House, was not yet ready to admit guests. Though open for business, it was still a resort-in-progress. We were offered a room in the Workers' Quarters instead, a cluster of new thatch-and-bamboo bungalows built on the foundations of the long-gone slave huts down by the Distillery, which, according to the brochure handed out at the desk, would eventually function as an educational exhibit to demonstrate the entire process of turning sugarcane into rum.

Not sure we could sleep peacefully on top of the graves of the slave huts, we turned down the Workers' Quarters and sprang instead for one of the more expensive suites carved out of the original main kitchen, called, naturally, the Kitchen, a low, narrow stone building tied to the half-restored Great House on the hill by an open passageway and terrace. With a separate structure for each domestic function—cooking, sleeping, dining, entertaining, maintenance, and so on—all of them linked to the main building with passageways and terraces and porches, the layout reminded us of the nineteenth-century great camps of the Adirondacks. Except for that sticky business about the African slaves.

The hotel grounds were spacious and inviting: crisscrossed by meandering walkways that passed through elaborate, overgrown, untended flower gardens along old crumbling walls and moss-covered brick terraces and fallen columns and dry fountains with soaring royal palms lining the long, curved drive. We dined in the Sugar Mill below, and afterward, before retiring to our suite in the Kitchen, we walked slowly back up the hill. On our way we passed through an unlocked side entrance of the Great House and wandered along the ground-level halls and crossed the parlors of the empty, unfurnished Georgian building and out to the columned veranda in front and stood there and took in the silver-green fields and the blackened sea beyond. As darkness came on, a full moon rose out of the sea.

Then suddenly the place went all eerie on us. Most of the restored plantation houses we'd visited so far had felt and looked like sets from the movie versions of *Captain Blood* or *Wide Sargasso Sea* or a Caribbean ride at Disney World, as harmless and unthreatening as kitsch. Soon Leyritz Plantation would be another romanticizing stage set, a slavery-days Potemkin village. But for now, tonight, up here on the hill by the Great House and Kitchen overlooking the glistening fields below, it was the real thing. The buildings seemed to have been only recently abandoned by the planter and his extended family, their slaves, like the livestock, left to fend for themselves in the forested hills above the fields or else swiftly captured and reenslaved by the absent planter's white neighbors.

We felt utterly alone in this ghostly, ghastly ruin. It was late in the season, and there was only a small, bare-bones staff. The other paying guests all seemed to have been housed someplace far from us. Probably down in the Workers' Quarters, I muttered. Except for the soft wind, it was silent. Silver moonlight carved sharp blue shadows on the lawns. I left Chase seated on a stone bench on the terrace outside the Kitchen facing the fields and the glittering sea and the pale moon and went to our bedroom and retrieved two glasses and the unopened bottle of Trois Rivières *rhum agricole* I'd purchased earlier in Fort-de-France.

I hadn't noticed, or perhaps had merely not admitted it to myself, but over the weeks I had begun drinking a bit too heavily in the evenings, shot by shot, usually starting before dinner at the bar with rum and a slice of lime and, when available, ice, and then a bottle of wine at dinner, continuing afterward with a different rum, neat, claiming that I was only sampling the local rums of all the different islands, as if I were a connoisseur or training to become one.

I sat beside Chase on the stone bench and poured us each a few inches of the clear liquid and thoughtfully sipped the Trois Rivières and pronounced it satisfactory. Chase left her glass untouched while I drank. She was growing concerned about my drinking and had mentioned it once or twice several islands back, offhandedly, as if in passing. But by now my drinking to excess was evident—although the reason for it was not—and undeniable, even by me.

That's when we started to hear them. Voices—faint voices in the wind. At first we thought that's all it was, the wind. And maybe it *was* only the wind, the soft Caribbean breeze unfurling from the sea. But they were human voices we thought we heard: we both definitely were hearing them—men and women and children in the distance, laughing, singing, then weeping close by, and now moaning—just behind us, right in front, on both sides of the terrace, coming from beyond the flower gardens where the dark shadow of the Great House filled the space between the two buildings.

We sat there for a while, silent and grieving, until gradually the voices, or the wind, subsided and eventually all was still. Chase shook herself free of the dream or vision or fantasy, whatever it was, and stood and said she was going to bed. I told her I was too sad to sleep and needed to sit here awhile longer alone. She seemed to understand, assuming that my sadness was due to the place, the ruins of the plantation and its ghosts, and gave me a hug and a delicate kiss and went inside.

I had not been this sad since leaving Jamaica ten years earlier, after Christine and our three daughters had gone back to the States a month ahead of me. The closer Chase and I got to Jamaica, where our courtship tour through the Caribbean was scheduled to end, the sharper and darker were my memories of that time and place. Christine's and my marriage had been in tatters the entire year, held together solely by our shared love of our children. In order to keep from quarreling, she and I had reached a point of barely speaking to each other, except to negotiate childcare and finances. We had decided that she and the girls should go back home for school a month early without me, while I finished my research on the Maroons, descendants of eighteenth-century runaway slaves living in the isolated village of Accompong in the nearly inaccessible hills of what was called Cockpit Country. The Maroons and Accompong and a white American academic researching their history were central to my novel, which eventually became *The Book of Jamaica*. I had convinced myself that I could complete my research only by residing for a month alone in Accompong in a one-room cabin loaned to me by a Maroon friend, a Rastafarian ganja grower who was accompanying Christine and the girls on their return to the States. He was a man I had come to trust and in many ways to admire. He hoped to find some kind of work in our New Hampshire neighborhood as a handyman, for he was indeed handy, and in a few months earn enough cash under the table from me and Christine and our friends and neighbors to support his family back in Accompong for a year or more. At least that is how he and Christine described the arrangement when it was first proposed.

Guilt mingled with anger creates sadness—at least for me it does. And unexpectedly the guilt and anger invoked by the ghosts of Leyritz Plantation, by the vivid tangibility of the plantation's history from slavery days to late-twentieth-century tourism, had somehow smeared over, or perhaps by emotional association had called back the guilt and anger I had felt a decade earlier in Jamaica, when my marriage to Christine was falling apart. Add to that the guilt that was still pummeling me for having left my third wife, Becky, for Chase the year before, mingled in turn with the anger I was directing against myself for having married Becky in the first place, and you have a man falling, or pushed, down a well of sadness. A man pouring himself another three fingers of Trois Rivières, shortly followed by yet another. Until finally, hours later, his fiancée appears at his side and helps him stand and walks him to their bedroom, where he falls into the sleep of the insensibly drunk.

The rest of our stay on Martinique, once we departed from Leyritz Plantation, turned surprisingly sunny and cheerful. In our yellow rented Toyota we wandered down along the many bays and out onto the narrow peninsulas of the east coast. We visited the Saint James rum distillery, naturally, and took the tour, lightly sampled the wares, of course, and became learned in the various gradations of rum. We ate well just about everywhere on Martinique. As was true on all the French islands, the breads were crisply crusted and chewy Parisian-style baguettes and country farm loaves. We almost always ordered the house special, no matter what it was called, because it usually turned out to be the day's catch and fresh local vegetables, prepared creole style, with plenty of hot peppers and onions. Most of the off-islanders we met were chic French vacationers, who, instead of driving their cars or taking a train to the Mediterranean, were increasingly flying here and to Guadeloupe, and we noticed an unusual amount of condominium and second-home construction, especially along the northeast coast. The island had Continental flair and energy—but it also had traffic congestion, the beginnings of air and water pollution, and, in the capital city of Fort-de-France, where class divisions were most noticeable, racial tension.

The next island on our itinerary, St. Lucia, is Martinique's nearest neighbor to the south, and although both islands are relatively large and volcanic, and have rain forests, beaches, and jagged coasts, the two could not be more unlike. The Caribbean's turbulent history, in which all the islands were pawns in wars fought thousands of miles away on the European and North American continents, accounts for much of their similarity today, but also their surprising diversity. In order, citizens of Spain, Great Britain, France, the Netherlands, and Denmark met here and promptly went to work exterminating the Taino and Arawak and Carib natives. Then they enslaved Africans to work the plantations and, after ending the slave trade, imported East Indians to till the fields. For four centuries, the Europeans stole and swapped and sold the islands to one another, until finally in the twentieth century the colonies became too expensive to rule and too impoverished to fight over, and one by one the islands, in particular those controlled by Britain, were allowed to become deeply indebted, independent micronations or, like the Dutch and French islands, distant dependencies more or less on the dole from their mother countries.

After sophisticated Martinique, St. Lucia seemed sleepy and backward. With 150,000 people, most of them of African descent, it was one of those independent British micronations abandoned by, and in perpetual debt to, its master. Nearly half the total population resided in and around the deepwater port of Castries. Settled originally by the French, St. Lucia wasn't taken over by the British until 1814, fairly late, which accounts for the mostly French place names, the patois spoken by the natives (although English is the official language), and the very good creole cuisine. In the late 1980s, when we came ashore, St. Lucia was still an agricultural island, with bananas the main cash crop, but tourism was coming up fast, especially along the northwest coast.

Although the island, for its size, felt crowded, the interior mountains were still inaccessible, except to the most intrepid of hikers and the last 150 jacquots on earth, a rare green Amazon parrot. In a last-ditch effort to save it from extinction, the jacquot had recently been designated St. Lucia's national bird. Too little, probably too late—like so much of Caribbean wildlife. The beaches and new resorts above Castries were no better or worse than those on most of the islands, so it was here, below the town of Soufière, in the southwest corner of the island, that one would lay over, especially if one was eager to see the magnificent Pitons, two half-mile-high volcanic peaks that rise abruptly, dramatically, from the sea; or if one intended to visit the Sulfur Springs at Diamond Baths or climb the dormant volcano, named, like the volcanoes on Montserrat and Guadeloupe, La Soufrière.

All of which we did—viewed the Pitons, bathed in the Sulfur Springs, climbed La Soufrière.

My walking stride had been reduced to a head-down trudge, and my drinking was getting worse by the day—or rather, by the night. Chase's concern was now serious, although she did not reveal this to me until many years later, when my drinking no longer worried her or me. As I trudged from island to island, always circling in on Jamaica, I remember thinking, So this is what depression feels like.

It was no longer just the final few years of my marriage to Christine and the year in Jamaica that were beating me down. By now I was being tumbled by breaking waves of memories of Becky, my third wife, memories of the pleasures of a low-intensity love affair with her, such a relief after those turbulent, sexually fraught years with Christine and our explosive divorce, and then memories of marrying Becky and living with her for five years in New York City, and memories of going off alone for a semester as writer-in-residence at the University of Alabama and meeting Chase there, and memories of having to return to Becky at semester's end and having to choose whether to tell her that I had fallen in love with another woman, or lie and begin conducting a clandestine love affair, which would have permanently contaminated my love for that other woman, or say a permanent good-bye to that other woman, who, it was clear to me, would be the love of my life for the rest of my life.

I told Becky that I had fallen in love with another woman.

There are probably no more painful words for a husband to say or a wife to hear, especially a wife who loves her husband more than he loves her. Especially when the man in fact loves the woman, yes, he does—just not as much as she loves him. Until I chose to say the words to Becky, I had not been obliged to say them to anyone. When I was twenty-one and my marriage to Darlene foundered and sank, there was no one who had displaced her in my heart. And after fourteen stormy years of melodrama, growing incompatibility, betrayal, frustration, and rage, when my marriage to Christine finally shattered, as if tossed by the storm against the cliffs of our warring self-interests—everyone overboard, fathers and mothers first—there was no one waiting in a nearby lifeboat with open arms and heart for either of us. At the end of my first and second marriages I was not already in love with another woman.

I said to Chase, Perhaps with Becky I simply fell out of love instead and then met you in Tuscaloosa.

No, I'd remember that and anyhow would not have left any of the three women for that alone. Especially Darlene.

Okay, so maybe I never loved Darlene or Christine or Becky in the first place, I said to Chase.

No, definitely not true. Or, Reader, I'd not have married them.

Possibly I did not love them enough, I told her.

Not that, either. I loved Darlene and Christine and Becky, too, more than most men love their wives.

Or maybe—and this gets closer to the truth—I had finally

realized that I could never make any of them happy. Except by my
absence.

Though I had no words or understanding for it then, with great
reluctance I had concluded that I simply could not meet my first and
second and third wives' seemingly insatiable needs—needs that I'd
been trained since childhood to find irresistibly seductive. For they
had been put to me as desires that only I could satisfy. Problems
that only I could solve. Conflicts that only I could resolve. Needs,
problems, conflicts that in the end no man, no other human being,
could satisfy, solve, resolve.

Just as I was incapable of making Darlene or Christine or
Becky happy, I had been unable, boy and man, to make my mother,
the primal wife, happy, either. No one on the planet, boy or man,
could satisfy her bottomless, hydra-headed hunger for attention and
control. It was a hunger so ravenous and impossible to sate as to
be an essentially metaphysical contradiction. None of us was aware
of it at the time or had access to words for it—not my mother, not
Darlene, not Christine, not Becky, and certainly not I. But theirs
was not merely a psychological or emotional disorder, a neurosis
or minor mental illness that could be treated with psychotherapy
and pharmaceuticals and kindness. Or by the love of a good man.
Through no fault of their own and, if I may say, no fault of mine,
either, I was doomed, boy and man, to fail to satisfy their simple
unchecked hunger for universal centrality. As a consequence they
grew angry. They wailed and gnashed their teeth and beat their
breasts and clawed at their tear-soaked cheeks. Their grief and rage
were caused by the irreducible nature of human reality. It was as
if I were humanity's sole male representative on earth, and not
merely a son or a husband, and for their satisfaction those needs
were directed at me alone. Each woman was manacled to a bottomless, contradictory, impossible need to exist as both the center of the
known universe and its encompassing entirety, too.

At sixteen, with Dario Morelli in his dad's Olds 88, I was
running from my mother's frustration and rage over my failure

to resolve that contradiction for her; and again at eighteen, when I insulted the pleasure and pride she took from my scholarship at Colgate, it was the same set of causes and effects that sent me running. At twenty, when I abandoned Darlene and Leona, and at thirty-seven, when I violently disassembled the fourteen-year-long marriage and household I had shared with Christine, and at forty-seven, when I left Becky for Chase, it was the same old, by now all-too-familiar flight from grief and rage generated in the women I loved by my inability to resolve the fundamental contradiction of their needing to be both the center of the universe and the universe itself, and their inability to acknowledge any metaphysical difference between the two. It was as if the solar system were simultaneously Ptolemaic and heliocentric, and the sun revolved around the earth and the earth revolved around the sun, too.

When, four years after my divorce from Christine, I settled into a life in New York City with Becky, I thought it would be entirely different. And, indeed, in the beginning it mostly was. It seemed clear that Becky was no narcissist, and at first she made no demands on me that I couldn't meet. Nor was she angry at me for failing to make her both the center of the universe and its surround as well. Not at first. She was a calm, some might say placid, woman ten years younger than I, previously unmarried and childless. She was originally from Fort Worth, Texas. Slim and pretty and tough in the benign, adaptable way of a nineteenth-century American pioneer woman, she was blond and green-eyed and very pale-skinned, possibly the whitest woman I have ever known. With a curious mixture of embarrassment and pride, she sometimes said of herself, I'm like white on rice. She was. She'd struck out early for a life different from her parents'—her father was an electronics engineer and her mother a retired schoolteacher—and had gone east for a life more glamorous and artistic and risky than theirs. She'd taken a graduate degree in creative writing and ended up a few years later running a national writers' organization based in Norfolk, Virginia.

Then—at an unfortunate time for both of us, as it turned out—

I sat on one of the panels at the annual meeting of her organization, and we met and quickly slept together. It should have ended there, probably. I was recently divorced from Christine and still trembling from it, struggling to withdraw my forces from the field of battle, but obliged nonetheless to continue fighting a rearguard action over childcare, money, and the true narrative of our long marriage and its dissolution. Becky had endured some childhood traumas—her parents' divorce, her father's mental illness and hospitalization— and had recovered from a couple of serious adulthood shocks to her system: the suicide of a lover, an assault by a home invader. But she spoke of these events with cool detachment, almost as if they had happened to someone else.

She seemed to me more stoical than merely repressed. Or depressed. She was calm and rational, undramatic and unaffected, and flexible in all ways—the apparent opposite of my ex-wife Christine. And she seemed to be very independent. She was lonely and terminally bored and frustrated by her job. As it happened, I was about to quit my teaching job in New Hampshire for a position to be split between Columbia and Princeton and base myself in New York City, and Becky wanted to get out of Norfolk. She had abandoned her desire to become a fiction writer, but she was well trained and understood fiction writing from the inside out. Maybe she'd try to become an editor in a big New York publishing house.

The novelist Nelson Algren used to warn younger men never to sleep with a woman whose troubles are worse than their own. Which applies as much (or as little) to the men women choose to sleep with, too. Algren was a mentor for me, and when I was in my early twenties he was a friend, and I probably should have listened more closely to him and remembered his advice when, in my early forties, I started sleeping with Becky and gradually learned that her troubles were worse than mine. Her ability to distance herself from them, however, and, with a wry, self-deprecating smile and shrug, file them under *Dysfunctional Family* and *Long Ago* (her childhood and adolescence) and *Far Away* (Fort Worth, Texas; Fayetteville, Arkansas; Norfolk, Virginia), gave me license to sleep with her and still credit myself with having followed Algren's advice. And because that went well, the sex, and she seemed to get along easily with my four daughters, and gave evidence of wanting to be married to me; and because it appeared that she needed me in order to be made happy; and because it looked as if finally a good woman's happiness could actually be achieved through marriage to me—yes, Reader, once again, I married her.

From St. Lucia, the next logical stop was a long eastward hop to Barbados. The transition was sharp, however, and not pleasant. More than any island Chase and I had visited so far, Barbados had successfully transformed itself into a full-blown resort. As Gertrude Stein reportedly said of Oakland, there was no there there. Except perhaps on the northeast coast, where the Atlantic winds constantly blew and the surf was too rough for swimmers. It was where the Bajans themselves went on vacation. Farley Hill National Park, in the north-central region, and the Andromeda Garden, over near the fishing village of Bathsheba, provided some refuge for the harried traveler, although both places attracted picture-snappers hauled out from the hotels in huge air-conditioned buses.

The whole of Bridgetown and the length of the west coast, where the famous white beaches were located, seemed to have been given over entirely to extracting money from foreigners. Bridgetown's streets were narrow and congested and littered and loud. Hotels lined the beaches hip to hip, and even the sea was crowded—paddleboats, rubber rafts, pirate ships, and hundreds of loudly buzzing Jet Skis, like snowmobiles on water, driven early to late by young Bajan men and boys in wild loops and circles in and around the bathers. Vendors selling trinkets, snow cones, drugs, or sex roved the beaches. Whatever you want, mister, we got it.

We fought off the throng of hustlers and took the first LIAT flight to St. Vincent, where we booked a room at the Grand View

Beach Hotel, fifteen minutes from the E. T. Joshua Airport. True to its name, the hotel was perched on a rocky cliff with a beach below and a grand view—of a Texaco oil tanker pumping its black cargo into storage tanks on the shore just beyond the white sandy beach.

The Grand View Beach Hotel was an old-time English seaside inn—clean, modestly appointed, with the hush of a hospital and a courteous, reticent staff and terrible food. But we welcomed the change. On Barbados it had been impossible to be a traveler; one was forced to be a tourist. On St. Vincent it was easy to be a traveler, but not impossible to be a tourist. The island still possessed its virtue, but, uncertain of its true value, was only a shy flirt. There was one ambitious, large-scale resort hotel called Young Island and several smaller operations trying to expand, but little else in the way of typical tourist accommodations or diversions. Serious change seemed unlikely.

St. Vincent is small, eleven by eighteen miles. With the forty Grenadines and barely 120,000 citizens, it is one of those independent British Commonwealth micronations. Like Dominica, it rises abruptly from the sea to steep lush mountains, with few beaches. It, too, possesses an active volcano named La Soufrière, which, like Martinique's Mount Pelée, last erupted violently in 1902, killing sixteen hundred people. But now St. Vincent was essentially a quiet, peaceful fishing and agricultural island, exporting coconuts, bananas, and spices by boat from its excellent deepwater port at the capital, Kingstown.

One day we boarded one of those boats, a freighter heading down the Grenadines carrying rum, ax handles, cinder blocks, buckets, push brooms, crates of Glow-Spread margarine, Dole sliced pineapples, and a half-dozen passengers to Bequia. Probably the best way to cruise the Grenadines is by charter sailboat, a mode of transportation that I myself, a nonsailor and an incipient claustrophobe, shirked. I preferred to loaf in the sun on the top deck of an old, fat, dripping freighter chugging its way south, surrounded by talkative Small Islanders wearing their good clothes and new shoes and shouldering boom boxes for the trip home from St. Vincent, the Big Island.

Bequia and the other Grenadines are a sailor's dream of the Caribbean—if not mine—come true. It's all sea and sun and sky; almost no people, almost no land. Bequia is an old boatbuilding and whaling center with a small protected harbor and extensive repair facilities for yachts in Port Elizabeth, the one settlement on the island. In recent years it had become a magnet for scuba divers. There were a few private vacation homes in the hills surrounding the harbor and several laid-back inns and small hotels—this on a strictly barefoot island, seven square miles in area, with forty-five hundred residents. Beyond Bequia, the Grenadines only got smaller, less populated, and casual to the point of seminaked somnolence. Port Elizabeth was about as far as you could go in the group and still find a professionally cooked dinner and fresh coffee and unspoiled wine. From here on, unless you planned to drop in on Princess Margaret or Mick Jagger on Mustique or check into the resort islands of Palm Island or Petit St. Vincent, it was roasted breadfruit, catch of the day, and warm Heineken. Which was fine by us.

On our second day on Bequia, while waiting to catch the freighter back to St. Vincent and our flight from there to Grenada, over lunch at a dockside café Chase brought me back to my account of the decline and fall of my marriage to Becky. It was an unstated clause in Chase's and my courtship contract, one of my tacitly agreed-upon obligations, that before she and I married, I would explain the end of the three marriages that preceded ours—as if I were applying for a job and needed to explain why I hadn't lasted in my three previous places of employment. She already knew, perhaps too well, having participated in it herself, the story of the fall of my third marriage following my return to New York from Tuscaloosa. But not the story and causes of its decline, which had presumably preceded and precipitated the fall.

Chase had not set out to seduce me in Tuscaloosa, nor I her; in fact, we had both gone to great lengths to avoid falling in love with each other that winter and spring. We were temporary English department colleagues who played tennis once or twice a week and went out to dinner a few times and gradually became "just friends" and surely could have left it at that. Sex was not yet a tie that bound. So there must have been something rotten in Denmark to start with, or in New York City, where Becky and I had been living together as husband and wife since 1982.

The truth is, there was nothing about my marriage to Becky that deserved complaint. It was calm and mutually satisfying and supportive. Many of our friends found it enviable. But the force that holds a couple together is like the force of gravity, spinning the pair in orbit around each other through decades of having and holding from the first day forward, for better, for worse, for richer, for poorer, in sickness and in health, loving and cherishing till death them do part. But sometimes the gravitational attraction between two bodies is sufficiently weakened by a difference in mass or momentum, or both, so that the faster-moving of the two bodies breaks free and sails off into outer space alone, or the smaller of the two crashes like an asteroid into the surface of the larger. Perhaps because my love for Becky depended on her need for me, my love contained less measurable mass than her need and greater momentum. Escape velocity was inescapable. And from the day our separate orbital planes first crossed, I knew it. And for the rest of my life I will regret it—not the difference in the force and momentum of Becky's and my love for each other, but that I recognized it at the time and took the measure of those differences at the beginning, yet nonetheless behaved as if I had no idea such differences even existed. There should be a corollary to Nelson Algren's advice to young men: Never marry someone who needs you more than you need her. Or him. You'll cause her, or him, more troubles than your own.

By this time in our journey—Chase and I were still on Bequia in the Grenadines—I could see clearly that my courtship narrative and this peripatetic voyage through the archipelago ran parallel to each other in ways both exculpatory and condemning, the one reflecting, enabling, and explicating the other. A memoir is like a travel book: whether short or long, it's a radical reduction of remembered reality and is structured as much by what it leaves out as what it puts in. Just as in my life I must seem here, boy and man, to have only briefly, if serially, touched down in love and marriage, managing throughout to evade both permanent commitment and trivial pursuit, to the reader of this account of my cruise with Chase through the Antilles I must seem less than a travel guide to the islands and more than a tourist. All true, and thus the mutually reinforcing parallelism of its structure—more like a double helix than a string of chronologically ordered narrative beads. And thus, at Bequia, I temporarily abandoned my account of the demise and fall of my marriage to Becky, and we returned to St. Vincent, the Big Island, and moved on from there to Grenada.

One could not approach the Point Salines International Airport on Grenada in 1988 without imagining how the island must have appeared from the air to the American invasion forces spearheading Operation Urgent Fury in October 1983. Grenada is a glittering green jewel, only twelve miles wide and twenty-one long, about the size of St. Vincent, with not as many people, mountainous in the center and heavily cultivated along the coastal plain with cinnamon and cloves and ginger, the spices for which it was once so famous. There is a small horseshoe-shaped harbor and one town, St. George's, the capital, a picturesque cluster of old brick buildings spreading from the waterfront up the sides of several steep hills. Grenada is a small place, as Jamaica Kincaid said of Antigua, and pretty, and invading it hardly seemed worth the trouble—never mind the American, Grenadian, and Cuban lives it cost. When our de Havilland Twin Otter DHC-6 taxied up to the large glass-fronted terminal, we checked out the size and length of the runway, built by the Cubans whose presence on Grenada had stoked the Americans' urgent fury. It made our plane look like a toy. Perfect for

Reagan's locked-and-loaded U.S. Air Force C-141s and C-130s back in 1983, however. And now a perfect fit for the American Airlines Boeing 747 warming its engines to carry three hundred American tourists back to New York.

There was a great deal of building going on in Grenada, hotels, mostly, and what appeared to be private villas, especially along Grand Anse Bay, where the best beaches on the island were located. This was not yet Barbados or St. Thomas, but you couldn't say they weren't trying. We rented a car and in a day circled the whole island, passing through and stopping briefly at a half-dozen crossroad settlements. In a sense, most Caribbean country villages look alike—unpainted one-room houses, dirt yards, a rum shop with six or eight bored adolescent males standing around outside, a bunkerlike cinder-block schoolhouse in the middle of a bare field, a crumbling nineteenth-century cut-stone church. Caribbean country villages were almost all poor, but some, like these, seemed poorer than others.

One did not need to take this drive, of course. One could enjoy the beautiful waters and sands of Grand Anse instead, as we frequently did. There were a number of fine hotels bellied up to the beach, including the elaborately renovated Ramada Renaissance, which had replaced the old Holiday Inn, used in 1983 as a barracks for the occupying U.S. troops. One might avail oneself of some truly fine West Indian food at Mamma's, served out of Mamma's own home near St. George's—around $30 for two hungry people, ten or more courses, which may include tattou (armadillo), manicou (possum), lambi (conch), flying-fish fritters, rice and beans cooked in coconut milk, and, when available, roasted green monkey.

Disinclined to hang around St. George's waiting for the availability of roasted green monkey, we packed our bags and moved south to Tobago, a source of Robinson Crusoe's story—Defoe's fictionalized version. In 1988 Tobago was still laid-back and sparsely populated, with lots of well-fed, nearly feral goats roaming the hills, and if today the relationship between Crusoe and Friday seems some-what more equitable, it's only because Crusoe eventually hitched a ride home to England and Friday's descendants managed to sue successfully for the deed to the island.

Going to Tobago was like returning to St. Vincent, except that Tobago, with Trinidad hulking next door, was the Small Island. And a beautiful island it was, too. Like all the volcanic Antilles, it was mountainous in the middle, with fertile coastal plains, plentiful rivers and streams, numerous bays and small harbors, and, on the leeward side, several brown sand beaches. Tobago was and still is where Trinidadians go to get away from the madding crowds and pollution of Port of Spain and the industrialized west coast. There were some new, self-contained resort hotels—notably Mount Irvine Bay, Kariwak Village, and Arnos Vale—with more under construc-tion, suggesting that in a few years Tobago would go the way of many of its sister islands. But without the white sandy beaches so mysteriously loved by the white foreigners, the limits to tourism here, as on St. Vincent and Dominica, were probably built-in.

By now, having opened the chapter on my third marriage, I was traveling beneath the full shadow of my separation and divorce from Becky, and it almost didn't matter where I was, white beach or brown or black, Big Island or Small, resort hotel or B-and-B. I was like Joe Btfsplk, Al Capp's depressed comic book character with the gray rain cloud permanently hovering above his head. I had tried to avoid the subject, but once opened, it was hard to close. Chase wanted to know, she deserved to know, why I had been so inclined to fall in love with her, even though at the time I was happily mar-ried to Becky.

I knew the answer but didn't like it much. One marries for love, and sometimes one divorces for a greater love, as I did, and one is punished for it with a burden of guilt, which one knows is far easier to bear than the pain and humiliation borne by the wife or husband who was betrayed and abandoned. Knowledge of that difference only adds yet another layer of guilt. The wife I left behind may someday forgive me for having fallen in love with another woman, and that will help me forgive myself and alleviate the weight of the guilt I carry to this day, almost thirty years later. But she can never know and therefore can never forgive me for the crime at the heart of the crime.

Darlene and Christine eventually forgave me for giving up the attempt to make them happy. They both knew by the end that it was hopeless and that I had loved them at least as much as they had loved me and possibly more. Darlene, when she grew older and wiser, forgave me for being too young to marry and too naive and neurotic and egotistical and without any useful self-knowledge. She would find another man who was none of those things. Christine forgave me for being angry and self-protective and afraid of being controlled by her several forms of power. She, too, found another man with none of those limitations and flaws. And possibly, by now, after three decades apart, Becky has forgiven me for falling in love with Chase, and I hope that she, too, has found a man who resembles me not at all and is currently growing old with her.

For most North American and European visitors to Tobago, on their flight in or home, Trinidad's Port-of-Spain is just an urban airport stop twenty minutes away, where they switch between an Airbus 380 with five hundred seats from the States and a Twin Otter DHC-6 with nineteen based in Tobago. But in our journey down the Antilles, Chase and I had booked for Carnival, Trinidad's annual homage to the erotic-sublime. Departing from Tobago, we joined a mob of fellow celebrants headed for Port-of-Spain and made the quick flight over and checked into the Hilton, which, like the entire city, was already packed with revelers from all nations.

Officially, Carnival is celebrated on the two days preceding Ash Wednesday, when Lent begins. It has pre-Christian European roots in the annual cycle of death and rebirth and in Dionysian rites from the Mediterranean, as well as more recent, colonial-era origins in the slaves' attempt to preserve African religious, artistic, and social forms within a society intent on suppressing them. Carnival in Port-of-Spain, as in New Orleans, Rio, and elsewhere in the Afro-Latin world, is public and communal, with little distinction made between performers and audience. There's no fourth wall, and it is deliberately ecstatic—which is to say, Carnival is one hell of a party.

For me the timing was perfect: I sorely needed a party. For Chase it was different. Her depression, which saps her of energy and laughter, is clinical; mine was purely situational, the depression of a narrator telling a story about a man a lot like himself that causes him pain and makes him feel guilty all over again for long-ago crimes. So while Chase only reluctantly went along with the spirit of Carnival, I hit the streets with alacrity and relief.

For these few days, social, racial, and even sexual differences are set aside. You can wander the packed streets of Port-of-Spain in a business suit, a costume made of green bananas and tinfoil, or stark naked, and people smile affectionately at you, as if your very ⸰humanity delights them. There were parades and all-night and all-day jump-up performances of calypso and soca bands throughout the city, but especially in the huge central park, Queen's Park Savannah, where there were comfortable viewing stands for those who didn't wish to march along with the bands.

The bands themselves were enormous, with five hundred to five thousand members, each crew more or less organized and costumed on a theme and led by a mass of musicians, usually on steel or brass, or by a deejay and a flatbed truckload of two-thousand-watt boom-box speakers playing at ear-shattering volume the three or four top entries in the song competition. The trophy for that year's top band was awarded to Hero-myth, although I myself preferred the costumes of Tush in the Bush and the concept behind Alkebulan, Reflection of a Sailor's Vision, which I deconstructed for

Chase as a dramatization of the European encounter with Mexico. I agreed with the judges' choice for Carnival queen, Nicole Cobham, a stunning beauty costumed as a black Pallas Athena, Queen of Spades, but my choice for king was second-place winner Roderick Snell, who, as Hammurabi, the Star Gazer, wore only a silver cape and thong and marched inside an enormous slow-turning silver gyroscope like a hamster in a laboratory treadmill. The winning song, soon after sung all over the United States, Canada, and England, was the soca "Free Up" by Tambu, fought to the wire by Crazy's "Nanny Wine."

One normally could not care less about such things, but at Carnival, for a few days, one cared passionately. And afterward one somehow felt better for it—one felt freed of one's Yankee seriousness, at least for a while. How can one return to being so somber and self-important and self-analytical and guilty when one has just spent three days dancing ridiculously through the streets with a million or more of his fellow human beings?

On Ash Wednesday, with shocking ease, everything returned to normal. The city was cleaned up, people, most of them nursing colossal hangovers, went back to work, and the Hilton emptied out. We, too, took our leave, heading for Curaçao, Aruba, and Bonaire, the cluster of Dutch islands located way to the west, a few miles off the coast of Venezuela.

As I write this, I've recently turned seventy-five, and while I'm not close enough to death's shore yet to see the waves break, I hear them smack the sand. The mountains in the background loom large and dark. Like a lifelong sailor, I find myself wondering, now that the end of my final voyage is in earshot and sight, how and why I ended up where I have ended up. How did I wash ashore here, instead of somewhere else? It wasn't intentional, part of a carefully charted plan. And it's not as though I've been on some decades-long Odyssey and am finally returning to my home in Ithaca, to my old arthritic dog, my grown son and beleaguered wife, looking for a land-locked spot to plant an oar.

My wife Chase's given first name is in fact Penelope, as Clive Cravensbrooke knew, but despite even that connection, the strained Homeric analogy breaks down. Nowadays I have two homes, neither of them in Ithaca, and am reluctant to call either of them home. Nor are they merely safe harbors or stops on the way to someplace else. While I can easily answer the questions *What's your hometown?* (born in Watertown, Massachusetts, raised in New Hampshire small towns and suburban Boston) and *Where do you live?* (Miami, Florida, and the Adirondack mountain village of Keene, New York), when I'm asked, *Where is your home?* I have no answer. Miami and Keene are not my homes. Simply, they are where I ended up; they are where in my mid-seventies I seem to have washed ashore. One place is located almost as far south in the United States of America as I can get, and the other as far north. Both lie at the edge of wilderness, the Everglades in the first case and the Adirondack Mountains in the second.

That's not a coincidence, I suppose, but it's not intentional, either.

Since I was eighteen years old, as if caught by an ocean current, I've been drifting south in the direction of Miami, pulled toward the Gulf of Mexico and the Caribbean by a New England Protestant white boy's eroticized fantasy of semitropical history and geography and climate and culture and race. How and why I lately ended up wintering over more or less permanently in South Florida is a long, circuitous story of stops and starts, like an imagined current pushing stubbornly south against the northbound Gulf Stream. It's a coherent story, though, one that I pretty much understand now— a classic, or at least an old-fashioned, American male quest story. I started fictionalizing its early chapters back in the early 1960s, and one day I'll get around to telling it for its own sake. Perhaps that's one of the things I've been doing here.

Meanwhile, for the last twenty-eight years I've lived seasonally and sometimes year-round in a tiny, remote village in the High Peaks region of the Adirondack Mountains of New York. When asked, *How did you happen to pull up and drop anchor there?* I don't have a reliable ready answer or a long or short story to explain it. Not the way I do for Miami. When I arrived in the Adirondacks in the late 1980s, I was following no romanticized vision of the place, no mythologized, projected version of its history, the way I was when I first drifted south to Miami; I wasn't on a quest and in fact had little knowledge of where exactly the Adirondacks were located and what kind of people lived there. No prior fantasy or projection drew me there from wherever I was before—which happened to be New York City, where I was living with my wife Becky, and Princeton, New Jersey, where I was employed as a professor. I came to the Adirondacks purely by accident. Serendipity. On a rainy night in June 1987.

I should say that I was following a woman. It would be the basic truth. As I confessed earlier, I'd done it before, back in the early 1960s, when, crazed with love, I followed the young woman named Christine south from where I was working as a restaurant dishwasher in Massachusetts to her family home in Richmond, Virginia. Eventually, as young lovers do, we quarreled, then betrayed each other, and I moved on to Boston, the Florida Keys, San Diego, ending in New Hampshire, where this time Christine followed me, and we forgave each other our trespasses and for fourteen turbulent years lived as husband and wife and raised our three children together.

Now, twenty-five years later, I was crazed with love for the woman named Chase—she whose given name is Penelope—who was in thrall to her Connecticut family's multigenerational, transcendental, forest-and-mountain Adirondack fantasy. Her male ancestors were mostly clerics and academics, and for generations the family spent long summers and fall and spring breaks and winter holidays in the Adirondacks. It was the place where she had enjoyed something like a happy childhood, a respite from the rest of her childhood. It was the only place on earth where, as an adult, she felt at peace with the world. Her reasons for settling there make a different story from mine, which I leave for her to tell someday.

I followed Chase to the Adirondacks, then, she who had a good, perfectly understandable, familial reason for living there. Start with that. And for nearly three decades I have lived with her in a house perched on the shoulder of a mountain, a house that she bought at the age of thirty-seven as a summer retreat for herself alone, when she was a professor in Tuscaloosa, less than a year before I arrived on the scene. I might have just hung around as a summer vacationer, a middle-aged, love-besotted houseguest, and departed sadly in the fall to teach my classes at Princeton, and she might well have followed me, instead of me following her—as indeed she did many years later, when I wanted to continue my lifelong drift south and end it in Miami, for which I bless her. But I instead stayed on with Chase in Keene. And in addition to living with her down in Miami now, I live up there with her, too.

And where is "up there"? It's a six-million-acre sprawl of mountain and muskeg, marsh, river, and pond, a land of cool, abbreviated Mongolian summers and long Siberian winters, bordered on the east by the Champlain Valley, on the north by the Saint Lawrence watershed, on the south by the valley of the Hudson, and on the west by the gently rolling hills and valleys of New York State. It's a "howling wilderness," as the first white settlers called it, and from the beginning has been viewed as a kind of Ultima Thule.

It's a true borderland, a place between places, which in a sense is what has preserved it more or less intact into the early twenty-first century. Which may account for its continuing attraction for so many writers and artists and philosophers and clerics and professors, people whose lives depend for their meaning on standing slightly outside the world. People without year-round jobs. People, I suppose, like me.

From the wood engravings that portray Samuel de Champlain's tentative first encounter with the North American wilderness to the svelte, four-color, fantasy-ad inserts of Ralph Lauren; from the writings of James Fenimore Cooper to E. L. Doctorow's *Loon Lake;* from the transcendentalists' Philosophers' Camp to the U.S. Army's northern outpost at Fort Drum: the word *Adirondack* has over the centuries evoked a variety of conflicted images and meanings. Translated into eighteenth-century English, the word means "bark eater" and refers not so much to the natives' diet of choice as to one of the more unpleasant consequences of being condemned by hostile and more socially organized neighbors in more favored regions beyond to reside in a land that everyone, Algonquin, Iroquois, European, Quebecois, and Yankee, regarded as uninhabitable. That is, you will grow so hungry there that, like the starving deer in winter, you'll eat the bark off the trees.

Following the Revolutionary War, the financially strapped American Congress surveyed the land, financed a narrow corduroy road through the forests, and offered wide swaths of the Adirondacks to New England and New York soldiers as a veteran's benefit. Despite the undeniable natural beauty of the place—haunting mountain passes and waterfalls, splendid primeval forests, glittering chains of lakes, and north-flowing rivers and streams—there were very few takers. Too cold, too dark, too much snow and ice for too much of the year, too many black flies and mosquitoes in spring and summer, too little arable soil and too short a growing season to farm it.

Landless veterans preferred to pay a pretty price for softer Vermont acreage or simply trekked west and south to homestead in Pennsylvania and Ohio and beyond. The Adirondacks they left to hunters, fur trappers, hermits, and, in time, to bluff and hearty millionaires on seasonal safari helped by local servants and guides, roughing it in Victorian comfort and splendor in their huge, elaborately furnished and decorated great camps. Behind them came those artists and philosophers and writers I mentioned, along with clerics and academics like Chase's ancestors, looking for a scenic hideaway located in the mostly unsettled far corner of the soul-stealing, newly industrialized, fallen world of urban New England and New York.

I'm not sure if this is background to my story or foreground. But it's my nature to see myself and everyone else as contextualized by the warp and woof of history and place, by geology and climate and economics, by culture and class and race, before I see myself or others as individual human beings. It's a way, I suppose, to delay facing what baffles and distresses me.

But I knew nothing of this and held no beliefs or opinions regarding the place when, late that night in June 1987, having left one good woman for another, my third wife for the woman who would become my fourth and final wife, I drove my ten-year-old diesel Mercedes sedan north for six hours and arrived sometime after midnight in the village of Keene, nestled in the valley of the Ausable River at the center of the forested wilderness known as the Adirondack Park. It was blackout dark, and a heavy late-spring rain pounded the car roof and hood. I knew nothing of the history or ecological fragility of where I had arrived; it could have been anyplace at the dead end of an unpaved lane a six-hour drive from the Manhattan apartment I had abandoned that night; it could have been someplace in West Virginia, Maine, or Pennsylvania. As has happened so often in my life, I didn't know where I had gone. Only that I had gone *away*, that I had left someone, someplace, something behind.

It was long after midnight, and the house in Keene was dark when I arrived. The diesel engine clattered to a stop. The rain pounded down on the car. I asked myself, What have I done to myself? What have I done to the good, loving woman I have lived with for nearly five years and now have left behind, and to the equally good, loving woman I have followed into this unknown wilderness? For the last six months the woman I left behind had ridden the F train every day to her Manhattan office, returning to our apartment alone every night, while I casually, more or less innocently, befriended Chase in faraway Tuscaloosa, Alabama, while I

was the visiting writer-in-residence at the university and Chase was
a professor in the English department. Not until nearly the end of
my one-term residency did we realize that, despite all our best and
honorable intentions, we had fallen in love—suddenly, unexpectedly, as if one night in May on a dance floor at a literary party in
Chattanooga we had simultaneously, spontaneously gone insane.

    This was not, of course, the first time I had gone crazy with
love for a woman. It happened with the teenaged girl I married
when I was nineteen in St. Petersburg, Florida, and again, a few
years later, in Richmond, Virginia, with the woman who became
my second wife, and yet again in New York City with the woman
who became my third wife. And it was not the first time for Chase,
either. When it happens to you, when you go crazy with love, there
is no advance warning, no point ahead of time when you can merely
move to higher ground and evade what's coming. Suddenly you are
obsessed, totally fixated on another human being, and it's as if you've
been hit by a tsunami, and you find yourself flailing wildly, upside
down and tumbling heels over head, carried off by an overwhelming wave whose irresistible force has been generated at the bottom
of the sea hundreds of leagues away and thousands of feet below by
vast, unpredicted tectonic shifts.

    The living room light came on, and then the glow of a porch
light cut a pale wedge through the rain and the darkness, and she
walked onto the porch wearing a tattered pink cotton bathrobe and
stood in the light and waited for me there. Her left index finger was
wrapped in a thick bloody bandage, which she held in the air like a
beacon.

    The house, now that I could see its outline, was not a farm-
house or a summer cottage and certainly was not a great camp. It
was a long, low structure that seemed to have been built in stages
over generations for a large, steadily growing family, as if every few
years a new wing and roofline had been added onto it. It seemed
much too large for one person or even two or three. A towering pair
of pine trees stood like sentries near the porch stairs. I got out of my

car and beneath the pouring rain jogged across the dirt driveway and climbed the half-dozen steps to the porch, and we embraced. She kept her bandaged finger in the air above our heads. Probably she quietly said, Welcome, for that is what she almost always says when someone arrives at our house for the first time. *Welcome.*

Welcome to the Adirondacks. Earlier that evening she had sliced so deeply into her finger that she'd rushed it for stitches to the emergency room of the hospital in Elizabethtown fifteen miles away. She'd cut into it while standing on a wobbly stepladder in the kitchen stripping the wire of a broken overhead light fixture with a pair of fingernail scissors.

This all happened nearly thirty years ago. It was the summer before our courtship tour of the Caribbean. She still wears a thin white scar like a piece of string across her left index finger between the second and third knuckles. Whenever it catches my eye, everything about that night returns to me—the wild, uncontrolled plunge into betrayal and abandonment and the emergence of a new connubial adhesion and the total reconfiguration of my life; and the rain, the porch light, the pink bathrobe, the bandaged finger in the air; and the all-too-familiar burden of shame. And sprawled out there, invisible in darkness, as if it were an ocean and there were no end to it, the wilderness.

As must be apparent by now, Chase is a gambler. She was definitely gambling on me, a thrice-married man with four daughters, scratching out a living as a novelist and part-time teacher, and who, having just left his third wife, was essentially homeless. But she was also a card player whose reputation had preceded her when she first arrived at graduate school in Iowa and later when she went to Alabama and held weekly card games at her house with only the most dedicated players among the faculty sitting in. I had never known a woman who was a serious, deliberate gambler, and it attracted me. She owned a beautiful set of poker chips. She also owned a set of drums and had played in a rock band in her twenties and still worked out on her drum set alone in the garage. That attracted me, too.

Thus, all along, on Sint Maarten and Antigua and now on Aruba, wherever we found them, Chase and I had been hitting the casinos, seated shoulder to shoulder with the package tourists at the blackjack, craps, and roulette tables, and in spite of the glitzy bustle and smoke, the cynical exploitation of greed, fantasy, and addiction that casinos foster in an island culture, we enjoyed it. It helped that we were both winning at the blackjack tables. Back then Caribbean casinos were nothing like those in Las Vegas or Atlantic City. They were generally small, a little tatty, and on the amateurish side, like the depressing Oneonta and Mohawk Indian reservation casinos in upstate New York. Some of them were more like church bingo parlors than the Sands or the Mandalay Bay, and rather pleasant for that. Especially on Aruba, at the Alhambra Casino on Eagle Beach north of Oranjestad, the capital, where Chase tried the roulette table for the first time and cleaned up and I continued to do just fine, thank you, at blackjack. We dressed fancy and cashed a bunch of traveler's checks and let ourselves be good-time Charlies, and we stayed lucky for several nights running.

Until recently, Aruba had been a prosperous offshore oil refining and transshipping point. In the late 1970s, the whole island had been an Exxon and Shell company town. When, in the early 1980s, the oil companies cut back production in the region, it devastated the economy, and Arubans responded by rapidly, single-mindedly, developing large-scale tourism. By 1988 almost all the hotels, and there were many of them, were large, new, full-service resorts. The town of Oranjestad was a free-port shopping mall with newly constructed, cutesy neo-Dutch buildings stuffed with tax-free liquor, lace, china, and jewelry. Aruba was once again prosperous. The environment suffered less now from oil pollution than from overbuilding—it's a small island, arid, low, without much fresh water, and with little capacity for handling waste. Aruba appeared to be turning itself into a beached cruise ship, and one felt that one was a late-arriving guest at the end of the final party there.

The saddest irony in the Caribbean is that without large-scale tourism the islanders starve; but with it, the islanders destroy the very thing they promote and package—beaches, coral reefs, wildlife, mountainous rain forests, desert landscapes, natural wonders that have filled visitors with something like religious awe for thousands of years, since the first humans paddled north along the chain from the Orinoco basin. The whole archipelago, from the Netherlands Antilles just off the shoulder of South America north to the U.S. Virgins, is a highly complex and fragile ecosystem. The vitality and warmth of the people and the beauty of the land and sea and sky are what draw and heal us. Yet our very presence in the numbers that almost every island needs for economic survival contaminates the source. The people become dead-faced dealers and their land and sea and sky a shabby, second-rate, smoke-filled casino.

Aruba's closest neighbor, Bonaire, may well one day walk the same big-time tourist path to environmental and cultural degradation, but it will be years before the necessary infrastructure and trained personnel are available. Meanwhile, it remained perhaps the best island in the Lesser Antilles for serious scuba diving. But not much else.

Like Aruba, Bonaire is parched and flat, with long coral beaches and low hills in the hinterland covered with cacti. Because Bonaire was the only island in the region where it was forbidden to fish with spearguns or remove coral from the fabulous reefs that surround it, the shoreline waters were essentially an unspoiled underwater garden. There were endangered species of birds and lizards that thrived here and nowhere else, and more than 13,500 acres had been set aside in the Washington Slagbaai National Park. As a result, until recently, the usual visitors to Bonaire were ornithologists, marine biologists, and serious scuba divers. But in the late 1980s that was changing rapidly, and in spite of numerous gov-

ernment and private studies urging restraint, there was a whole lot
of beachfront building going on.

The third in this trio of Dutch islands, Curaçao was the most
cosmopolitan and populous. It has a long history as a transshipping
point—first, slaves (nearly half the slaves destined for the Caribbean
passed through Curaçao, where they were "rested" and then distributed to the other islands); then goods from the Dutch colonies
in the Pacific brought through the Panama Canal; then Venezuelan
oil; and now free-port luxuries. Owing to its location and the aridity
of its soil, Curaçao has always been more of a trading outpost than
a producer and exporter of goods—a quiet, calculating middleman
among the islands.

When we were in Curaçao, there was an ambitious, ongoing
attempt to develop tourism, especially along the southwest coast
below Willemstad, and there were some wonderfully diverting
attractions up and running, such as the Curaçao National Underwater Park and the Seaquarium. But the beaches were short and
often man-made, and most of the hotels seemed better suited to
the needs of business conventioneers than families on vacation or
couples gone a-courting.

For us, after Aruba's beach-resort glitz and Bonaire's rus-
tic simplicity, the city of Willemstad on Curaçao was a welcome
change. It was a real international city, a deepwater port, one of
the largest in the world, with good restaurants, mainly French and
Indonesian, attractive seventeenth- and eighteenth-century town
houses and public buildings, bustling narrow streets that wound
around the port and crossed from one side to the other on lovely
bridges. All day long, people of all races, from all continents, pushed
along the crowded sidewalks with an urgency you rarely saw in the
Caribbean—there were deals to be made here, goods to buy and
sell, numbers to move from one column to the next.

But then night fell, and the city of Willemstad turned into a
quiet, languorous Caribbean port where folks strolled slowly past
their neighbors' doors under moon-silvered palms or sat and gos-

siped over rum in dimly lit taverns or, later, before bed, opened the shutters of their rooms to the cool evening breeze and gazed across the sea at the dark coast of Venezuela's Paraguaná Peninsula and the continent beyond and contemplated the tangled, bloody history and destiny of the tropics. I imagined Arawak families, fishermen and farmers, emerging from the South American continent's muddy rivers and deltas and crossing the silvery sea in their long canoes in a northerly direction, moving island by island up the chain, building villages in the bays and worshiping their gods in secret hillside caves. I watched the fierce Carib warriors come along behind them, conquering and pillaging and eventually being absorbed by the culture of their victims. Soon, from the east, came the Spanish in their galleons, searching for gold, enslaving the people they mistakenly called Indians, for they were lost and thought they had landed in India, and in their blind lust for gold they soon exterminated the entire native population. Behind them came the privateers and corsairs of other European nations, some of them landing and setting up as traders and planters, but most of them sailing farther west to steal stolen Spanish gold and topple Spanish power on the continent. Gradually, the Europeans agreed to divide the islands among themselves, and they enslaved and imported Africans, and began to plant spices, tobacco, coffee, and then sugar, one of the most labor-intensive industries known to man, requiring more and still more slaves to work the fields and turn the green cane into white powder and rum, until the entire region was caught in the eye of a cruel economic storm that swirled from Africa to the Caribbean to North America back to Europe.

In time, the North Americans and Europeans ceased to need the Caribbean for sugar, and the storm broke up; the African slaves, replaced by impoverished workers from India, were no longer transported here, and the long decline into desuetude and abject poverty began; until modern times, when the islands became small, more or less independent nation-states themselves, and once again a new economic storm began to swirl, and the region filled with

North Americans and Europeans again, not conquerors this time, but visitors whose needs could be met only to a point before they threatened these azure seas and emerald-green isles, destroying their environment and dissipating their culture.

Who can bear this history? Who can stand it? My heart fills with admiration for the people of the Caribbean, who have loved and clung to these islands and insisted, against all odds, that this place is no dream, no fantasy, no self-indulgent racial or sexual projection, for in this place they are at home. As much at home as I in my Adirondack village and the city of Miami. Or more.

Chase and I had come to the end of our passage through the Lesser Antilles, this long, complex voyage that had reconnected my imagination to the part of the world that I once loved more than any other. We had but one island left to visit, Jamaica. I knew as we boarded the plane that in returning to Jamaica I was going back to where I first learned how to do that, to love a people and a place other than my own. It was where my imagination first revealed itself to me. It was what I meant by the very term *imagination*.

All over the cavernous, crowded terminal at the Sangster Airport in Montego Bay there were uniformed soldiers carrying automatic weapons. Their cold eyes scrutinized us as we passed through. Was there some danger of invasion that I somehow hadn't heard about? I thought suddenly of Grenada and Operation Urgent Fury. Then remembered: Jamaicans had recently held an election, and after nearly a decade Michael Manley and his left-of-center People's National Party were back in power; and as Manley had learned last time, to stay in power he had to depend on Washington's goodwill. He was showing the Americans and possibly the ganja growers and dealers that this time he was obeying his master's wishes and had gotten serious about "cutting drugs off at the source," as they say.

We drove southeast from Negril to Ocho Rios along the north

coast and saw little evidence of the previous year's devastating hurricane. But it soon became apparent that since I was here last, other
terrible things had happened. There were many more undernour-
ished wandering children and unemployed young people, and they
all seemed to have come to the cities, Kingston and Montego Bay,
and to the resorts where the tourists were waiting for them. And
there was much less money now than there had been in the 1970s.
No one had any money at all. No one. Except us, the outsiders. But
since so many of the children and young people were trying desper-
ately to sell us ganja, or more often cocaine and crack, one tended to
conclude that the problem was drugs, not economics.

It was easy to confuse effect with cause. The Jamaican dollar
was worth two-fifths its value of a few years before, less than $0.20
U.S. and dropping. Manley was dealing with a $4 billion U.S. foreign
debt that annually cost 51 percent of Jamaica's foreign exchange.
He had been forced to eliminate a tax on the banking industry and
make it easier to import cars from nations that manufacture cars; at
the same time, he had removed price supports from flour, cooking
oil, and other basic foodstuffs. All this pleased the business community and the International Monetary Fund and the World Bank. But
the minimum wage hadn't increased, and the people were enduring
price rises of up to 50 percent.

So there was a desperate quality to the selling, especially in
the touristed areas of the north coast. Whether it was drugs, souvenirs, sex, or food, there was little room for dignity in any kind
of exchange. People stood by the side of the road with a handful of
bananas or scraps of colored cloth and thrust them out to our car as
we sped past. When we stopped at a light in Ocho Rios, our car was
surrounded by kids calling, "Ganja, mon, me got good sens, mon,
lamb's-breath! Crack. Anyt'ing you want, mon, me got it!"

Chase and I settled in at Port Antonio, once a favorite haunt
of mine, on the eastern end of the island at the foot of the Blue
Mountains, where there were few beaches and consequently few
large hotels. And, no surprise, the frenzied selling abated. We

stayed at the DeMontevin Lodge, an old down-at-the-heels Victorian manse in the residential neighborhood of Titchfield, at the edge of town. The previous owners had died since I was last here and had been replaced by a young black couple. Except for the presence of a continuously running television in the living room, little had changed. It still seemed to belong in a Graham Greene novel, where the guests were conscience-stricken oddballs and international itinerants.

My few friends in the town, it turned out, had all gone. Port Antonio looked the same, however—an old United Fruit shipping point and fishing and sailing port, with a string of bars and brothels along the waterfront, a central marketplace that my friend George Smith used to run, Navy Island in the harbor, won by Errol Flynn in a poker game, now operated as a cottage-and-cabana resort hotel, and steep hills rising swiftly toward the Blue Mountains behind. Out at the edge of town, Rastafarian squatters had taken over Folly Point, but they had already started camping and holding their "sessions" there in the mid-seventies anyhow. There was a sweet, sad quality to the place, as if I were visiting my own reluctantly abandoned past.

But Port Antonio had always seemed deliciously melancholy to me; it was an essential part of the town's charm. It was the New Orleans of Jamaica, where tropical lassitude and international intrigue wound together in darkly baroque ways. By comparison, Kingston, the capital, was the New York City of Jamaica—huge, bustling, as rich as a large industrialized city can be and as poor as any third-world ghetto, with little in between but chain-link fences and guard dogs. That was something you could do with ease in Jamaica—compare one part with another, one kind of town or city with a different, contrasting kind. The island was so large and complex and varied that no one place or person or group of persons could be said to characterize it. It was the United States of the Caribbean, perhaps.

In fact, everything that could be found on individual islands in the Lesser Antilles could be found on Jamaica as well. The long white sand beaches of Negril were still stunning, and often nearly as empty of bathers as the beaches of Anguilla; the towering Blue Mountains were as overwhelming and impenetrable as the mountains of Dominica. The full-service resort hotels east of Montego Bay and in Ocho Rios were as luxurious and private as any you could find on Martinique or Aruba. Small guesthouses in the hills of St. James reminded us of the inns of Nevis. Charter fishing and sailing out of Port Antonio, scuba diving off Negril, windsurfing in Ocho Rios, compared nicely with what we had found in the U.S. and British Virgins. If one was attracted to the historic sites and restored plantation houses of Antigua and St. Croix, one might want to visit Spanish Town and Port Royal and Good Hope and Rose Hall in Jamaica. And if one liked the multiracial intensity of Port-of-Spain, one would love Half Way Tree in downtown Kingston on market day. If Carnival in Trinidad had loosened us up, we could try the Reggae Sunsplash festival in Montego Bay. In all ways, perhaps even the sad and painful ways, Jamaica was the Caribbean.

We had one last journey to make before leaving the Caribbean altogether—to Accompong, the Maroon village in Jamaica's nearly inaccessible Cockpit Country of Trelawny, where, back in the mid-seventies, I had spent some of the loneliest and most enlightening days and nights of my life. The descendants of the Maroons, escaped slaves, had fought the British to a standoff in a seventy-year guerrilla war during the eighteenth century and had lived in the area's limestone pockets ever since. There were three such villages on the island, the other two in the east, but Accompong remained the most isolated. Mostly small farmers and artisans who owned their large tract of land communally, with an elected "colonel" to wield civic authority and a "prime minister" to keep the old British treaty and Maroon tales and lore alive, the Accompong Maroons were a remnant people who for more than two centuries had preserved much of their history and significant elements of their West African culture against all attempts to assimilate them. They had also, with perverse humor and argument and outrageous financial demands, resisted becoming a tourist attraction.

It was clear to me, as our rented car chugged up the last hill to the tiny settlement, that in the years since my last arrival in Accompong very little here had changed. A rooster crowed, a dog barked, and a child ran to find an adult to come greet the visitors. The afternoon light fell softly in planes against the leaves of the banana trees and splashed off the whitewashed walls of the small houses and cabins scattered along the narrow lane. Accompong was timeless, a fitting end to our journey. Martin Luther Wright, nervous and officious, just as I remembered him, was still colonel; the hundred-year-old rascal Mann O. Rowe, loquacious and tricky as ever, remained the prime minister.

I introduced the two men to my fiancée. All three smiled self-consciously without showing their teeth and looked down, as if discovering as one that Christine was no longer my wife. Suddenly it was as if I were a stranger to Chase and my two old friends, and they to me. I was simultaneously alive in the past and alive in the present, but disassociated from both, a nonparticipant, a member of the audience, as if I were watching the same scene from two different films shot in two different time periods on the same location and with the same actors. They were not my actual fiancée, Chase, or the two old Maroon friends I had fictionalized in my novel, *The Book of Jamaica,* but famous actors, movie stars, portraying them. In both films, Chase was played by a woman who resembled Jamie Lee Curtis. Morgan Freeman and Don Cheadle, heavily aged by make-up, had been cast as Martin Luther Wright and Mann O. Rowe. I myself was not in either film, not as character, not as actor. I was an unglamorous bystanding stranger, that's all—I was not even Russell Banks, that little-known American writer who back in the late 1970s had nearly become a citizen of this village. Nor was I the somewhat better-known writer twelve years later courting the woman who would become his fourth wife on a two-month island-hopping cruise through the Caribbean—I was not him, either.

The scene, both versions, faded out, and Chase and the two old men disappeared from the screen, and then Chase and I walked arm in arm about the village together, and it was as if I had never left and twelve years had not passed and I would never leave again. But it was also in some mysterious way as if I had never really been here before, never touched down, and was only passing through on my way to somewhere else. As if it were a flyby.

I told Chase as much. I said I felt like *Voyager 1*.

She didn't quite get it.

I explained that ten years previously, when I first read about *Voyager 1*, I had felt an immediate affinity and affection for it—not quite an identification with the spacecraft as an appropriation of some of its essential character and capacities that seemed to apply to my own peripatetic life so far. Perhaps especially to my marriages and several other close, lasting relationships with women. Over Chase's and my nearly three decades together, starting that winter and spring in 1988, when we were still courting each other and touring the Caribbean together, I have tried from time to time to explain this to her without making me sound cold and detached and fearful. Although, when I was falling madly in love over and over again, until I met and married Chase, I had indeed been all three—cold and detached and fearful.

From the start, I was attracted to the language and terminology used by scientists and NASA officials to describe the mission of *Voyager 1*. The words and phrases were metaphorical to me, I said, connoting way more than they denoted. When, on September 5, 1977, around the time I returned from Jamaica and left Christine's and my home for good, and the Titan rocket carrying *Voyager 1* blasted off from Cape Canaveral, Florida, we were told by NASA that the satellite, once separated from the rocket, was programmed not to go to a planet or moon, but to bypass all the planets and their moons

and eventually exit our entire solar system. Out there it would encounter what's known as termination shock, a condition that occurs when the stream of high-speed ionized particles ejected from
the sun's corona—the solar wind—slows to subsonic speeds. After
termination shock, the satellite would pass into the heliosphere, a
pear-shaped region created by the collision between the solar wind
and what's called the interstellar wind—electrons coming from beyond our solar system. Then, when it reached a point 10.8 billion
miles beyond the sun, *Voyager 1* would enter the heliopause, the
zone where the solar wind shifts its axis to the horizontal plane and,
no longer colliding with the interstellar wind, is absorbed by and
merges with the interstellar plasma. Eventually, the satellite would
pass into cosmic purgatory, where the number of charged particles
emitted by the sun declines by half, and the interstellar particles in-
crease one hundredfold. The outer extension of cosmic purgatory
is called the heliosheath. And just as planned, on August 25, 2012,
thirty-five years after liftoff at Cape Canaveral, thirty-five years after
my divorce from Christine was finalized, *Voyager 1* would pierce the
heliosheath, cross out of cosmic purgatory, and at last enter the interstellar medium—outer space. Coincidentally, that date, August 25,
2012, was also Chase's and my twenty-third wedding anniversary. At
the time, I did not make a connection between any of these events.
I made them only when I began making notes for this book, and I
merely offer them here.

There is aboard *Voyager 1* a gold-plated audiovisual disc with
photos of our planet and many of its life-forms, a small library of
scientific diagrams and mathematical formulae and humanistic
and religious quotations and artistic imagery, recorded greetings
from President Jimmy Carter and the secretary-general of the UN,
and a medley of "Sounds of Earth," including selections of music
by Beethoven, Blind Willie Johnson, Chuck Berry, and Valya Bal-
kanska, who sings the ancient Balkan folk song "Izlel e Delyu
Haydutin"; plus, among many other sounds, the mating calls of
whales and crying babies and thunder and barking dogs. The gold

disc was designed to contain the contents of a fairly well-educated late-twentieth-century human brain. Astronomer and television host Carl Sagan was responsible for it, so maybe it's the contents of Sagan's brain. My brain would have included different individual items, quotations, and songs, perhaps, but a very similar mash-up.

The satellite was aimed at Alpha Centauri, the hoof of the centaur, the star system nearest to our sun, 4.37 light-years, 25.8 trillion miles, from home. At *Voyager 1*'s present speed, an Alpha Centauri flyby is scheduled to occur in about forty thousand years, a time frame that in human terms is almost unimaginable: it is highly unlikely that our species will even exist forty thousand years from now. *Voyager 1* might as well be aimed at heaven or hell or some other purely imaginary place, some other land of the dead. But that, too, along with the metaphoric language deployed by the scientists, attracted me. The whole project was a Blakean construct to me. And, naturally, it possessed certain moral implications.

Here are a few that held particular meaning for me. Before a satellite could exit our solar system and reach termination shock— something we all must expect to face eventually—it had to make its way along a carefully calibrated path around and between the planets that orbit our sun, following a route designed to keep it a sufficient distance from the planets' gravitational fields, so as not to be drawn into orbit around one of them or crash onto its surface. It also had to pass close enough to the two largest planets, Jupiter and Saturn, to pick up a spinning, gravity-assisted slingshot that would hurl the satellite into space at escape velocity, the speed needed for breaking free of the sun's gravity—another intriguing metaphor, for hadn't I spent most of my life traveling at escape velocity?—or else it would eventually circle back toward the sun and be incinerated. Having reached escape velocity, blown across the interstellar medium by the interstellar wind, *Voyager 1* is expected to continue sending data back to earthlings until 2025, when its three radioisotope thermoelectric generators (RTGs) run out of power to operate its scientific instruments. In 2025 I will be eighty-five. Barring fatal accident or illness, my RTGs, too, will have about run out of power. From then on, there will likely be nothing but silence. And, except for the glow of Alpha Centauri forty thousand years in the distance, darkness.

Are we poor forked creatures, all of us, as solitary as that sad satellite, deliberately programmed by the god of evolution to sail off into darkness, silent and alone, receiving and transmitting data until our batteries dim and die? Or is that fate merely my peculiarity alone? Against all my hopes, never to be truly known and never to have truly known another seems inescapable. Yet we keep on revealing our secret selves to ourselves and to one another, even to strangers—receiving and transmitting data back to earth—by writing books like this. As if revealed secrets somehow make us known to one another.

In the winter of 1988, the afternoon when Chase and I visited the Maroon village of Accompong, we walked to our rented car to start back to our hotel in Montego Bay, and a pair of bulky, sunburnt white men in their mid-thirties waiting beside the car stepped forward and approached us. They were short-haired strangers with a serious purpose, clearly. But what purpose? I was frightened and, remembering our savaged Corolla on St. Thomas, put myself between Chase and the two men, who now stood squarely between us and our vehicle. Both men wore Boston Red Sox baseball caps and loose, untucked polo shirts and Bermuda shorts and running shoes. American tourists? Harmless? Maybe not. We, or at least I, had spent two months demonizing white American tourists, radically differentiating between them and us. Maybe they had finally seen us as we had been unable to see ourselves—condescending, ironic snobs—and had followed us to Accompong to have it out with us. Maybe they were Boston Irish mobsters, pals of Joker, hunting me down to shut me up for talking loose in public about the old days in the Keys. Or maybe they'd been sent from Dominica by Clive Cravensbrook (who surely had a copy of our itinerary) to report back on our last stop in Jamaica.

But it was nothing as fanciful or absurd or threatening as any of those possibilities. The nearer of the two men said, "Excuse me, sir, but the old man over there, Mr. Rowe, he told me who you are."

They were from Dedham, Massachusetts, a Boston suburb, on vacation in Jamaica with their wives, he explained, who were waiting for them back at their hotel in Ocho Rios. They each had a battered paperback copy of *The Book of Jamaica* that they claimed to be using as a travel guide and had found their way to Accompong by following the trail of the narrator of the novel. They wondered if I'd be willing to autograph their copies of the book.

Relieved and surprised, I agreed and signed the title page of both books, which made them very happy. The two men read the signature over several times and grinned. "Dolores isn't gonna believe this!" one of them said. "She said we were nuts coming way out here in the boonies without a guide or anything, except your book."

"It's a novel," I told them. "You know, fiction. It's not a guidebook."

CODA

In March 2003, forty-four years too late for the revolution, I finally made my way to Cuba. I even got to meet Fidel Castro. I was there by official invitation to attend the Havana Book Fair, invited because one other American writer, my friend the novelist William Kennedy, and I had agreed to let the Cubans translate and publish our work, even though, thanks to the Helms-Burton Act, we would never receive a penny in royalties. We were assured, however, that our novels would be distributed free to every high school in the country and made available to the general public for the rough equivalent of one American dollar.

As it turned out, Kennedy and I were able to spend most of our second day in Havana interviewing Castro in his private office. You don't really "interview" El Commandante; you try to get a question in before he delivers another speech. Although when I asked him if, after forty-four years in power, he regretted anything, he answered quickly and efficiently: "Yes. Two things I regret," he said. "I thought the revolution would eliminate racism, which it hasn't. As you can see, everyone in a position of authority looks like me. But we're learning from you Americans," he added, "by promoting affirmative action." *Touché*. "And second, I never should have trusted the Russians."

Around 6 P.M., he said, "You boys must be tired." Kennedy was edging up on seventy-five, and my Medicare was about to kick in; no one had called us "boys" in half a century. But we were tired—nine hours in close quarters with Fidel Castro is exhausting, and we had been up the night before till 3 A.M. at the dinner he'd hosted for the cadre of visiting writers, all of them, with the exception of me and Kennedy, from the Caribbean and Central and South America. Castro had zeroed in on Kennedy and me, however, the only gringos present at his dinner, ignoring the writers we'd come there to meet. It was a few weeks before the American invasion of Iraq, and Fidel seemed unwilling to believe the Bush administration was crazy enough to do it. We assured him that it was. When Kennedy's wife, Dana, became ill from the hovering blue cloud of cigar smoke, Castro ended the dinner. As we were leaving, he invited us to interview him alone in his office the next day. Hard to say no. It was the eve of Shock and Awe, the full-scale American invasion of Iraq, with Cuba one of the eight countries on the U.S. State Department's list of state sponsors of terrorism, and El Commandante hoped, no doubt, for a puff piece by his left-leaning American literary guests in the *New York Times* or the *Washington Post*. Kennedy and I privately agreed that we would not write about our meeting with Fidel Castro, and until now, neither of us has.

The interview done, Castro called for a map, and a secretary unrolled a huge map of Cuba and spread it across the desk. Castro pointed at the Bahia de Cochinos, the Bay of Pigs. "This is where I go when I am tired," he said. "It's a national park now," he added. He pointed to an unlabeled harbor where he said a secret naval base was located. Tomorrow morning a car would carry us across Cuba to the base, where a boat would be waiting to take us to his personal retreat on a tiny island named Isla de las Rocas, also not on the official map. We were to stay overnight at his guesthouse. He told us to fish. Swim. Rest.

The Bay of Pigs has been a rigorously protected nature preserve since April 1961, when the Cuban exiles and their CIA trainers and the Miami-based gangsters—colleagues of Joker, my old Boston gangster pal—famously tried and miserably failed to launch the counterrevolution. Now it was the Caribbean as it was before the arrival of Columbus, before the arrival even of the Arawak and Carib native people. Birds literally darkened the sky, and fish seemed to leap willingly into our boat, and there was no sign of human habitation—except for the Cuban naval force escorting me and Bill Kennedy and his wife, Dana, to Castro's Secret Hideaway. We were aboard one of two small cutters, Russian castoffs fitted with Cold War–era .50-caliber M59 machine guns and manned by ten or twelve young sailors per boat. During the forty-five-minute ride, without baiting our lines, Bill and I managed to haul in nearly fifty fish, often one and two at a time, mostly red snapper, which we were assured would get shared out with the crew. Socialism at sea.

The difference between being just plain dumb and being reckless is between doing a dumb thing by accident and doing the same dumb thing with conscious awareness that it may cost you your life. I had done many dumb things over the years, but very few that were truly reckless. I was about to do something truly reckless. Enjoying an al fresco lunch of grilled red snapper and fried plantains and avocado salad on the pier at Castro's Isla de las Rocas with the Cuban naval captain and his officers wasn't reckless. Drinking liberally from several bottles of mind-numbing, palate-pleasing, smooth-as-butter Cuban rum wasn't reckless, either. Neither was following up with a few chilled bottles of '01 Celler Gramona III Lustros Brut Cava from Spain. Getting as seriously drunk as Hemingway in his

prime in the middle of the afternoon on a tiny island a few miles
outside the Bay of Pigs wasn't reckless. Not really. Until the captain
asked us if we'd like to go scuba diving for lobster.

Bill and Dana shook their heads no, they needed a nap, and
staggered off for the small guesthouse a few hundred yards beyond
Castro's modest getaway cottage. The steep-roofed cottage faced
the open sea and was painted blue, and a string hammock on the
deck swung in the offshore breeze. The Caribbean glittered under
the unrelenting sunlight. I was drunk. Very drunk. I had scuba
dived in shallow water a few times in the Seychelles and on Bequi,
but had never shot a speargun before. And I had never dived while
drunk. I said, "Capitano, I'm there, man."

A half hour later, over forty feet of water so clear you could see
the wavering antennae of the dozens of lobsters snoozing on the
white sand below, I balanced on the rail of the cutter, wearing only
my Calvins and swim fins, and strapped on tanks and a weight belt
and hefted the speargun. And stopped. And said to myself: Wait a
minute. I have a loving wife and four daughters and a granddaughter, my ninety-year-old mother whom Chase and I take care of, and
many dear friends. They are all going to be very pissed off at my
memorial service. They won't feel sorry for me. They'll say, Russell
was drunk. Russell had never dived in forty feet of water before or
shot a speargun. Russell was reckless. He deserved to drown.

On either side of me, four young Cuban sailors were strapping
on their tanks and weight belts, and I thought, There's no way these
guys will let me drown. They'll have to report back to El Commandante that they let the old gringo writer drown in the Bahia de
Cochinos. No, Fidel's sailors will save me from my reckless self. I let
go of the gunwale and leaned back and entered the sea, shoulders
and backside first, the way I'd seen Lloyd Bridges do it on television.

I shot three lobsters that afternoon, more or less by accident,
and got grinning thumbs-ups from my fellow divers. And then
missed two. Then, suddenly exhausted and dizzy, I realized that I
was swimming in small circles, lost beneath the sea. Not *beneath* the

sea—I was *inside* it, afloat in a transparent ether that filled endless space between the firmaments above and below. The other divers had disappeared. I was alone. I was not frightened or confused. I was almost happy. I had moved in widening spirals out from under the long shadow of the boat, and when I looked up now saw only the soft bright light of sky, but I could not mark where the sea ended and the sky began.

The boat had abandoned me, or I had abandoned the boat: at that moment I didn't care which. Below, like the surface of an ancient, airless planet, the white rippled bottom of the bay faded into darkness on all sides and disappeared at the distant horizons. As if enticed to map the planet's cold, permanently dark side, I tried swimming toward the horizon that happened to face me, but it receded and was swallowed by a farther horizon. Swimming in the opposite direction, it was the same. There was no north, south, east, or west; no up or down, in or out. Without a sun or stars overhead to navigate by, or familiar landmarks below to calculate my place and movement in time and space, I was simultaneously located nowhere and at the exact center of the universe. I was nothing and everything. It terrified me. But there was a strange, almost irresistible, vaguely familiar pull to this awareness, one that I had never felt before. I did not think it then, but I realize now that for a few moments, lost in the Caribbean Sea, I had finally imagined and penetrated the poetic mystery of my mother's consciousness, her experience of being, and therefore had entered Darlene's and Christine's, and in its diminished form, Becky's, too. For a few precious moments, I was able to grasp the story of my life so far.

Until the sailors found me and hauled me back aboard the cutter like a gaffed marlin. That night at the Isla de las Rocas the cook grilled the lobsters over an open fire for me and the Kennedys. "Russell, you are a goddamn idiot," Bill said. "But the lobsters are grand."

PART TWO

PILGRIM'S REGRESS

THE RETURN OF THE CHAPEL
HILL THREE HUNDRED

Fourth of July weekend, 1986—Liberty Weekend, it was called—and on Governor's Island in New York Harbor Ronald Reagan opened a national celebration of the freshly renovated and scrubbed Statue of Liberty, a televised orgy of American self-love designed to leave participants standing tall as Marlboro men and brimming over with enough weepy narcissism for a beer ad. José Feliciano sang the national anthem, Neil Diamond followed with "They're Coming to America," Frank Sinatra warbled "The House I Live In," and Elizabeth Taylor told us how much the statue meant to her. I was in eastern Pennsylvania piloting a rented RV, a beige slab-sided twenty-seven-and-a-half-foot-long Southwind recreational vehicle, a $50,000 condo on wheels. My passengers and I were a gaggle of middle-aging college classmates, heading south on Route 78 as if in flight from the wretched excess taking place in New York Harbor.

We were on our way to Chapel Hill on this stifling weekend to what the North Carolina papers were already calling a "hippie reunion," a gathering of one of the scattered tribes from the Woodstock nation. My old friend and classmate Alex McIntire was more responsible for the event than anyone else. It was he who'd called for the reunion—an anti-reunion, actually, for alumni who wanted no reunions and had never been to one, and it was he who'd compiled the nearly eight hundred names and addresses of Chapel Hill outriders from the sixties—all those civil rights workers and anti-war warriors and poets and painters and folkies and rockers and druggies and leftist journalists and hangers-on and god-seekers and sandal-makers and communards and utopians, all those antiestablishmentarians who had passed through Chapel Hill as students, enrolled and non-enrolled, at the University of North Carolina between 1962 and 1970.

Sometime in the early 1960s, the chancellor and trustees and the administration of the University of North Carolina had decided to transform the place into the Berkeley of the South. To turn a sleepy, if distinguished, southern state university located halfway between Durham and Raleigh into a major, highly competitive, research-oriented institution like Michigan, Chicago, Columbia, and Berkeley, they had to beef up their faculty with old lions and young Turks, seek out graduate students from the hot centers, admit women and blacks, and recruit actively for undergraduates in the top public and private high schools of the North and East.

In the 1960s, Chapel Hill was the first choice after Harvard, Princeton, and Yale of the graduating classes of Andover and Exeter. Allard Lowenstein was radicalizing the political science department, while Forrest Read, O. B. Hardison Jr., Louis Rubin, and William Harmon made people nervous in the English department. It was like that all over campus and in town, where students and faculty joined CORE and SDS and took beatings and got arrested integrating restaurants and movie theaters and lined up outside the post office every day to protest growing U.S. involvement in Vietnam. The best and the brightest, one might say, and frequently the most radical and often the most creative young men and women coming out of northern schools were heading south to UNC, where they met their southern counterparts, and where both met up with veteran civil rights workers, black and white, and a nascent antiwar movement. By the mid-1960s, Chapel Hill was being excoriated as a hotbed of communism, libidinous excess, facial hair, and racial agitation, condemned most rabidly on WRAL-TV in Raleigh by a newscaster who looked like a sneering woodchuck—a man named Jesse Helms, who flailed Chapel Hill with the passion and rhetoric of a Bible Belt preacher.

By then drugs had appeared, the traditional grass and speed, but also LSD, and in enormous quantities. And almost before anyone knew what had happened, there was a full-blown sixties scene on Franklin Street in downtown Chapel Hill, mostly in and around a dim, scruffy New York–style bar and deli called Harry's where everyone hung out early and late, at the Tempo Room, a grungy basement bar, and in various beat houses scattered across town and old abandoned sharecropper cabins in the rolling Piedmont countryside, where people freaked out at 3 A.M. and put their fists through walls or walked stoned off roofs or argued till dawn about the inevitability of revolution, the politics of Herbert Marcuse and John Lennon, the wisdom of Timothy Leary and Meher Baba. The UNC trustees got their Berkeley of the South, all right, but it wasn't exactly what they'd bargained for.

There were six of us in the van so far, with four more to pick up in Virginia. Everyone had heard rumors that there would be hundreds of us descending on Chapel Hill, from up in Michigan and out in Mill Valley, flying in from Hollywood, driving down from Washington and up from Mississippi. But secretly all of us in the van feared that we would turn out to be the only people present at the reunion. Surely everyone else thought the whole idea was silly. We'd seen *The Big Chill* and *The Return of the Secaucus Seven*. We knew how we looked.

We were four men and two women, close friends two decades

ago, and in recent years, after extensive side trips, friends again. Flopped across the bed in the stateroom way at the back of the van, in deep sleep since the Verrazano–Narrows Bridge three hours earlier, was Kathy Fehl, who at sixteen had been one of the youngest freshmen at Chapel Hill the same year I, at twenty-four, was one of the oldest. We met in orientation, got bored filling out the Minneapolis Multiphasic Personality Index, and ducked out for a beer at Harry's, which Kathy, as a precocious, rebellious faculty brat, knew all about. I was a recently married ex-plumber from New Hampshire, a provincial young man preoccupied with his marriage and his growing literary ambitions, and Kathy's presentation of her pals and CORE associates at Harry's provided my first exposure to the sixties.

Twenty years later, I was divorced, remarried, and a working novelist, and Kathy Fehl was an actress and playwright and the founder and artistic director of the Pelican Theater in New York. Tall, rangy, with astonishing blue eyes and a hawklike face, Kathy was a person who worked and thought and spoke and connected in recklessly intense bursts, loud explosions of energy, followed by equally intense periods of recuperative withdrawal—silence, melancholy, sleep, dreams. This morning she was in recuperative mode.

Sprawled in the passenger's seat next to me, reminiscing about the year he ran a bar and lived in a Greek cave with Joni Mitchell, was Carey Raditz, a banker in a Panama hat, muscle shirt, and Mexican peasant pants, a trim man with a movie star's grin, the urgency of an EST trainer, and the good-humored abandon of a beachcomber. Nowadays Carey arranged loans in the Middle East for a major New York bank, but like so many members of our generation, at least fifteen years of his adult life were close to unaccounted for, years he wandered in Africa and Haight-Ashbury and Turkey and the Lower East Side. Joni's song "Carey" blasted from the deck, and Carey was deconstructing it. The song, of course, was about him.

Behind me and Carey, seated around a fold-down table as if

at a booth in Harry's in 1966, were Lucius Shepherd and Dave Forster and Dave's wife, Dale. Lucius was a giant of man who looked
more like a retired defensive tackle for the Chicago Bears than a
rock singer come in from the cold to write novels set in the jungles
of Central America. He'd gone from being all-Florida high school
fullback to poet-prodigy at college to kisser-of-the-sky living for
months off LSD like Saint Theresa living off the Host to commu-
nard up in Michigan, where, with nothing more than a decent sense
of rhythm and a pleasing tenor voice, he formed a band. He went
on the road, and after enduring the usual highs and lows, touring
with Dr. John and other outlaw bands and singers back and forth
across the country, going through a split-up with his wife, in his late
thirties he finally abandoned all that and switched over to writing
fiction with a dark, futuristic, highly political vision of the world.

Dale Forster, a development officer for the Metropolitan
Opera, sat next to Lucius, who was explaining how cocaine is free-
based. She did not attend Chapel Hill, was a few years younger than
us, and was almost literally along for the ride. She was smart and
attractive, regarded us with amused, affectionate tolerance, and
asked the right questions, the questions that set us to arguing over
what really happened the night the Ku Klux Klan shot up the party
at Ed Causey's house in Carrboro, and who was that kid who kept
bringing in kif from Morocco in diplomatic pouches, and who was
with Dave Snelling the night he tried to fly on acid.

Dale's husband, Dave, had become a successful importer of
luxury table linens, supplier to the White House, among other
fine houses. Dave, too, had about fifteen years of his adult life that
were nearly unaccounted for, years spent on a farm with Lucius up
in Michigan, in Bolivia, on a commune in Arkansas, doing a turn
in Africa in the Peace Corps, before he returned to New York and
entered the family business. He was a reticent man who pursed his
lips before he spoke, then spoke slowly and precisely. He still possessed all his sixties records, an amazing feat, and it was he who'd
prepared the sound track for this trip, professionally engineered

tapes of songs we all knew all the words to, even the harmonies, and we sang along joyously as the huge blond van careened down the highway, a family of aging hippies on a family outing, staving off mortality with battle songs we hadn't sung in years. *"How does it feeeeel, to be on your own, with no direction home, a complete unknown, like a rolling stone?"*

A few miles south of Harrisburg, we pulled over for gas. I remembered hanging out now and then at Merritt's Shell Station, located on South Columbia Street just outside Chapel Hill, near where I lived in a small rented house with my wife Christine and our baby daughter. As often happened on a hot and humid fall night, Christine and I would quarrel—we could not know it, but we were then just starting the long, painful guerrilla war that would lead ten years later to divorce and partition—and I would head up the road to Merritt's to cool down with a cold beer. The place was in fact a country beer-bar, only disguised as a filling station, and sometimes James Taylor, a local teenaged folksinger, who was a friend, or one or another of his brothers hung out—their parents, Ike and Trudy Taylor, and their musical brood lived nearby then—but the regulars at Merritt's were good old boys, local workmen who sat around night after night watching Carolina basketball on the black-and-white TV set on the counter.

On this particular night, none of the Taylors was there. I bought a Miller's, leaned against a far wall, and took a look at the TV. A larger crowd than usual had gathered more intently than usual around the screen, and it was hard to see, but after a few seconds I realized they were watching James Meredith, the first African American to attend the University of Mississippi, walk from Memphis to Jackson to encourage voter registration by African Americans. It was called the "March Against Fear."

"Damn nigger," someone growled. "Look at that damn struttin' nigger." The talk got tougher, tighter, and then I heard the sniper's gunshot, and Meredith went down, and a cheer went up, a triumphant roar of joy, as if for a winning basket at the buzzer. "Kill that nigger! Shoot all them bastids!" There were calls for instant replay, and the network obliged, and then more cheers, as I edged silently toward the door and slipped into the humid North Carolina darkness.

By late in the afternoon we were in Virginia, sailing down the Shenandoah Valley. The Blue Ridge Mountains—softly rounded humps running north and south in parallel waves—turned from deep green to slate blue as the sun drifted toward the horizon, and I was trying to remember clearly the night I first met Ray Kass, the man whose house in Christiansburg we were headed for.

It was in September 1964, my first week in Chapel Hill, and my infant daughter and Christine were still up in Richmond staying with Christine's parents, while I matriculated at college like the rest of the incoming freshmen, almost all of whom were six or seven years younger than I. I was also supposed to be renting a house and preparing it for us to live in. Someone from Harry's, I can't remember who, invited me to come along to a party in the country, and when I arrived, it looked like a lot of college parties I had been to back in Boston and even in New Hampshire—mostly white kids with a couple of black kids dancing and standing around and listening to records and smoking grass and drinking beer and cheap wine and joking and flirting with one another. We were crowded into a small cinder-block bungalow surrounded by brush and short, tangled trees with a scrawny woods of tall, skinny pines separating it from several similar houses, whose lights I could make out dimly through the trees.

Around eleven o'clock the shooting started. I ended up under the kitchen table with a tall, skinny blond kid who, when I asked him what the hell was going on, explained with astonishing aplomb in a suburban Long Island accent that, because of the black kids at the party, we were being attacked by the Ku Klux Klan. He introduced himself as Ray Kass and told me he was an art student and started describing his paintings to me as if I owned a gallery.

The paintings actually sounded pretty interesting, but I was getting a little anxious about the shotguns blasting away from the yard, smashing windows and blowing straight through the tiny house and out the other side. Soon it became clear that a couple of people from our side were firing back—handguns, from the sound of it—and under cover of the return fire lots of folks were leaving the party by the back door, squirting across the backyard to their cars, and roaring down the rutted driveway to the dirt road and away. Ray refused to move, fascinated by what was happening, as were a dozen or so others, me included, who didn't believe yet in our own mortality or even that there were people who wanted to kill us. While the guns blasted over our heads, we went on talking about art.

At Blacksburg, a few miles south of Roanoke, I took the exit off Route 81, and Ray drove down from his house in the hills to lead us back along a winding, quickly rising country road to his home and studio. At last, the van was still—ticking quietly as it cooled, dripping, sweating, squatting like a huge airliner parked outside Ray's carefully terraced house that looked over a broad valley where an evening mist rose like golden breath from the trees.

At dinner, sprawled around Ray's living room with him and his companion and colleague Jerri Pike, a soft-spoken woman with the kind of skepticism and tolerance and good humor necessary for hanging around Ray for very long, we regressed, put on our faces and voices of long ago, and drifted backward in time in a fugue state that was as seductive as it was threatening. Besides Ray and Jerri there were two new additions to our crew, Chris Munger, who'd been a brooding actor at Chapel Hill and was now a brooding documentary film director about to take off for Cambodia, and Saundi Mercier, who'd been one of the first women admitted to UNC as a freshman in 1963 and worked now as a therapist in Baltimore.

We were survivors, and after traveling circuitous routes to get here, we were comparing notes and maps, recalling turns we'd made at crucial junctures, companions we left behind or naming who turned right when we turned left, who turned further left when we went straight, friends who kept on diving when we came up for air, people who disappeared into the darkness beyond, just as we turned back. The list of the dead was long, much longer than actuarial tables say it should have been, and the causes of death over and over again were drug overdose and suicide.

Someone recalled the night Chris Munger strolled into the Chapel Hill police station in his droopy, tattered drawers and torn T-shirt and arrogant, red-lipped snarl and with a bad check bailed out twelve friends arrested during a sit-in. "Now that was acting!" Kathy said, and we laughed, and Chris tried his old snarl on and got it just right. Because of his baldness and scruffy beard, he looked even more like Brando in *One-Eyed Jacks* now than he did in college. He probably hadn't worn that face for a decade, not even as a joke.

We were all balder and fatter and grayer and more careful than we were then, but tonight we seemed to have been yanked out of our forty- and forty-five-year-old bodies and poured back into the bodies and the faces we'd worn twenty years ago, as if to join our friends who died back then—Jim Rossman, Dave Snelling, Cliney Lea, Wyatt Hart, John Dunne. The list went on, and it was long, too long.

I looked around the room, cluttered with empty wine bottles and overflowing ashtrays, and I saw on our faces the strain and the pain of remembering. It was long after midnight, early in the morning of the Fourth of July, 1986. In less than twenty-four hours, President Reagan would flip the switch, and Lady Liberty, our copper-clad national goddess, would glow red, white, and blue in New York Harbor. Let the celebrations begin.

I was wakened by sunlight streaming through the van's stateroom window and loud static hissing from somewhere in the front of the van. The static, evidently coming from the tape deck, abated, only to return, an irritating, nasty, electronic scratch. I sat up and yelled, "What the hell's wrong with the tape deck?"

Shirtless, showered, hair slicked back, and eyes bright, Carey performed a slow set of yoga exercises. "Isn't that great?" he said.

"What the fuck is it?"

"It's the surf off Dakar at dawn. I taped it last year."

"Jesus, Carey." I got out of bed and realized I was hungover and stumbled toward the bathroom.

"Wait till you hear the dog bark. Russ, it's fucking awesome," he said and went back to his yoga.

Somewhere near Fancy Gap in the Blue Ridge Mountains, heading southwest into North Carolina, we pulled over at a filling station and country store for a pit stop. The RV gobbled gas like the Concorde, forty gallons a shot, and I stood there pumping gas and having flashes of trips I'd all but forgotten, when Christine and I owned a beige-and-aqua VW microbus, the ultimate sixties vehicle, and regularly packed together a bunch of friends and lit out for the territory—a Rolling Stones concert in Raleigh, the beach at Cape Hatteras, a long weekend at the Union Grove Old Time Fiddlers' Convention in the mountains. I always drove; Christine was the navigator.

I topped off the tank and paid the watchful attendant standing next to me at the pump, and one by one my passengers returned from the country store across the road lugging Cokes and beer and jars of honey and jam and potato chips and pretzels. Lucius carried a huge watermelon.

"You can't squeeze all that stuff into that little refrigerator," I said. "Especially the watermelon."

"Relax, man," Lucius said. "I'll just rearrange the chardonnay."

It was a little after noon when we exited Route 15-501 onto South Columbia Street and rolled past Merritt's Shell Station and entered Chapel Hill. In the last fifteen minutes everyone had gone silent, even Ray, who'd been unfolding his Roy Cohn theories—Cohn as thousand-year-old vampire, whose imminent death, Ray predicted, would only be Cohn's usual way of getting out of trouble for a while. "Roy Cohn doesn't die, he just lies low for a few years."

The streets were lined with live oaks and tall pines. Tulip poplar, wisteria, and magnolia trees surrounded sprawling homes in large, shaded yards where lawn sprinklers twirled slowly over grass green as mint. A few of the homes were antebellum white-painted brick with wide verandas and columns, but most were Craftsman faculty houses built in the early years of the century and maintained impeccably by residents who for generations had been consistently genteel, leisurely, intelligent, and tasteful. I realized all over again how truly, almost sexually, desirable the town was.

The interior of the van looked and smelled like an airliner that had been hijacked by terrorists—food wrappers and watermelon rinds and empty wine and beer bottles and sleeping bags and newspapers and dirty clothes. The air conditioner had been busted since Winston-Salem, and it was as hot inside as the Beirut airport. Everyone was sweating uncomfortably and thinking shower, air conditioner, gin and tonic. We pulled into the parking lot of the Carolina Inn, a neo-Georgian brick hotel adjacent to the campus where the parents of UNC students used to stay.

An hour later, we regathered in the hotel lobby, and almost grimly we marched across the west end of the old campus, past the Ackland Art Museum, toward Franklin Street and the Carolina Coffee Shop. Possibly for the first time since proposing this journey, we realized that it was not an impulsive casual jaunt, not just a spontaneous Fourth of July weekend party.

The coffee shop was packed with people, all the booths filled. There was barely room for me to stand and signal the others to fight through the crowd and join me here in the middle. Their proximity had suddenly become important to me, since I didn't think I knew any of the people who surrounded me. Except for my traveling companions, they were all strangers in early middle age, ordinary citizens who looked like they had ordinary problems. I didn't know them, and I didn't particularly want to. I wanted to go home.

But then I recognized one man who at twenty had looked forty, and he still looked forty. It was Newt Smith—and there was his wife, June—and they were talking to Steve Hawthorne, who was next to Bob Bottomly and Nancy Sasser, who were at a table with Rick Doble and Bill Hicks, and suddenly I was swept up as if in a dream of faces, all of them smiling eagerly, whirling around me as I spun through the room like a gyre wobbling around a point that was located somewhere in my forgotten past, the point where . . . what? Where innocence ended? Where the dreams started to fade? Where divorce and disillusionment and the steady dying began?

Years disappeared in seconds. Time collapsed. Faces were simultaneously youthful and middle-aged, smoothly naive and closed against suffering and pain. People came up to one another, stared into each other's face for a few seconds, struggling to get the overlays right, to get rid of the double exposure that kept them from truly recognizing one another, and then one or the other said his own name, and the image suddenly came into focus. They fell into one another's arms, hugged each other's thickened bodies fiercely, their grins becoming painful grimaces. Many of them were weeping. We were like a group of Vietnam veterans at a memorial service, survivors recognizing others who'd lived through the same trauma, remembering those who didn't make it and realizing all over again how close we ourselves came to not making it. For a moment there was a kind of intimacy among strangers, as when the family gathers and grief turns to joy and joy back to grief.

Later that afternoon and into the final hours of the night, there was a party and barbecue at Bob Brown's farm a few miles south of town—Robert V. N. Brown, rasp-voiced activist and former editor of the radical quarterly *Reflections: The Free South Review* and later *The North Carolina Anvil,* a tough, physically ugly, in-your-face kind of weekly paper that somehow kept afloat until 1983, then perished as its left-wing, counterculture, university-based readership drifted away.

At the party Brown was, as always, an impresario, greeting people with embraces and old jokes as we ambled down his long dirt driveway from the field filled with parked cars. Brown steered us on toward barrels packed with ice and beer and soft drinks and the food spread over tables and grills, where dozens of groups of people, ten and twenty to a clot, stood around yakking intently at one another. Peacocks screamed from trees or stalked the pathways of the elaborately designed flower gardens, and beyond the flowers several blond horses sniffed the air and edged along the corral toward the gate as dusk settled and the light softened and tinted everything in pale amber. Children of various ages picked their way through the crowd to the food, then retreated to where they could watch the horses and talk about the funny-looking grown-ups, many of the men bearded, with long hair tied back in ponytails, and women in peasant blouses and granny dresses.

It was a beer party, what you'd expect at a Lions picnic, except for the unusual abundance of soft drinks. Not exactly a heavy-drinking crowd. Not anymore. And there seemed to be no dope at all. No cocaine, certainly, but not once was a joint passed on to me. I couldn't even pick up the sweet smell of it, which was somehow jarring, running against my visual sense of the event. The music, loud and endless, of course, was pure Woodstock—Jimi Hendrix, Janis Joplin, the Doors, the Rolling Stones, Aretha, Dylan, the Band.

Harry and Sibyl Macklin, the owners and proprietors of the old Harry's Deli, had come up from their retirement home in Margate, Florida. Wearing Bermuda shorts and drip-dries, tanned and looking very much like the elderly retirees they had become, Harry and Sibyl smiled and greeted the middle-aged men and women who treated the couple like a favorite uncle and aunt. It was Harry and Sibyl who'd supported the kids who kept getting busted by local and state cops for trying to convince Chapel Hill businesses to serve blacks alongside whites, the only grown-ups who would bail the kids out of jail, let them bus tables when they got broke, run a tab and work it off during the hours after midnight. Most parents were horrified by what was happening to their children over at Chapel Hill, and the university itself washed its hands of them, even though officials knew exactly what was happening, tracked every sit-in, every demonstration, every arrest, with the kind of diligence and surveillance that made the FBI of that period notorious later.

Slowly, I started looking around for my fellow RV-riders. It was late, and I was exhausted, as much emotionally as physically, and I was starting to feel a strange, unexpected loneliness and frustration. The closer I got to this place, the more I realized that it was gone, it wasn't here—all those young friends and all those rough farmhouses in the North Carolina pinewoods and those warm nights filled with music and delight and those bright flashes of moral clarity, all of it gone.

Saturday morning at breakfast in the Carolina Inn dining room, I ran into Ben Jones, the actor-politician, who had arrived late the day before after a day kissing babies at Fourth of July picnics in his rural Georgia district.

Ben looked good. In a way, he looked better than he did twenty years ago, before jogging, tanning salons, hair stylists, designer glasses, and stone-washed jeans, back when Jack Kennedy was the only politician who seemed to know how to look like an actor. Then as now Ben was tall, broad-shouldered, dark, and square-featured, but in college he had an off-center bulk and physical recklessness about him that made him seem strangely vulnerable. He'd lost that, which was no doubt to his cosmetic advantage—he probably looked better on TV now—but he was harder to reach in conversation, seemed distracted, as if looking for the camera, while we strolled down East Franklin Street onto the old campus.

Soon, however, the familiar beauty of the place cast its spell, and we both found ourselves listening to each other describe himself twenty years ago as a naive country kid with luck and pluck who was essentially faking it in a world that intimidated him. Ben and I both had been bright, talented poor boys, he from western North Carolina, me from the hills of New Hampshire, who through marriage had the great good fortune to be picked up along the way by wealthy benefactors. His story matched mine. I hadn't known that about him, had always thought of Ben as somehow well-off, and, of course, he had thought the same of me. We passed the famous Old Well and the half-dozen buildings dating back to the university's founding in 1795, and strolled south across the wide Sargasso-green lawn toward Wilson Library, catching each other up on our marriages and divorces, our children, our failures and ambitions.

I asked Ben how he expected to have a political future with his ragged personal life, drug use, and activist political past. He looked his age to me now, was walking in his old off-centered way, a hillside lope, and his tinted designer glasses no longer hid the pain a man feels when he knows he's hurt people he loved—people he would not hurt today if given the chance, but he knows he hurt them so badly they will never give him another chance, and he thinks about it every day.

"When it was first suggested to me that I run for Congress, I told them about everything, the wildness, the political activism, the drugs, the divorces. Everything, Russ. Even the parts I can't remember. Took it all out of the closet and dumped it in front of them. They said fine. Down here folks understand a reformed sinner, and they deeply mistrust that feller throwing the first stone. A good thing, too," he added.

Deep in the arboretum behind Morehead Planetarium, we came upon a small bridal party, girls in their pastel-colored dresses like huge wobbling chrysanthemums and big-boned sunburnt boys in tuxedoes looking like they were headed to a sports awards banquet. The group stood in a clearing among rosebushes with a wall of mountain laurel curving around behind, and in the center, under an arbor covered with yellow roses, the bride and groom were being photographed by the best man. Off to one side, the parents and the preacher and several other adults had gathered together, as if advising one another on how to live without the children now.

Ben and I moved quickly, silently, past, a pair of old soldiers, slightly grizzled, home briefly from the foreign wars and finding out that everyone they once knew and loved had died or moved on or else had simply forgotten their names and faces. No one's here now but strangers.

There were numerous informal, spontaneous get-togethers all over town that morning and afternoon. The only organized function was a combination Alcoholics Anonymous/Narcotics Anonymous/Overeaters Anonymous/Gamblers Anonymous meeting that turned out to be surprisingly well attended. Or maybe not so surprisingly. I talked afterward to three friends who were at the meeting, and they seemed oddly clear-eyed, relaxed, as if a great, protracted tension in their lives had been resolved. "It was an important meeting," one told me. "Really important, Russ." But he said it as if it had been the opposite of a meeting, a coming together; as if instead it had been the occurrence of a much-desired severance.

Later that afternoon, there was another bash, this time at Rachel Brousseau's house, north of Chapel Hill in Carrboro, where redbrick bungalows and modular homes and trailers appeared out of the kudzu along the winding country road with open fields of corn and melons out behind and a black ridge of North Carolina pines at the horizon. Cars were parked on both sides of the road for a half mile.

"Not one stretch limo," Ray sadly observed, as we squeezed past the rows of beat-up VWs and Hondas, secondhand station wagons, campers and pickups. It was hot—midafternoon, midsummer, Piedmont hot—but the air conditioner in the RV had come magically back to life again, so I eased the van around the sawhorses at the end of the long driveway and rolled past the strings of people walking in from the road like pilgrims making their way to a shrine, and when I arrived before the house begged Rachel Brousseau to let me park the thing on her lawn. She shrugged, Why not? I shut off the motor and switched on the generator and left the air conditioner running. Four or five bottles of the original case of chardonnay remained in the fridge.

A pair of pigs was roasting over a wood fire, and a huge parachute tent had been set up in the pinewoods behind the white ranch-style house. Music blasted from speakers set on the ground among the trees, and an enormous crowd milled around the tables of food and iced barrels of beer and soft drinks. An American flag ten feet high and twenty feet long with the peace symbol superimposed over the stripes had been attached to the side of the house—a sad but still powerful, time-shattering image, like the music wailing across the fields all the way to the road and the sight of Paul Hutzler sitting cross-legged on the ground in front of a speaker zoned out by the thump-thump-thump of the Moody Blues and the hickory smoke and vinegary smell from the roasting pigs and the half-dozen couples slow-dancing on pine needles and the shirtless kids named America and Starr wandering around at the edges of the crowd— and suddenly I knew that I'd had enough. Whatever I came here to say and do couldn't be said or done; whomever I came to see couldn't be seen.

Lucius was laid out in the van working on his novel and a bottle of chardonnay, and Chris and Saundi were on the sofa talking about the future. Dale was reading her book, and Jerri was napping in the stateroom in back. Carey was off somewhere, last seen following an extraordinarily attractive dark-haired woman he said he was scared of, and Ray and Dave were being interviewed and video-taped by Elva Bishop for a local TV documentary. Kathy I hadn't seen since last night at Bob Brown's, when she went off with the Honigmanns to swim in their pond.

I said to Lucius, "Enough?"

He looked up for a second. "Plenty."

It was Sunday morning, July 6. In New York they were sweeping up a million tons of trash. We'd checked out of our rooms at the Carolina Inn and were waiting around the lobby for Carey and Kathy to phone in and tell us where to pick them up. Then word came to the front desk that they'd meet us at noon at the picnic brunch at Ralph Macklin's. We groaned—not another crowded barbecue in the midsummer sun. We were thinking very seriously about Monday morning already, and it was an eleven-hour drive to New York.

Macklin's was indeed just like the others, only hotter. But there was a lake, we were told, and "lots of folks" had gone down there swimming. The lake turned out to be a recently constructed Corps of Engineers basin with the skeletons of hundreds of drowned trees sticking up like ghosts and a wide, dark red, dried-mud aureole encircling it. A few people were actually swimming in the tepid water, but most stood in the sun along the shore, smoking cigarettes and talking in low voices. The party was truly over.

I rounded up my scattered passengers one by one, then said good-bye and walked back out to the road, where the van sat, cool and waiting, like the F train to Wall Street.

Everyone accounted for, I was about to join them, when I heard someone call, "Hey, Russ, wait a minute! Got something for you." It was Tucker Clark, a man whose face, when we were both in our early twenties, so closely resembled mine that coeds who had spent the previous night with Tucker would come up to me on Franklin Street and bat their eyes and tell me what a great time they'd had. It was uncanny and often embarrassing, but I thought Tucker was a good-looking guy, so didn't really mind. Today he looked less like me, but then so did I.

Tucker took me aside for a second and handed me a folder of photos, large black-and-whites. "I dug these out and meant to show them to you all weekend. There's one I wanted you to have," he said, poking the others out of the way, most of which seemed to be of old girlfriends of Tucker's. "There, there she is," he said proudly and plucked a five-by-seven from the group and handed it to me.

It was a black-and-white photograph of Christine, my ex-wife, standing alone and smiling in her tight-lipped, witty way, gazing directly into the camera. Instantly I recognized the place, the Union Grove Old Time Fiddlers' Convention, and time, early summer, 1965. I stared at her face, and my hands started to tremble, and then

I felt myself falling helplessly into the picture. This was the face I came here to see, the one person I came back to meet and talk with. Christine was the person I needed to walk with across the campus greens and through the arboretum, to stop off at the Carolina Coffee Shop and reminisce with, to hang out at a party at Bob Brown's farm in the dusky rose light watching the fawn-colored horses move nervously back and forth against the split-rail fence, while behind us the peacocks screamed from their perches on the dogwood trees. In the picture she was only a girl—a slim, open-faced girl, trusting and impish and smart—and all the things that truly, lastingly, hurt a person had yet to happen to her or to anyone she loved.

I handed the picture back to Tucker.

"Keep it," he said, and I did. I turned and walked alone back down the dry, hot lane to the road, where Carey, Dave, Dale, Kathy, and Ray waited impatiently to return to New York.

And I thought, Good-bye. Good-bye, my darling. Good-bye.

PRIMAL DREAMS

When you fly into Miami International Airport from Newark and drive south and west for two hours on Florida's Turnpike, you travel through the early twenty-first century in North America. Condos and malls and housing developments like orange-capped mushrooms spring up from horizon to horizon. Fast-food outlets, trailer parks, used-car lots with banners crackling in the breeze, and, in Homestead, the lingering wreckage of last year's hurricanes—stripped live oak trees, decapitated palms, boarded-up buildings, temporary housing—give way to tomato and sugarcane fields where migrant workers from Jamaica and Mexico toil under the subtropical sun. It's the inescapable present.

But then, suddenly, you drive through the entrance to Everglades National Park, and it's as if you've passed through a gate into another time altogether, a distant, lost time eons before the arrival of the first Europeans, before even the rumored arrival of the Arawak in dugouts fleeing the Caribbean archipelago and the invading Caribs. Out on the Anhinga Trail, barely beyond earshot of the cars and RVs lumbering toward the lodge and marina in Flamingo, at the southern end of the park, the only sounds you hear are the wind riffling through the saw grass and the plash of fish feeding on insects and one another and the great long-necked anhingas diving or emerging from the mahogany waters of a slug-gish, seaward-moving slough. You hear a hundred frogs cheeping and croaking and the sweet wet whistle of a red-winged blackbird. A primeval six-foot-long alligator passes silently through the deep slough to the opposite side, coasts to a stop in the shallows, and lurks, a corrugated log with eyes. An anhinga rises from the water and flies like a pterodactyl to a cluster of nearby mangrove roots and cumbrously spreads and turns its enormous wings like glisten-ing black kites silhouetted against the noontime sun.

A rough carpet of water lilies—clenched, fist-size buds about to bloom—floats on the surface of the slough, while just below, long-nosed gars luff in threes and fours, and bass and bluegills col-lect in schools, abundant and wary of the next upper link in the food chain, but strangely secure, like carp in a Japanese pool, as if here they have no unnatural enemies. A large soft-shelled turtle hauls herself out of the water and patiently begins to lay her dozens of eggs in the gray limestone soil, depositing them like wet vanilla-colored seeds. Farther down the embankment lies the wreckage of an old nest broken open by birds, the leathery shells smashed and drying in the sun. A dark blue racer snake slides into the brush. Mosquitoes gather in slow, buzzing swirls. The sun is high and it's hot, ninety degrees, with a slight breeze blowing from the east. It's mid-May, yes—but what century?

In our time, much of travel that is freely elected by the traveler is time travel. We go to Paris, tour Venice, visit Athens and the Holy Land, mainly to glimpse the past and walk about the cobbled streets with a guidebook, a sun hat, and a furled umbrella—emulating as best we can Henry James in Rome, Flaubert in Cairo. Or we fly to Tokyo, Beijing, Abu Dhabi, perhaps, for a safe, cautious peek into the future. Sometimes, for both the past and the future at once, we make our way to cities like Lagos, Mexico City, Lima. It's time travel, but it's strictly to the past and future of humanity that we've gone.

For some of us, that's not enough. We want to travel even farther in time, to view and imagine anew the planet without billions
of human beings on it. For this we get up an expedition and float
down the Amazon on a raft or we go off to Africa and clone ourselves a Teddy Roosevelt safari and shoot the large animals with
cameras instead of guns. Some of us traipse off to the Arctic or to
uninhabited deserts or to mountaintops—journeying to the last
remaining places where a traveler can be alone, more or less, and
view the planet as it was before we started killing it.

But who can afford that? Who has the time? With only a week
or two available and a modest amount of cash in hand, most of us are
obliged to look for places closer to home. For me, when in search of
this type of time travel, one of the most satisfying places to go is the
Florida Everglades. The reasons are many and complex. Of no small
importance, the Everglades is easy to get to, especially for a traveler
living in the eastern United States. The park is a smooth seventy-
mile drive from downtown Miami. And it is vast in size; you can get
lost there. It is the second-largest national park in America outside
Alaska—twenty-two hundred square miles, an area approximately
the size of Delaware. And despite its proximity to one of the most
densely populated regions in America, it is, for its size, one of the
least visited parks in the system, especially from April to November.
You can be alone there, or nearly so.

But more to the point, every time I climb into my time machine
(usually an air-conditioned rental car picked up at the Miami International Airport) and travel into the Everglades, I journey to a place
that has a shivering personal resonance for me. I almost always go
by myself. It's less distracting that way, and I don't want to be distracted, because, once there, my imagination is instantly touched at
its center, and all the world seems significant and personalized, as
in a powerful dream. It's my dreamtime, and I don't want anyone,
even someone I love and trust, to wake me.

Most people, if they're lucky, have a place or two where this
happens, but for me it occurs in the Everglades. Who knows why?

Childhood visions of pre-Columbian Florida and the Caribbean, maybe, induced by stories of Columbus, de Soto, and that master of time-travelers, Ponce de León, in which I helplessly identified with the wide-eyed European conquerors. Followed years later by adolescent pilgrimages to the Keys in naive search of Ernest Hemingway's source of inspiration—as vain an enterprise as Ponce's, maybe, but who knew that then? And over the years, repeated visits to the Glades, by accident or casual circumstance, building up a patina of personal associations, until now I enter the park with an expectancy based on nostalgia for a lost self—nostalgia for the New England boy reading about the Arawak Indians and Columbus, for the youth trying to become a novelist, for the reckless young man footloose in South Florida.

It's an expectancy that is almost always met. I park my time machine and walk out onto the Anhinga or the Gumbo Limbo Trail, step by step moving along the catwalk of my own personal time line. I keep returning, and with increasing clarity I see more of the place and more of my past selves. And more of the past of the planet as well.

Beyond any other national park, the Everglades bears repeated visits, justifying a traveler's return trips, but maybe requiring them, too. Without intending it, over the years I've acquired from these visits a gradual accumulation of information—about my layered self, I suppose, and, more important, about the place—which has helped me learn to look at the Everglades and see it for what it is, instead of what it isn't.

The first few times I didn't get it. There are no high mountains, no rushing cataracts, no grand panoramic vistas. There's no rain forest, no powerful continent-draining river, no rocky seashore. The Glades is quiet and low and slow, a shallow, almost invisible river of grass, an intricate, extremely fragile subtropical ecosystem that seems shy and difficult of access to the human eye, which is, of course, one of the reasons humans have come so close to destroying it—and may yet succeed.

To see the Everglades for what it is and not what it isn't, you have to develop a kind of bifocal vision, as if you were floating down the Mississippi on a raft with Huck Finn. You have to learn to switch your gaze constantly from the concrete to the abstract, from the nearby riverbank to the distant sky. You need an almost Thoreauvian eye for detail and for the interrelatedness of nature's minutiae. It's a 1.5-million-acre Walden Pond I'm talking about here, the largest wetland in the United States. From November through May there are between fifty thousand and a hundred thousand wading birds in the Everglades. More than one hundred species of butterflies have been identified in the park. Fifty species of reptiles, including twenty-six species of snakes and sixteen of turtles. Eighteen species of amphibians. Three hundred forty-seven species of birds. Forty species of mammals. More than one thousand species of plants. There are fifty-two varieties of the small striped Liguus snails that you see clinging to the trunks of the live oaks along the short Gumbo Limbo Trail, where, as you stroll, you can catch the skunklike smell of opening white stopper buds, used in ancient times by the Arawak and the first white settlers as a specific against dysentery.

The Gumbo Limbo Trail winds through great, twisted old live oak trees with epiphytes clinging to the trunks and upper branches, and dead-looking brown resurrection ferns at the roots that burst greenly into life after a rain. The trail is circular and begins and ends at the hundred-foot-tall royal palms of Paradise Key. The key is a hummock, a gentle, almost imperceptible rise in the blond watery plain, more like a solidified limestone sea-swell than an actual key or island. The majestic palms, which these days tower photogenically in front of Miami hotels and cluster around the old Bebe Rebozo compound on Key Biscayne and a thousand other estates, appeared first on the continent here in the Everglades, their seed carried by wind and water from the Caribbean thousands of years ago to catch and eventually prosper on this very hummock. A short way off the trail, I notice a small, still pool of water covered

with bright green slime—duckweed—which, seen up close, turns
into a glistening skin, as clean and beautiful and serene as snake-
skin over the dark, turbulent, fecund water below. I lean down and
look closer and imagine I can see into the thrashing molecular soup
of life itself.

But the swarming details of the Everglades can overwhelm
you. It's almost too much to absorb and organize. In this finely delin-
eated and particularized landscape, to gain perspective you have to
step away from time to time and abstract it. Along with Thoreau's
eye, you need to develop an almost Emersonian appreciation for the
vast circular canopy of blue that stretches unbroken from horizon
to horizon and the broad watery swale under your feet. It's as if you
are at sea and stand upon a shimmering grassy plain that floats like
a Sargasso between the firmaments, above and below. The light is
spectacular and shifts constantly as clouds build and dissipate and
build again. The intensity of the light and its movement are dizzy-
ing. To steady yourself, you shift your gaze almost involuntarily
back to what's close at hand, clinging to it as if to the rail of a ship.
In so abstract a landscape, to ground yourself you have to look again
at the details.

And so it goes—back and forth, the long view and the short, the
abstract and the concrete—for here you are situated in an infinitely
complex world whose parts and the tissue of connections between
them can be seen only if the viewer keeps shifting his focal point. By
comparison, the city of man, the anthrosphere, from nearby Miami
to distant Mumbai, seems stilled, frozen, caught in a snapshot in
relatively recent time, serving either as all foreground or all background, with no movement between them. The central figure, the
subject, is always us; humanity is the figure and the ground; we are
content as well as context. In the Everglades, the central figure is
the ancient planet itself and its immense plenitude.

Sometimes, instead of visiting the southern end of the Everglades, I drive out from Miami along Route 41, the old Tamiami
Trail, cross through the Miccosukee Indian reservation, past the

airboat rentals (banned inside the park but ready to rent all around it) and the solitary fishermen sitting by the canals built by the Army Corps of Engineers, to reach the north side of the park and spend the day at Shark Valley. It's less a valley than a broad, shallow slough twelve miles wide, a one- to three-foot-deep scimitar-shaped depression in the limestone bedrock that carries the overflow from Lake Okeechobee in a tectonically slow drift south and west at barely one hundred feet per day, sliding the fresh, nutrient-rich waters across the saw grass plain to the mangrove estuaries of the Gulf of Mexico. Out here, South Florida seems freshly emerged from the ocean, still dripping and draining back into the Gulf, as if the Ice Age ended only yesterday. Its highest point is barely eight feet above sea level, but from it you can see for miles.

At the Shark Valley Visitor Center there's an open, rubber-tired tram that carts tourists into the Glades a ways, with a Park Service guide on a loudspeaker who'll describe what you're seeing. There's a bike-rental shop and a fifteen-mile bike path to an observation tower and numerous trails where you can walk in silence. In a half hour, I'm under the hot May sun a few miles out on the bicycle path, pedaling the wobbly old one-speed bike I rented next to the visitor center. I'm finally far enough into the Glades that I can no longer hear the visitors or their cars and RVs or the guide on the tram, so I pull off the path and stop.

Purple pickerelweed is flowering everywhere, and bladderwort, like yellow stars, blooms against the dark water of the slough. Deerflies cruise by and then swerve hungrily back toward me, a new warm-blooded mammal, and hairless, too. All I can hear now is the clank of the links in the food chain. Herons and egrets stand knee-deep in water, waiting motionless, like the fishermen I saw earlier alongside the canal on the Tamiami Trail, and now and then I hear the splash of a gar or a bass busting the air for a low-flying dragonfly. For a long time, without making a ripple, a six-foot alligator on the far side of the slough stalks a spindly white egret, drawing closer and closer, undetected, until suddenly there is a great furious roil and splash of water, then feathers floating, and silence as the gator slides away.

Later, out at the observation tower, I pause halfway up and look down, and in the copse below, a rust-colored fawn with pale spots across its belly lies curled and hidden by its mother. Intent only on protecting her offspring from the huge gator snoozing in the slough fifty feet away, she obviously has not considered aerial reconnaissance, especially by a human. Down below, the fawn lies as still as a statue in the cool shade of the copse. I feel oddly invasive for watching and resume climbing to the top of the tower. There I gaze out across the watery veldlike plain of saw grass. In the west a bank of cumulus clouds piles up above the Gulf near Everglades City, promising rain. For a moment I consider hurrying back to the car, but then decide no, let the rain come down. And within the hour it does, and as I walk my rented bike the eight miles back to the visitor center, I feel finally invisible, lost in time and space, afloat inside a dream of a lost and coherent world.

Crossing Shark Valley by foot in the warm torrential rain, it's almost inconceivable somehow that my points of departure—Keene, New York, and Miami, Florida—are in the same time zone as the Everglades. Not just longitudinally, as on a map, but literally, as on a calendar or a wristwatch. Here and in Keene and Miami, today's headlines and stock quotes are the same, the historical facts still hold, and thus all three places bear, at least abstractly, the same relation to the onrushing millennium, to its ethnic cleansings, genocidal massacres, famines, global floods of refugees, men and women and children gunning one another down with automatic weapons, wanton destruction of the planet—everything that drives a modern man or woman nearly mad with grief and despair, so that finally all one wants is to get out of this time zone. "Anywhere, so long as it's out of this world," said Baudelaire. And here I am, out of that world. Astonishing!

Later in the day, after the rain has passed east toward Miami and the Atlantic, I drive out on Route 41 to Everglades City in the northwest corner of the Everglades, where there is another visitor center and a marina located at the entrance to the Ten Thousand Islands, a vast spray of mangrove islands that stretches about forty miles from Marco Island in the north to Pavilion Key. It was Ponce de León who guessed there were ten thousand islands, but the modern count, via satellite, is 14,022. The number keeps changing, because most of the "islands," even those several miles across, are built on clustered red mangroves and are constantly being broken apart and restructured by hurricanes.

It's close to five o'clock, though midafternoon bright at this time of year. The sky is washed clean of clouds, and the still surface of the cordovan-colored waters of Chokoloskee Bay is glazed with a taut silvery skin. In these calm tidal waters there is an abundance of snook, tarpon, redfish, blue crabs, and bottlenose dolphins, feeding and breeding and being preyed upon by one another, by the thousands of cormorants and ospreys and cranes and pelicans and egrets and ibis that flock year-round on the mangrove islets and rookeries, and by the sport and commercial fishermen from the tiny villages of Everglades City and Chokoloskee as well. They're not preyed upon in such numbers as to endanger them yet— except, of course, for the elusive, mysterious manatee, that fifty-million-year-old watery relative to the elephant, a seagoing cow with flippers. The manatees are protected, but their death rate may exceed their birth rate: these gentle two-thousand-pound animals are being decimated and cruelly wounded by the propellers of the fishing and pleasure boats that roar up and down the waterways here. Nine out of ten of the remaining eighteen hundred manatees bear ugly prop scars on their smooth backs. There are about seven hundred thousand registered powerboats in Florida, and thanks to persistent lobbying in Tallahassee by their owners, there are no speed limits in these peaceful, secluded waters. The boats race along the thousands of interlaced channels and crisscross the myriad unnamed bays at thirty to fifty miles an hour, chopping through anything too slow or confused by the noise to get out of the way. Generally the manatees keep to the channels among the islands, feeding on sea grass in waters so darkened by the tannin from the roots and dead leaves of the red mangrove that the animal cannot see the bottom of the boat approaching; nor can it hear the roar of the motor until the boat is nearly on top of it, and thus cannot flee in time to elude death or maiming.

There's enough daylight left to tempt me to rent a canoe at the visitor center. I push out into Chokoloskee Bay and paddle slowly along one of the scores of channels that cut into and around Sandfly Island in the general direction of the Turner River Canoe Trail, the start of the Wilderness Waterway that winds for ninety-nine miles through the most extensive mangrove forest in America, all the way to Flamingo and Florida Bay in the south. All I want today, however, is a few hours of solitude on the water, a closer look at the cormorants and the frigate birds and the tricolor Louisiana heron I glimpsed heading low over the bay toward Sandfly Island.

Halfway out, barely a quarter mile from shore, a pod of bottlenose dolphins, maybe four or five, swimming a short way off my bow, notice the canoe and slice through the water to investigate, their dorsal fins racing toward me like black knife blades. After circling the intruder several times, they move off again, apparently satisfied or bored, but the last in the pod—an adolescent, probably—makes a show-off's grinning leap. It practically stands on the water and plops over, splashing me and rocking the canoe, and then cruises back to join the others.

I move out into the bay another half mile. Atop many of the channel markers, ospreys have built their nests, turning the poles into tall, branchless trees. They are incredibly stable birds, mating for life, and they use the same nest year after year. Off to my right a ways, one of the smaller islands has been converted into a rookery by a huge flock of fork-tailed frigate birds. There seems to be a great flurry of activity, so I paddle over. Fifty or more parent frigate birds are huddling protectively over their fuzzy gray hatchlings, while another fifty make a great racket and fight off dozens of predatory, sharp-beaked cormorants screeching and hungrily diving for the offspring. I draw near in my canoe and watch the fight for a long while, an invisible witness to a savage siege and great acts of parental courage and sacrifice.

To let you see what's there, most national parks get you up high on a mountain or make you gape into a canyon or a gorge, playing with scale and fostering delusions of human grandeur without your even having to leave your car. "This car climbed Pikes Peak, Whiteface Mountain, Mount Washington," and so on. In the Everglades, though, you're kept on the same plane as the natural world. You can't see the Everglades at all, really, unless you get close up and keep it at eye level, which humbles you a bit. "This car drove through the Everglades" is not much of a claim. This sort of viewing is interactive, and your travel backward in time to the continent's beginnings is all the more convincing for it.

Maybe it's especially true for Americans—we whose present is too much with us, we whose future looks worse and whose past is increasingly paved over or deliberately erased—that, for our emotional and intellectual well-being, for our moral health as well, time travel has become more essential than ever. Maybe it's this need that explains the growing popularity and proliferation of historical theme parks, the desire to build a Disney World near a Civil War battlefield, for instance. Or the whole *Jurassic Park* concept, which surely, as much as the animated dinosaurs, accounts for the extraordinary popularity of the movies. It's the idea of safe passage to the distant past that appeals. This idea may also account for the rapidly increasing popularity of our national parks. The total number of visitors is up 10 percent overall in the last decade, and it's much greater in some parks (70 percent in Yosemite, for instance), bringing—especially in the parks located within easy striking distance of urban areas—traffic jams, environmental damage, graffiti, crime: all the woes of life in the here and now that we're trying to escape.

The Everglades, which is more demanding of its visitors' imaginations than most other parks, has not yet suffered as they have. The greatest danger to the Glades comes from outside the park, from the agriculture industry and real estate developers, who for generations have been blocking and draining off its freshwater sources in central and southeastern Florida for human use and polluting the rest with chemical fertilizers and runoff. In recent years, the National Park Service, the state of Florida, and the U.S. Army Corps of Engineers have begun cooperating to restore the old flow of water from Okeechobee as much as possible and to control with great rigor the amount of pollutants allowed to enter the system. In 1994, Florida governor Lawton Chiles signed the Everglades Forever Act, a complicated, expensive compromise between the environmentalists and the agricultural interests, brokered with the assistance of Interior Secretary Bruce Babbitt. The bill requires the state to construct forty thousand acres of filtration marshes around Lake Okeechobee at a cost of $700 million, with the farmers paying a third of the costs and the rest coming from Florida taxpayers. No one is happy with the deal, which suggests that it's as good a deal as anyone is going to get right now. This act sets a temporary clean-water goal of fifty parts of phosphorus per billion parts of water, which means that the pollution from chemical fertilizers, though diminished, will nonetheless continue. But saving the Everglades is an ongoing, extremely costly fight, and for some species it may be too late. One of the thirty remaining Florida panthers was recently found dead inside the park, and its body contained mercury at a level that would kill a human being.

The sky in the west has faded to pale rose. Ragged silver-blue strips of cloud along the horizon glow red at the edges, as if about to burst into flame. I turn my canoe back toward the marina and paddle fairly energetically now, for I don't want to get caught out here after dark among ten thousand islands and ten million mosquitoes. You could easily get lost in this maze of channels and not be found for days and be extremely ill by then. I'm reluctant to leave this primeval world, however. Once again, the peaceful, impersonal beauty of the Everglades has soothed and nourished my mind and heart and has restored some of the broken connections to my layered selves and memories. It's time to return to the anthrosphere.

Then, suddenly, a few yards ahead of my canoe, I see a swelling disturbance in the water. It smooths and rises, and the water parts and spills, as first one, then two large, sleek-backed, pale gray manatees surface and exhale gusts of mist into the air. They slowly roll and dive. A second later they reappear, and this time there is a calf the size of a dolphin nestled safely between them. I can hear the three animals inhaling huge quantities of air, and then they dive again and are gone. The water seethes and settles and is still. A low-flying pelican cruises down the channel ahead of me and disappears in the dusk.

For a long time I sit there in my canoe, thrilled by the memory of the sight, feeling unexpectedly, undeservedly blessed. Jurassic Park, indeed. This is the real thing! For a few wondrous seconds, a creature from the Paleocene has let me enter its world and has come close enough almost to touch. It's as if the old planet earth itself contained a virtue, a profound generosity of spirit, that has allowed it to reach forward in time all the way to the twenty-first century in North America, and has brought me into its embrace.

HOUSE OF SLAVES

Arriving at a so-called Developing World capital from the so-called Developed World can be metabolically disruptive: a familiar logic displaced suddenly by an unfamiliar one. It jangles one's body as much as one's mind. Compared with landing in Lima or Djibouti, however, my arrival at Dakar from New York via Brussels was orderly in a familiar way. There was, of course, the expected military presence—tall, pistol-packing Senegalese youths with aviator sunglasses and mustaches and batons—but the passport check was swift and efficient, and my baggage showed up quickly and intact, and taxis into the city were waiting patiently in a line outside.

Nearly half my fellow arriving passengers were white European tourists, mainly French and too young to feel even vaguely postcolonial. The rest were returning upper-crust Senegalese, elegantly tall and slender, many dressed in traditional, elaborately embroidered boubous, and a large number of middle-aged African Americans on package tour, most of them somewhat overweight, wearing stone-washed jeans and brightly colored dashikis—somber men and women on a serious, roots-finding mission to West Africa. I was here on business, one might say—research for a novel requiring use of the archives at the Gorée Institute, a Pan-African think tank and conference center on Gorée Island, a few miles offshore. I had a second reason for coming to West Africa, but didn't know it yet. Before departing Gorée, I would learn that, despite being a white American, I, too, was on a roots-finding mission.

A twenty-minute ride through the treeless, sun-baked sprawl of cinder-block suburbs brought me to the congested heart of the capital. Dakar was thronged, a hustling, bustling city of more than a million and a half people and growing way too fast to adjust. The main drags were jammed with cars and smoke-belching trucks and buses. The entire downtown seemed to be one big open-air market. On Avenue Blaise Diagne, as in midtown New York and the Marais in Paris, smiling Senegalese sold genuine Rolex watches for twenty bucks or, for five, a Lacoste shirt guaranteed not to shrink. The streets and sidewalks were packed with pedestrians, fully half of them selling—everything from Bic lighters to pirated videos and CDs and knockoffs by the thousands of carved wooden figures and tribal masks—the other half arguing good-naturedly over the prices.

My host, John Matshikiza, a South African writer and head of the humanities department at the Gorée Institute, got us aboard the last ferry to Gorée just as it left the terminal at the eastern end of the port, where a half-dozen rusting freighters and tankers under a Panamanian or Liberian flag lay wheezing at anchor. The double-decker ferry was filled to the rails with island residents returning from the mainland, most of them women chatting and arguing cheerfully in Wolof or simply resting from a long day's work before beginning the night's. As the sun set, a group of muscular teenaged boys wailed away on drums, while the rest of us, helpless to resist, swayed in time and gazed at the fading skyline of Dakar silhouetted against the blood-orange sky.

The island faced the open Atlantic like a medieval fortress, and on its approach, the ferry swung wide to avoid a buoy. Matshikiza explained that late in World War II an English freighter thought to be carrying General de Gaulle was sunk by Vichy guns on Gorée.

"The gun placements are still there," he said, pointing to the north-ern end of the island. "Deactivated, of course. Although there are three thousand French soldiers stationed on the mainland. In case de Gaulle finally shows up, I guess," he said and laughed. "History's not dead in Africa. It just gets recycled."

Gorée Island was tiny, an islet barely a mile long and half as wide, crowded with crumbling old warehouses and two-story stuccoed stone residences and the empty, decaying mansion of the long-gone colonial governor of French West Africa. Other than the elegantly restored and renovated buildings owned by the Gorée Institute, there were a few guesthouses, one small hotel, one res-taurant, and several seaside cafés—for the intrepid French tourists escaping for a day from the heat and crowds of Dakar and picnicking Senegalese and for the African Americans, usually in couples—my countrymen and -women.

I checked into my lodgings immediately, a two-room tile-roofed cottage off a village lane facing a large, multilevel courtyard with flower gardens and swaying palms and baobab and acacia trees enclosed by a high wall. My quarters were clean and bright and comfortable. There was a kitchen galley and a large tiled bath, a sit-ting area, and a desk. Perfect. I unpacked quickly, then headed out for dinner at the restaurant of the Hotel Chevalier de Boufflers—grilled fish, rice, good French bread, a decent French country wine, and a splendid view of the moonlit Atlantic from my table.

Later, following the main lane back through the village to my cottage, I passed an alley and from the darkness heard drumming and the high-pitched ululations of a choir of women. Following the music, I ducked into the alley and turned onto a square with an ancient cottonwood tree at the crossing and came upon the boy drummers from the ferry and two lines of beautiful tall girls and women leaping in time, turn and turn again, dancing brilliantly in torchlight. I stood awhile, enthralled, and not until the dancers and drummers broke up and walked off in pairs did I finally head for my quarters.

In the morning, after a long night of hard-edged, jet-lagged dreams, I looked around and saw that my lodgings were from paradise. From the window I could gaze on hibiscus and bougainvillea and ferns and tall Norfolk pines. Seedpods hung from the bare arms of baobab trees like small bombs. A rooster crowed; ground doves cooed. From beyond the courtyard wall came the thin bleat of goats and voices of children at play and the liquid vowels of Wolof as women exchanged greetings and in the distance the thrum of the engine of the first arriving Dakar ferry. Far off, a muezzin called the faithful to prayer, and closer, the bells of a Catholic church rang out. I made myself French coffee and a breakfast of bread and butter and a fresh orange, and toyed with the idea of staying here for the rest of my life.

Gorée Island is about as close as you can get to the Americas and still be in Africa. It's a preindustrial locale: no cars, no bicycles, even; just handcarts. It's easy to get lost in time. With its narrow, unpaved streets and sandy lanes and early colonial-era stone warehouses and shops and houses with courtyards enclosed by high walls, the island looks very much as it did in slavery days. From time immemorial, the Wolof people of what we now call Senegal—a region situated neatly at the crossroads between Saharan and Equatorial Africa and between the rich interior kingdoms of Mali and the sea—have been a trading people. From the mid-fifteenth century, when Portuguese privateers first hove into view, Gorée Island has been a trading station. And with the arrival of the Europeans, there came a hunger that quickly grew insatiable and lasted for nearly half a millennium. I speak, of course, of the hunger for black African slaves.

The traders on Gorée who built these warehouses facing the sea and the handsome, now crumbling residences were first Portuguese, then Dutch, French, and, for brief periods, British. The black Africans they traded for or captured on their own, those that survived transport, ended up in Brazil, Guyana, the Dutch Antilles, Martinique, Guadeloupe, Haiti, Louisiana, South Carolina, Virginia, and beyond—peopling in time both American continents and the Caribbean archipelago between.

Farther down the coast from Gorée, in Banjul, at the mouth of the Gambia River, and on the coasts of Guinea and Ghana and south to Angola, other European slave-trading stations were built, and the same process of trade or capture and transport of black Africans to the Americas was established. Today, one can without difficulty travel to these points along the coast of West and Equatorial Africa and visit renovated and restored warehouses, docks, and dungeons built by the European slave traders. There is usually a local guide who will lead you from chamber to chamber, exhibit to exhibit, artifact to artifact. He will explain the use of the chains and manacles and collars and other instruments of confinement and torture.

My first day on Gorée, I learned that here, too, there is such a place. It's called La Maison des Esclaves, the House of Slaves. It's the reason those African Americans had come all this way.

One can tour the entire island in a day. Then one either heads back to the mainland or else, as in any small town, one goes inward—which is what I did. Gorée is perfect for that. I visited the Institute library daily and read and made notes and strolled the isle. I lunched at seaside cafés, took my evening meals at the Hotel Chevalier de Boufflers, and chatted with the locals. There were enough day-tripping tourists to make beggars of the children, a thing sad to see, but most Goreans were friendly, soft-spoken, hospitable, and happy to try out their bits of English. The natives of this place did not appear to want to live elsewhere. Understandably. And the women were stunningly beautiful. There are few islands left in the world like Gorée—the Caribbean island of Dominica, perhaps, or the Seychelles. One hopes they'll never be colonized by the soul-stealing industry of resort tourism. One feels guilty even writing about Gorée, and thus I leave out of this account more than a mere passing mention of the beaches.

My time on the island passed all too quickly, and then one afternoon, a few days before my scheduled departure, I passed along a quiet side street, intending finally to visit the House of Slaves. For vague and unexamined reasons, I had been putting it off, as if my presence were somehow not warranted. Halfway there, I noted for the first time a small collection of craft stalls side by side in an open courtyard with a wide banner overhead flapping in the breeze. The words on the banner were in English: WELCOME TO THE FIRST FAIR OF GORÉE ISLAND // BLACK HISTORY MONTH FROM 1ST TO 28TH FEBRUARY.

I puzzled over the words for a moment, the only English-language sign I'd seen on the island, then hurried on. Later, as I stood outside the gates to the House of Slaves, waiting behind a group of fifteen or twenty African Americans just off the ferry and a claque of French tourists, I still wondered about the sign. Whom was it soliciting? Certainly not the French tourists. Not the Africans from the mainland. Not me. I looked at the crowd of my countrymen and -women about to enter the House of Slaves. Of course, the *other* Americans. And said to myself, I shouldn't be here, and quickly left.

That night, at the Hotel Chevalier de Boufflers, I got into an intense conversation with the bartender, Mamadou, a tall, hand-some Wolof who knew the history of his people. In my bad French and his bad English we discussed the collaboration between racism and slavery in the sixteenth century, how for the Europeans and Americans racism had become the moral justification for slavery, and as we talked, I remembered Shakespeare's *The Tempest*, set on an island not unlike this, and my favorite lines, Caliban's Curse:

> *This island's mine by Sycorax, my mother*
> *Which thou tak'st from me. When thou cam'st first,*
> *Thou strok'st me, and made much of me, wouldst give me*

Water with berries in't, and teach me how
To name the bigger light, and how the less,
That burn by day and night, and then I lov'd thee
And show'd thee all the qualities o' th' isle,
The fresh springs, brine-pits, barren place and fertile:
Curs'd be I that did so!

I remembered the passage well enough to recite most of the lines, and Mamadou smiled broadly to hear them. I paid my bill, and as I moved for the door, Mamadou asked if I'd visited the House of Slaves yet.

"No. Not yet."

"Should check it out. Teach you some things," he said.

Walking in the darkness to my cottage, I wondered if I'd been avoiding the House of Slaves solely to keep from having to stand in that baleful place alongside my black fellow Americans. It wasn't merely to sidestep racial guilt. There was something else, something I'd only begun to understand. The African Americans had come to Gorée to be where their black ancestors had stood in chains, to meditate and reflect upon their ancestors' and their own connected fates and histories. If I stood there, it would be for a reason only slightly different—to meditate and reflect in the literal, physical place where the American imagination, and therefore certain distinguishing aspects of my imagination, too, was born. It wasn't born at San Salvador when Columbus dropped anchor in the Caribbean Sea; nor at Jamestown, Virginia; nor at Plymouth Rock; nor at Cumberland Gap looking westward-ho across the continent. No, the American imagination, at least as I was coming to understand it, was born right here on the coast of Africa where the African diaspora began. It was here that Othello, who was merely different, became Caliban, who was Other. To ground my imagination in historical reality, to know myself, I needed to stand in the place where that transformation had occurred.

The links between the specious, socially constructed concept

of race and its corollary, racism, and the history of the African diaspora created a chain that, even today, binds all Americans. It binds
us regardless of our skin pigmentation or any other so-called sec-
ondary racial characteristics, regardless of our ethnic backgrounds,
even regardless of the date of arrival in America of our ancestors—
whether they came in 17,000 B.C.E. from Siberia in pursuit of the
woolly mammoth or 1975 C.E. in flight from having backed the losing side in a civil war in Vietnam. The story of race is the story of
America. "My inheritance was particular, specifically limited and
limiting," James Baldwin wrote. "My birthright was vast, connecting me to all that lives, and to everyone, forever. But one cannot
claim the birthright without accepting the inheritance."

As I arrived back at my cottage, I reminded myself that the
point of travel is knowledge, not information. Its purpose is to create new thoughts. Tomorrow, before I leave for home, I will visit the
House of Slaves.

I approached the gated, head-high wall of the House of Slaves at the
same time as a large tour group of African Americans. I could hear
the ferry returning to Dakar for the next load. While I stood waiting at the rear of the group for the gate to open, I noticed a large,
middle-aged black man looking at me with idle curiosity. The others seemed pointedly to ignore me.

"American?" I asked him.

"Yeah," he said. "From D.C. You?"

I said, "Yes, American. From New York."

He raised his eyebrows in surprise. We shook hands politely.
His name was MacDuffy, and he was here with his wife and son,
who were just ahead of him in line and watching me now with
interest. He nodded toward the front of the line, where a half-dozen
white people were speaking French and checking their cameras.
"Not many white Americans here," he said. "Why are you?"

"I guess my history starts here, too," I said.

"Yeah," he said, almost sadly. "I guess it does." The line began to move forward then, and our conversation ended.

The gate to the House of Slaves opened onto a courtyard. I looked across the courtyard into several small holding chambers and cells and peered straight ahead along a narrow, darkened corridor on the far side of the courtyard that led through an open archway out of the building onto the remains of a stone pier. Beyond the pier I could see the glittering waves of the Atlantic. And beyond that, America. There were ghosts in this place, the ghosts of those who were enslaved, and the ghosts, too, of those who enslaved them. That was my inheritance, in Baldwin's sense. And I had to accept it before I could claim my birthright.

THE LAST BIRDS
OF PARADISE

I'd arrived at Seychelles' La Digue Island late the previous day by interisland freighter from the main island of Mahé. Then, early in the morning, I packed a bottle of water and some fruit and biscuits and, map in hand, walked from La Digue Island Lodge along the sandy lane of the village of Réunion, headed in a deliberately circuitous way for the hiking trail at the island's southern tip, three miles away.

I passed the Catholic church and a dozen small houses, and soon was out of the village. Farther on, simply to admire the graceful pitch of the thatched roof and the long, open veranda, I made a lingering stop at an old copra plantation house, and ended up staring at the surreal clarity of a pure white horse grazing among palms in the broad front yard with a high, rounded black granite outcropping looming behind the house and a deep blue sky hanging overhead.

Keeping to the well-marked but seldom-used seaside trail, I passed along a string of empty white sand beaches on the southwest side of the island, where huge pink and red room-size blocks of weathered granite lined the shore. They rose out of the water and powdery sand and palmy hillsides, mysterious and atavistic, like

Celtic circle stones or Easter Island heads, altars and gods from an ancient age—chthonic images that, like so much in these Seychelles islands, were strangely familiar, yet familiar in a way that I couldn't name.

Then I remembered reading a few weeks ago, before leaving the States, that these very beaches had served not as a site for pre-Christian religious rites but as locations for the filming of *Crusoe, Cast Away,* and *Goodbye Emmanuelle.* That's why they looked so oddly familiar. The shockingly white beaches and colossal red rocks were background shots in soft-core and long-ago-and-far-away films I'd seen, settings for stories of mythic desire and escapist myth. So much for atavism, then. Here, merely, was a modern man out for a morning walk, all alone and more than ten thousand miles from home, and in deep escape mode, gone to where fantasies begin. On location.

I held to the path and went from beach to beach, to where the path finally gave out and dwindled to a thin track, then disappeared altogether from my map and at my feet among rocks and jungle. On a hillside in the shade of coconut palms, I ate my breakfast and, more like a Phoenician castaway than Crusoe (this being the Indian Ocean, not the Caribbean), contemplated the wheeling frigate birds and petrels and terns and the endless luminescent sea below.

Suffering a mild case of burnout, I'd come here and had been island-hopping in the Seychelles for weeks now, diving in the clear, reef-filled waters, climbing black granite mountains, hiking through protected rain forests, and wandering alone along chains of spectacular, unsullied beaches. I was on the mend, but greeted the knowledge with ambivalence. Soon I'd be healed and would have to leave this place. I'd learned a lot and been seduced, but I hadn't gone over. In all the important ways, I was still the busy, harassed fellow who'd flown out of JFK fourteen days before.

Hiking back toward Réunion, I stopped at an old French cemetery located just off the road a short way beyond the copra plantation. The still-legible dates on the stones placed it in the mid-

1800s. I ducked under the low-hanging branches of a poinciana tree and sat on a moss-covered sarcophagus half-sunk in the sandy soil and lingered awhile, meditating, as one does at such a spot, on time and human history. When suddenly there it was! A paradise flycatcher—the male of the species, a jet-black bird the size of my hand, with beautiful long, glossy tail feathers—perched on a tree branch six feet from my face! This was an astounding sight. Before me was one of the rarest birds on earth. At last count there were but eighty left, and those eighty, I'd read, were nowhere else but here, on the tiny, isolated Indian Ocean island of La Digue, and even on La Digue one almost never saw them anymore.

No way to photograph it. I could only contemplate its beauty and singularity, its rare and fragile presence. It was a black, very intense small bird with a lovely warbling song and a brilliant stone-hard gaze. After a moment it flew off, keeping to the lower branches of the nearby trees. I waited, still stunned, standing motionless on the mossy grave, and five minutes later the bird returned and clung unafraid to the same branch as before, and for a few seconds that I will always remember, the bird and I studied each other—I one of more than six billion, he one of eighty. It seemed an almost irresponsible thought, but at such a moment inescapable. Who was worth more to the universe, I or this tiny black bird?

The answer did not cheer me.

To travel from New York City to the country of Seychelles, a scattered archipelago in the middle of the Indian Ocean, four degrees south of the equator and a thousand nautical miles from the east coast of Africa, is to venture almost as far from home as a North American can go and still be on the planet. It was eight hours in the air from New York to Paris. Then eight more on the ground in Paris. From Paris, it was nine hours more, by way of Djibouti. The plane was loaded with French military men and their families headed back to the islands of Réunion and Mauritius, with a few vacationers on their way to Seychelles—divers, apparently, judging from their carry-on equipment.

I myself was traveling light, outfitted for a few weeks of solitary hiking and tropical mountain climbing. Seychelles was known to me as a hiker's and naturalist's paradise. Nearly 40 percent of its mountainous land area has been nationalized and set aside in preserves laced with hiking trails; most of its coastline and coastal waters and reefs have been designated as protected, with some of the smaller islands given over entirely to bird sanctuaries. Tourism and development are carefully monitored and controlled, and new projects are allowed to proceed only after protection of the environment has been guaranteed. The country is the Vermont of the tropics, apparently. And though the government of this onetime British Colony is nominally socialist, it seems more green than red.

Seychelles, with just under seventy thousand people, is a micronation. Most of its citizens reside on the main island of Mahé and live and work in Victoria, the world's smallest capital, a town, really, of fewer than thirty thousand. The 115 islands that make up Seychelles are scattered over 150,000 square miles of ocean; altogether they provide only 171.4 square miles of dry land. Mahé, the largest island in the group, is shaped like a bright green bow tie, about seventeen miles long and five wide with a spine of mountains running north and south and hundreds of cays and bays and tiny offshore islets. In the distance, as the plane landed, I could make out the profiles of several of the larger outlying islands—Praslin and La Digue and the mysterious Silhouette.

I passed quickly through customs, and a short while later—after visiting a bank, a car-rental agency, and the Seychelles Tourist Office in downtown Victoria for pamphlets, maps, and trail guides—reconnoitered over a couple of SeyBrews, the excellent local beer, at the Pirates Arms. The café, a clean, well-lighted place with slow-turning overhead fans, was open to the busy street, a central spot where you can sit in the late afternoon and watch the small world of Victoria go by.

Something happens when you have passed over one ocean, a large sea, three continents, and then traveled a thousand miles into a second ocean. You realize that you have gone to where no one can reach you. The past is spatially so far behind you that your future, the rest of your life, seems for a moment entirely of your own making. You briefly feel that you can invent your destiny. All too easily, you can imagine becoming a permanent expatriate.

The denizens of the Pirates Arms were a heterogeneous mix of locals and tourists and a miscellany of Europeans and North Americans who looked like international adventurers or people who wanted one to think that that's what they were. Retired CIA operatives and out-of-work soldiers of fortune and treasure hunters and smugglers—that sort of exotica. More likely, they were upscale vagrants and expatriates hiding behind their designer sunglasses from no one but themselves. But in a seaside international-crossroads town like this, one never knew.

Posters on walls and huge orange-and-black banners strung across the streets proclaimed the presence of something called THE INDIAN OCEAN OIL PRODUCERS SEMINAR and kept me conscious of where I'd landed. But it wasn't easy. The flavor of the town of Victoria was not quite Caribbean, though a lot of that (the neocolonial architecture, the cruise ship in the harbor); and not quite coastal East African, though some of that, too (the relentless equatorial heat and light and the easy, ancient blend of African, Indian, Asian, Arab, and European complexions and features); not Mediterranean, either, but somewhat (especially the sight of young, hip couples on lavish holiday smoking Gauloises and pouting over menus). Victoria was the country cousin to old Beirut, maybe, where histories and races and languages and cultures mingled indiscriminately. There were scattered pairs of pale tourists wearing clothes from Kanye West's closet, and I noticed flocks of attractive local women, young, black, tan, and white women in chic blouses and skirts and high heels. I started to wonder if I myself, with a new pair of sunglasses, might not pass as exotic.

I'd taken a room at the Northolme, near the village of Glacis. Stuck on a high seaside point on the northwest side of the island, it was one of the oldest hotels on Mahé, small and quiet with soothing views of the mountainous coast to the south and the sea to the west, a good place to use as a base for my peripatetic operations. Compton Mackenzie, Ian Fleming, and Alec Waugh had stayed there, which seemed recommendation enough. It was a bit too bourgeois, perhaps, for Graham Greene, but fine for me. The rooms were large and airy, and there was a small cove below the dining room where one could take a morning swim. Above all, the place was quiet—a quarter mile off the road that wound uphill from nearby Beau Vallon, with its long beach and string of bars, restaurants, and shops.

Waking early the next morning, six thirty, on a biological clock that was eleven and a half hours earlier than my watch—or twelve and a half later, I couldn't decide which—I went out for an hour's walk along the road into Glacis, and the astonishing natural beauty of the island suddenly came home to me. This was how I imagine the Caribbean looked before it was discovered by tourism, the northeast coast of Jamaica before Errol Flynn sailed into Port Antonio. Kids were walking to school, fishermen were going out and coming back in small red pirogues, while beautiful young men and women waited for lumbering old buses to carry them to their jobs in town. Everywhere I looked, there were birds and glistening spiderwebs and morning glories and flamboyants and flowering trees—such an abundance of natural beauty that it almost frightened me. And it all came wrapped in endless, dense birdsong. I was hot and sweating in minutes, even this early in the day, and remembered that Seychelles is equatorial, whereas most of the Caribbean is merely subtropical.

Back at the Northolme, the sole diner at breakfast in the large open-air restaurant, I watched Silhouette Island twelve miles to the west glow like a hot coal in the morning sunlight and listened to the surf explode against the huge slabs of red rock below, rocks that seemed natural to the coast of Maine or Nova Scotia, not the tropics. Blue-throated sunbirds and scarlet Madagascar fodies sang and darted through the trees, while down on the leaf-covered ground turtledoves chuckled and cooed, and out on the water terns and gulls cruised past in calligraphic arcs and swirls. I'd spent years traveling in the Caribbean, and compulsively, automatically, I kept comparing this place with that place, these people with those—but Seychelles was different somehow, different in ways that mattered. I couldn't say how yet. It was a secret I knew existed but hadn't been told.

I had signed up the evening before for a demonstration scuba dive with a local dive master, Rick Howatson, a fast-talking, witty, barrel-chested Englishman around forty. Rick turned out to have a boat-dive scheduled with "some local bloke who's getting PADI-qualified," he explained, so I went out with his second-in-command, Tommy Tirant, a somber, wiry, coffee-colored Seychellois in his late twenties.

We suited up and like a pair of bipedal frogs clumsily flapped down the long stone stairway to the short, rocky beach below the hotel and entered the water there. Freed of the land, empowered by the sea, we were suddenly graceful as porpoises and swam straight out to the reef, fifty or so yards from shore. Seconds later, we were diving in the reef, parting dense wedges of brilliantly marked and colored fish, hovering above a huge chalk-white manta ray, passing alongside steep Gothic walls of coral.

The main dangers to divers and snorkelers in Seychelles are sea urchins, scorpion fish, and stonefish, the worst being the stone-fish because it looks like a stone, not a fish. The others look as dangerous as they are and consequently are not so dangerous. There are at least two hundred species of fish in Seychelles waters, and first Tommy and then I passed through clouds of them: bright yellow and blue damselfish, striped sergeant majors, parrot fish grinding coral to sand, batfish, pipefish. And of the 150 species of coral, we saw brain coral and fan coral and mushroom coral that, growing an inch a year, require ten centuries to grow thirty-three feet. When you dive you fall through time; you watch eons pass before you.

I had done a lot of snorkeling in the Caribbean and a little scuba, but I still felt fearful, especially at first, dropping down into this foreign, unknown world where surprising and dangerous thoughts could sweep over me and put me in serious physical danger. The warm, silent, shimmering undersea, like a deep dream of infancy, was seductive, inviting me to let go and descend still farther. I struggled with alternating fearful and soothing visions of the netherworld, gradually calming myself down, while Tommy swam ahead through beautiful blades of pale light, urging me to follow his disciplined lead, waving me back into line.

Too soon, of course, the dive ended, and when we'd staggered back to the dive shack, unloaded tanks, weight belts, fins, and masks and became human again, Rick showed up, accompanied by his grinning, dripping, newly qualified diver, and gave me the hard sell for the full course. No time, I explained. I was here to hike and see the country all over. Rick said fine and introduced me to the other man, Steve Ambrose—like him, British. Steve managed the casino at the Beau Vallon Bay Hotel just down the road. We chatted awhile and parted amiably, and I changed and headed into town in my rented Mini Moke, an open, low-slung, jeeplike car that, because of the narrow, winding mountainside roads, was the best means of transport on Mahé.

Later that day, I wandered into the botanical gardens, a short way south of Victoria. Visiting a botanical garden is an easy and pleasant way to learn the names and faces of the local flora fast, and Seychelles has an especially elaborate flora, most of it unfamiliar to me. The garden was large, sprawling, with paths that looped through dense groves of cinnamon, jackfruit, clove trees, and san-dragon, past stands of palm trees, huge ferns, mahogany, tacama-hac, and white flowering begonia trees. And all the while, of course, there was that envelope of birdsong.

Almost no other people were here, but deep inside the gar-dens, I ran into two mustachioed, dark-haired young men, Malay-sians working as advisers to the Ministry of Agriculture. They were agronomists, they told me. They were gathering up prickly, dark green fruits that had fallen from a tall, broad-leaved tree. It was a durian, they said, whose fruit is a delicacy in Malaysia. It was brought over here for the personal pleasure of Sultan Abdullah Khan of Perak and his retinue in 1875.

Under the British, the islands were used as a minimum-security political prison for generations, with King Prempeh of the Ashanti, Sa'd Zaghlul Pasha of Egypt, and Archbishop Makarios of Cyprus among their more illustrious prisoners. That Seychelles has long been home to exiles, and now expats and foreign advisers, is an important quirk of its history. Situated so far from all known sailing routes between Asian and African ports of call, the islands of Seychelles were among the last in the world to be settled. They were uninhabited, and except for rumored sixteenth-century Por-tuguese landings, were essentially unknown until the French sailed north in 1742 from their Mauritius colony, established a naval base, and used African slaves to set up a small number of struggling spice plantations in the 1770s. With the Treaty of Paris in 1814, Seychelles passed into British hands, the economy shifted over first to coco-nut oil and then copra, and the British started importing banished, deposed, and overcome politicians and leaders who had the effron-tery to oppose the empire elsewhere. None of the exiles seems to have complained of his time in Seychelles. The last was Afif Didi, sent out in 1963 after leading a secessionist takeover of the southern Maldives. In 1976 Seychelles became an independent nation, and the official exiles ceased coming.

I tasted the durian. *Foul!* Like an overripe brie marinated in vinegar. The taste wouldn't go away. It clung to my palate for hours, and even today, many years later, leaps instantly, viscerally, back to memory. "We even make durian-flavored ice cream!" the Malaysians told me, laughing at my discomfort. "A delicacy!"

The next day I set out on my first serious hike. I drove out Sans Souci Road from Victoria, past the U.S. embassy, the radio station, the forestry service headquarters, to the trail marker for the mountains called Trois Frères, where I parked the vehicle and began my climb. The trail led through a lovely section of the Morne Seychellois National Park. I found it helpful to have the *Trois Frères Trail Guide,* which I had purchased earlier in Victoria, and absolutely necessary to carry water, lots of it. The heat and humidity were of an intensity I had never before experienced. It was like climbing in full wet suit. The trail was nicely, intelligently marked and, like Adirondack or Appalachian trails, was deceptively easy at first, then very difficult. For several hours, I clambered up the mountain, crossing wide-open sheets of black granite, passing through fifteen-foot ferns and forests of cottonwood trees, thickets of cinnamon and wild vanilla and pineapple, mahogany groves and sisal, while mynah birds and bulbuls and sunbirds squawked and sang as I crossed below them. Not one person passed me. I was alone.

After two hours of steady climbing, I reached the top, exhausted, and sat back against a chunk of blue-gray granite. Just as I was about to enjoy the wonderful 360-degree view of the entire island, a heavy white mist moved in, bringing light rain and blocking off the world entirely, and I was suddenly locked inside a small white room. I could have been anywhere; I could have been home in Princeton, New Jersey. Several long, cold, lonely moments passed, and then it suddenly cleared again, and now I saw how far from home I'd come. An Asiatic jungle spread out below, the famous tea plantation, terraced, like Cambodia, and beyond that Morne Blanc and the whole long spiny ridge of mountains all the way to the distant, pale green flatlands of the south. Sooty terns and kestrels and fairy terns cruised along the passes hundreds of feet below my crag. I peered down and saw the town of Victoria and its harbor and the four isles of the Ste. Anne Marine National Park below in the east, with Praslin, Cousin, Round Island, and La Digue farther in the distance near the horizon. I saw the sea as a huge glistening disk, with me situated exactly in its center, the sky a blue celestial bowl above, and the sun a cosmic eye. Propelled out of time, I felt in touch with something ancient and primal that I couldn't name.

The geology of most of these islands is as old as Gondwana-land, the mother of continents. They are a Precambrian granitic archipelago believed to have been left behind in midocean when India split off from Africa and headed for its fated collision with Asia. They are the only granite islands in the world not tied to a nearby continental shelf. Despite the palm trees, rain forests, and white sandy beaches, the Mahé group has little resemblance, geo-logically speaking, to the coral islands of the Lesser Antilles or the volcanic islands of the South Pacific. Here was an island experience of another order, I mused, sitting on my mountaintop.

Later, after a shaky-legged descent and a long swim and shower at the Northolme, I drove down for a drink at the seaside bar of the Coral Strand Hotel, where sunset watchers off the Beau Vallon beach ritually gathered—the young and the restless, mostly. At the bar I ran into Steve Ambrose, the casino manager I'd met the other day. He came up and saved me from a dreary conversation with a young Australian settled in the south of Mahé, a thoughtful person, per-haps, but basically an idiot. We had been arguing politics. The aver-age Seychellois's monthly income after taxes is about $400, which the Australian thought was just fine, since they had free health care and free education and food falling off the trees and leaping from the seas into their pots. Never mind that prices for food, clothing, and shelter were about what they are in Westport, Connecticut.

Steve offered to buy me dinner. We went to a place called La

Perle Noire, and as we ate, Steve's own story came out. He was a working-class Liverpudlian, a guitar-strumming boy who'd done lighting for rock groups. He'd found work early as a croupier in Liverpool, then had signed on for casinos in Baghdad, South Africa, and Liberia, moving up with each job and leaving each country just before war or revolution struck. Except for Las Vegas and Atlantic City, he said, all the casinos in the world are managed by Brits. Must be the way they look in tuxedos, he said and laughed. Adventures in the tropics, Steve went on, had been a hell of a lot more interesting than life in Maggie Thatcher's England. He knew he was spoiled for normal life forever. Seychelles, especially, will do that to you, he said to me. Be careful, friend.

Grousing about town the next morning, trying and failing to make arrangements to get across to Silhouette Island, I finally gave it up, and at nine thirty at the Marine Charter dock talked my way aboard a day-trip boat out to the Ste. Anne Marine National Park, an island and underwater reef preserve located at the mouth of the bay a short boat ride from Victoria.

It was a hotel group, mostly Germans and some Italians, everyone loaded with cameras and video cameras. It cost me $73 for lunch on the beach, drinks, snorkeling, three island stops, fish feeding, and a glass-bottomed-boat tour that turned out to be in a glass-*hulled* boat, a brand-new Australian-built forty-seater, the *Nautilus*. The guide, who spoke as if he believed his audience was actually intelligent, which was a relief and a pleasure, was named Jancy, a smart kid who asked the Germans if they wished him to speak English or French.

The people of Seychelles, although generally shy and reticent and not at all worldly, seem linguistically gifted. They almost all speak fine French and better English, as well as their native Creole, a language vaguely resembling Haitian Creole but utterly incomprehensible to my ears, and many speak an additional language or two, depending on their off-island travels. The young guide's ability to move easily, happily, among several European languages, none of which was native to him, was typical.

The best part of the day trip was the stop at Moyenne Island, owned by Brendon Grimshaw, a man in his late sixties—another British expat, it turned out. Expatriates, most of them British and French, with a few Yanks, seemed to run the country. It's difficult, if not impossible, for a nation with fewer than seventy thousand people and an economy dependent on tourism, fishing, and agriculture to train its own management.

Grimshaw ran a small restaurant-bar and guesthouse geared to the party boats from Victoria. Over a cold beer he told me his story. He had been a journalist for the *Financial Times* of London and had bought his twenty-five-acre island in 1962 for ten thousand pounds. He was a past president of the local Rotary Club and for all intents and purposes a proper businessman, but he was also, like so many of the longtime expats, a rogue who'd settled in, a loud, somewhat theatrical fellow, very bright and energetic and wary. He was an old-time ward heeler whose ward was a tiny tropical islet in a bay, not an urban neighborhood. Like Rick, like Steve, the man had invented a life out here to suit his strange needs exactly. He'd survived thirty years on the island, while political movements and conspiracies and coups and palace revolutions whirled around him.

From what I'd gleaned of Seychelles' recent history, this was no small feat. From the mid-1960s until shortly after independence, in 1976, Seychelles politics was run by the flamboyant, even grandiose, James Mancham, the nation's first president and the leader of the Seychelles Democratic Party. Sir Jim was friend to starlets, to celebrities, and to Adnan Khashoggi and various petroleum potentates, many of whom had bought huge tracts of land and pushed for big-time tourism. Mancham's prime minister was France-Albert René, a left-leaning young lawyer who'd founded the Seychelles People's United Party (SPUP) and had formed common cause with

Mancham in order to obtain independence for Seychelles. Then, in 1977, while Mancham was in London attending a conference of Commonwealth leaders, René and a small force of Tanzanian-trained Seychellois carried out a nearly bloodless coup.

Under René, the economy foundered, capital fled the country, and tourism all but disappeared. In November 1981, there was a widely reported and badly botched countercoup attempt led by the ex–Congo mercenary colonel "Mad Mike" Hoare. A troop of British and American mercenaries entered the country disguised as a South African rugby team, carrying automatic weapons and grenades in their suitcases. There was a failed mutiny of NCOs in the Seychelles army in 1982, then several more coup and assassination attempts, but despite all, René stayed in power.

He was coming now to the midpoint of his third five-year term, which was all he was permitted under the constitution. Though he seemed less the Marxist dictator he was sometimes called than a paternalistic socialist unwilling to delegate power, clearly Seychelles government was his show and had been since 1977. His strong, far-seeing policies for preserving the precious and fragile Seychelles environment and carefully developing the tourist industry were as enlightened as those of any government anywhere. It was easy to see, however, that the government and René's SPUP were extremely involved in the daily business of every citizen, and not all of them liked it.

The following morning I took a long, easy walk, hardly a hike, from Bel Ombre, on the west coast of Mahé, to Anse Major. While I walked, I picked up mangoes and custard apples from the ground and stashed them in my pack. The trail wound through jungle and fields of rose apple, along high black cliffs overlooking the sea below. It rained off and on, but no matter, as I was soaked in five minutes from sweat anyhow. I had parked my Mini Moke in a yard where the road ended, then walked for two hours to reach the beach. The only people I met were a local man and his two small boys in the jungle gathering coconuts, splitting off the outer husks on a sharpened stake on the ground. The man gave me a nut, and I slipped it into my pack and moved on. Where's the serpent in this garden? I wondered, as I walked along a winding narrow path beneath towering palms. Silent, solitary hiking is practically religious. Once you're into it and tired, your thoughts gradually replace the world, and you become a transcendentalist.

At a perfect small arc of a beach, there was a palm-frond lean-to, and I crawled under it to get out of the rain, reading a week-old London *Observer* I'd found in Victoria that morning, and ate my mango and custard apple and coconut. Strange, but lovely, to be stretched out under a Robinson Crusoe–style lean-to eating a lunch of fallen fruit and nuts, reading about the Redgrave sisters opening in London in Chekhov's *Three Sisters,* a fine warm rain falling, waves crashing at my feet. Soon the sky cleared, and I dried my clothes on a branch, swam, read a bit more, and wandered the beach and rocks for hours. There was no one else in the world, and it was wonderful.

At some point that day, much later—time had started to melt for me—the *Blue Marlin,* a charter fishing boat out of Beau Vallon, pulled into my bay and anchored. A fat lobster-red man in shorts jumped into the water and swam ashore. He was a Colonel Blimp type, British, who popped his eyes with delight when he saw my *Observer* and the front-page photos of England in snow. He grabbed it from my hands and sat on my rock, cruising through the news. Then abruptly he plunged back into the water and swam to the boat, clambered aboard, jovially waved, and took off, leaving me to my lovely solitude for the remainder of the day. Leaving me to the natural world—sea and sand and rocks and trees. Birds and lizards and sand crabs were my only companions. I was becoming a misanthrope.

That night, after a late dinner alone at the Northolme, I sat out on the terrace listening to the sea break against the rocks in the darkness below and fell into conversation with Rick Howatson, the dive master, who had stopped off on his way home from the Japanese restaurant located north of Victoria on the east coast of Mahé. He was unusually white-faced. He told me that tonight after he'd finished dinner the restaurant owner had brought out a tray of liqueur bottles, each with an odd, organic-looking object marinating in the liqueur. Rick had chosen the one that looked least harmful, he said. In fact, it tasted fine, but when he had drunk it off he was told that he'd chosen the liqueur with sliced deer's penis in it. All the bottles had animal penises in them, different types—some whole, some sliced. Rick had blanched and gagged, but kept it down all right, he said, but he now felt the need for a party. One would soon be in full swing at his house.

At first I declined his invitation, but a while later, after he'd gone—confusing solitude with loneliness—I got into my Mini Moke and made my way to his house. It was a garish white hilltop palace with a pool, three dogs, miscellaneous cats, several local teenage hangers-on with guitars, the Australian I'd been talking to at the Coral Strand the other day, and his wife or girlfriend, a very young black Seychelloise woman. It was the sort of house you'd expect a successful rock group to rent and wreck in Laurel Canyon. There were Steve Ambrose from the casino, another dive instructor named Avi, who was a South African Israeli, and his British wife, who was very pregnant, and a half-dozen others who looked like Europeans and North Americans, not locals.

It was not a good party. For a few hours, folks stood around and drank SeyBrews or straight gin and mostly talked local politics, until finally people drifted away, and it was only me and Steve and Rick and an American woman diver named Pat Scott, a Red Cross worker from Illinois who'd just spent four weeks in Kenya and Tanzania and was out now "for a few weeks of R and R," she told me. I asked her what had brought her so far from Illinois. "It's simple," she said. "You got Bonaire, you got the Red Sea, and you got Seychelles. Those're the three best diving spots in the world. I've been to Bonaire, and I can't go to the Red Sea right now."

The following afternoon I finally caught an interisland boat to the tiny island of La Digue, some twenty-five miles away, a three-hour ride. It was a freighter with fifteen to twenty passengers, mostly school kids going home for a few days on holiday break, a few intrepid travelers, and a man I especially noticed, a tiny, very old man who I assumed was British. He spoke to no one, and his demeanor resisted conversation. He had a furled black umbrella and a crisp gray military mustache and around his wattled neck a pair of binoculars on a string. I pegged him as a lifelong, hopeful birder coming out to see, before he died, the paradise flycatcher on La Digue and the black parrot on Praslin, two of the world's rarest birds, and even here seen only infrequently.

The islands themselves, La Digue and Praslin, situated close to each other, are as unique as the rare birds that make them their last home. Several biblical legends have been associated with the islands, generated by the famous coco-de-mer, the towering palm that grows only on Praslin. It's a tree whose huge seeds of astonishingly erotic shapes have washed up for eons on the shores of India, Africa, and Indonesia, coming from a place so far off the map that, until relatively recent times, no one knew it existed. Inevitably, the rare and mysterious nut came to be regarded as an aphrodisiac, and naturally, Victorian Christians, once they discovered its source, decided that the place was the original paradise and that the coco-de-mer was surely the Edenic fruit that had caused so much trouble there and everywhere.

As our boat approached La Digue, the old man with the black umbrella tottered up and out of the cabin to the deck and began studying the shore through his binoculars, not missing one of the not-too-many moments he had left. His combined ferocity of pur-

pose and concentration and his physical fragility made him a striking sight, especially surrounded as he was by a gang of boisterous,
healthy Seychellois school kids who seemed to have no focus what-
soever for their enormous vitality.

The coco-de-mer aside, the island of La Digue, if not paradise,
was not far east of Eden. There were very few people, fewer than
two thousand, and almost no motor vehicles. No place was too
far to walk to. Bicycles and oxcarts were used for transportation,
though the oxcarts were mostly for hauling tourists from the jetty
along the single-lane dirt road to the one hotel in town. Réunion,
the town, was a tiny fishing settlement scattered along the coast,
facing Praslin a few miles to the northwest.

At La Digue Island Lodge, I was put in "the yellow house,"
which turned out to be a renovated, bright yellow colonial residence with a shady veranda and eight small neat rooms, each with a
spiral staircase leading to a large first-class bathroom below. There
was an abundance of elaborately carved woodwork everywhere:
banisters, doors, sashes, countertops—all of it beautifully crafted,
fitted, and finished.

It was the heat of the day, midafternoon, but I was so eager to
see more of this place that I unpacked quickly and went out for a
serious walk, forgetting my hat and neglecting to bring a bottle of
water.

Big mistake. I hiked north through the village, passing day-
trippers from Mahé and Praslin pedaling rented bikes out to the
beaches and now and then a scrawny dog who couldn't find a piece
of shade. North of town and then around the point, one incredibly
beautiful cove led to another, with no one there—nothing but lush,
equatorial foliage, flowers, white sand beach, pink and red granite
boulders eroding into fantastic shapes. Soon I'd gone beyond the
point of easy return to the village. But it was impossible not to keep
walking. The astounding beauty like a drug led me way beyond the
point of no return, until I was closer to circling the whole island

than going back over my tracks. So I kept going, despite the heat and my thirst.

At one point I caught up to a teenage girl walking barefoot in a red dress in the glaring heat and sunlight, over from Mahé, she told me, on holiday from school and on her way to visit her grandma. A Little Red Riding Hood who may have been a hallucination by this time, although she seemed real enough, and I certainly did speak with her as we walked side by side for several miles. I felt like the Wolf, disguised not as a proper woodsman but as a tanned hiker who, beneath his clever disguise, was all lupine gray and corrupted by the huge dark industrialized world beyond.

Finally, we came to a path that led to where she said her grandma lived, and the girl parted from me. A ways farther, my trail ended, became a narrow track in the bush, then disappeared among the rocks before my eyes, and I feared that with one more step I would be lost. With no choice in the matter, I turned back, staggering along the pathway to the single-track roadway, the sun beating straight down on me. I slogged on, dizzy and rapidly nearing the point of exhaustion and dangerous dehydration, genuinely frightened now, when suddenly a beat-up red pickup truck rattled along, coming from God-knows-where behind me, with a bunch of teenage boys in back. Was it a hallucination, too? It was red, after all.

But no, it was real—spewing exhaust and blatting and skipping along the rough seacoast road with the radio blasting and the boys in the back banging loudly on the roof of the cab in time to Bob Marley's "No Woman No Cry." Never so glad to see a motor vehicle in my life, I hailed the truck, the driver brought it to a stop, and I climbed aboard and rode back to Réunion, surely saved from serious sunstroke.

Two hours later, showered in my first-class air-conditioned bathroom, two to three quarts of water in my belly, and a short nap behind me, I was fully recovered and ready for action. There wasn't much action on La Digue, however. After dinner at the hotel restaurant, I walked in the dark down to Choppy's, a bar located in an old movie theater called the Odéon, where I talked awhile with a local fisherman named Michael and his German girlfriend, Karen, who'd been out here for eleven months now. At Michael and Karen's urging, and the bartender's compliance, I tried *baka,* a fermented fruit brew with a very high alcohol content, a local favorite since colonial days. The bartender kept it in a jug in a cooler behind the bar and offered "samples only," as she had no license to sell it. It wasn't bad, but very dangerous, like a strong planter's punch.

Later, Michael and Karen took me to *le disco* at the cinder-block community center, where we all danced furiously to very loud, very good dance music, mostly U.S. rap and Jamaican reggae, in a nearly dark hall lit by a single yellow bulb.

The next day was the day I sighted the paradise flycatcher out by the old French graveyard, and afterward, as if to recover my senses, I spent the afternoon reading Henry James alone at a beach. Coming back to Réunion, I noticed at the side of a small house a wire cage holding what appeared to be three house cats but on closer inspection turned out to be fox bats. They are regarded as a delicacy here and are eaten grilled, baked, or in a pâté. I stopped and examined them for a long while, fascinated to see them up close like this. Their bodies were indeed the size of a house cat, but when they spread their black, silky wings, they were as big as eagles. They had small canine faces with reddish hair covering their bodies, except for their wings. They hung upside down inside the cage, watching me alertly, keeping their faces toward me as I circled outside the cage, their claws clattering against the wires as they turned. They yawned now and then, like bored dogs, but their eyes were black and watchful, as if they knew what was in store for them.

That evening, I was standing by the hotel pool having a loony conversation with a bald-headed Russian who looked like Yul Brynner and was teaching his five-year-old daughter to write Roman numerals in the sand. He kept uttering pronouncements like "Twentieth-century literature is the literature of suicide" and "Christianity is only the second of the five levels of understanding," like a character out of Dostoyevsky. In exasperation, I rolled my eyes skyward and saw swooping over the tops of the trees, silhouetted against the rose-colored evening sky, four, five, *six* fox bats, stunningly graceful in flight. They were so much more exciting and beautiful than when caged, and powerful, frightening—flying like land animals with wings, not at all like birds. They flew exactly as we do in our dreams of flying—controlled floating, wheeling overhead, safely watching everything going on below.

To catch the six o'clock ferry to Praslin the next morning, I was up at five and arrived at the jetty just as the boat was pulling away—even though it was only five thirty-five. I leaped aboard, just making it, to the delight and laughter of the crew and the handful of local people on board. They do have schedules here, but nobody seems to pay much attention to them, and they're as often early as late. As we left the bay, the sun rose behind the black silhouette of La Digue, and the sky went from cream to pale rose to turquoise. The water turned glossy black, and the island was a purple carbon color. I watched in awe while the earth simply behaved as it must.

Coming out here, I'd had only a vague idea of the effect the natural world could have on me. I had been thinking beaches, mountains, a few serious hikes in the rain forest, flowers, ferns, birds—the usual set of tropical-island clichés. I'd been a little curious about the people, about society, politics, history, racial attitudes. But I hadn't been very curious about the place itself, the land and the sea and the sky above and what lived in them and on them. But with all this hiking, with my visits to the untouched reef and the schools of protected fish, the shifting white mists of Trois Frères, the spotless, solitary beaches, putting *myself* in and on the land and sea, with the sighting of the paradise flycatcher my first full day on La Digue and fox bats soaring above the palms against the evening sky—these sights, almost like visions, had deeply affected the quality and intensity of my emotions, radically altering the overall relation I bore to this place in particular and to the environment in general.

The natural world has been preserved here, yes, but seeing it this close makes you aware of your absolute need for it, and that can break your heart. The preservation of this tiny bit of the planet makes you realize that the rest of the planet has been destroyed and can't be made to come back. For me, the big event was seeing the paradise flycatcher. *That* did it—broke my heart. I couldn't get over the fact that there are only forty pairs left on the earth, all of them on the remote island of La Digue, and that one of the birds was twittering on a poinciana branch right in front of me.

And now I was headed to Praslin, home of the Vallée de Mai, where the legendary coco-de-mer palm tree grew and where the last twenty-six black parrots on earth were to be found. How many by today? Twenty-three? Up to twenty-eight, maybe? Did it matter? Peter Matthiessen trekked to the high Himalayas to see one of the last snow leopards on earth. For me, I guess, it's the last paradise flycatcher, the last black parrot. More modest, I suppose, than Matthiessen's quest, but no less significantly moving to me for that. Standing eye-to-eye with that little black bird in an old French colonial cemetery amid crumbling, sinking stones at the edge of the shore—that's adventure enough for my heart.

About as much as I can handle, actually. But that's what one needs, isn't it? Enough heartache, not to *save* the world, for that's simply no longer possible, but merely to keep from helping in its destruction. The elegiac mode is the only appropriate form for our attention now. The only one available to me, anyhow. Up to now, I'd not been wrong, just unimaginative, about the fate of the earth, and in that sense, which is an important one, I had been wrong. Those T-shirts worn by Seychellois teenagers with the motto BE AN EXAMPLE TO THE WORLD! don't look so chauvinistic and provincial anymore. Just too late.

At Praslin, after settling in at La Réserve Hotel, I took the bumpy local bus out to the end of the line at Anse Boudin, walked two miles farther to Anse Lazio, reputedly the best beach on the island, and, after a long swim, had a pleasant lunch at a little beachfront restaurant, the Bonbon Plume. There was more of the wonderful woodwork that I'd seen all over La Digue and in the rural parts of Mahé and that had come to seem the characteristic and most distinctive Seychelles art form.

That evening I walked out again from my hotel, where a Chinese buffet was being served, for a creole meal instead. A place called Café des Arts was recommended to me by an Italian couple I'd talked to on the boat from La Digue. I passed through a mile and a half, two miles, of tropical dark, with no light from houses, for there was no electricity out there, no streetlights, no passing cars. It was a palpable darkness, like being inside a black tent. I walked down the dirt road through the village and on out, past a seaside house walled against the road, when suddenly I heard the unmistakable sound of a tenor sax. John Coltrane playing "Giant Steps"! For a long while, as long as the tape or record played on the other side, I stood next to the wall and for the first time on this journey felt truly homesick. I'd obtained whatever I'd come out here looking for, and now I wanted to take it home with me, to apply it there.

The next day would be my last on Praslin, my next to last in Seychelles. I rode the bus over bumpy winding roads to the famed Vallée de Mai, where I got out and began the two- to three-hour walk through the park, following the trail markers and my guidebook.

The Vallée was truly Edenic—as advertised, as predicted, as reported and chronicled by awed visitors for the last two centuries. I expected to see a brontosaurus munching among the tree-size ferns, to look up and see pterodactyls instead of fox bats soaring overhead. The hundred-foot-tall coco-de-mer was as truly erotic as everyone had said, its nut the largest seed in the world, weighing up to forty pounds and shaped like a Brancusi sculpture of the female torso, anatomically exact, with the male plant owning a huge black penis, the two of them pornographic comic book versions of female and male genitalia. One could only gape.

I had never seen any place this densely green, with primitive plants blocking out the sun and a wall-of-sound of birdsong. I could understand why General Gordon, hero of Khartoum, having stopped here on the way home from his post in Mauritius, decided that the earlier visitors and theologians were right, this was indeed the original Eden, and rushed on to London with the news.

Then, once again, great luck! Just as I came to the end of the winding path through the park, I looked up at the umbrella top of a huge cola nut tree and spotted, jerking along a branch in characteristic parrot-walk, as if pulling themselves ahead by their beaks, two small smoke-gray parrots that were nothing special, of course, except for what I knew about them, which intensified them, literally singled them out—for these were two of the last twenty-six black parrots in this garden, on this island, on this planet. In this universe.

A friendly fellow bird-watcher had come up silently beside me as I stood gaping, and he saw them, too, and smiled. For as long as the black parrots remained in the tree, which was perhaps ten minutes, we stood there watching them. Then, at last, they flew off, and we moved on. My companion asked me to take his camera and snap a picture of him for his sister back home. He was an Anglo-Irishman named Steve Jenkins, a reasonable, friendly, laid-back sort who, as we walked and chatted, turned out to be a petroleum geologist. He added that he was working for a British oil company whose name he would not reveal. He was in

Seychelles to attend the government-sponsored Indian Ocean Oil Producers Seminar being held at the Plantation Club on Mahé, and he'd taken a day off to come over to Praslin to visit the legendary Vallée de Mai.

I politely asked further about the state of oil exploration in the region and learned that Amoco had already drilled three test wells here and that, owing to the peculiar and ancient geology of the region, there was indeed oil in the Seychelles continental shelf, referred to as the Mahé Plateau. These islands, he pointed out, are the mountaintops of a microcontinent, part of what's called the Mascarene Ridge, a remnant of the continent that existed before Africa and India split apart. The islands lie at least one thousand miles from each continent but have the basic 650-million-year-old Precambrian geology of both, which happens also to be the same as the very best oil-producing regions in the world, he explained.

Steve Jenkins was a nice, smiling man in his late thirties, with a mustache and a potbelly. A reasonable, modern man. He assured me that the Seychelles government did certainly desire to protect the environment, even as they explored for oil and made plans to develop it. "We won't make the same mistakes we made in Scotland," he told me with a broad smile.

Here, then, was the serpent in the garden. I'd met him. A smiling, well-intentioned European man working for an international oil company that, for security reasons, cannot be named by its employees, especially not to peripatetic Americans with backpacks.

My last afternoon in Seychelles, I was back on Mahé, in Victoria, and stopped for a sandwich at L'Amiral, which passes reasonably well for a brasserie. I noticed at a nearby table the old bird-watcher I'd seen on the boat going over to La Digue. He had his black umbrella, straw hat, tight gray British army mustache. I stopped at his table and said hello, and he invited me to join him. He had a story to tell, and he needed to tell *someone*. He was eighty years

old, had spent two years during the war in Kenya, and was an artist. "Semiprofessional, retired," he said precisely. He had reached
an age where he could see things now purely for the sake of seeing
them, he said. His wife, ten years older than he, had died a few
years ago. He'd then become friends, he said, with a Seychelloise
in England, a woman in her early fifties who, he added, had been
his and his late wife's housekeeper. He had always wanted to see
these islands and the rare and marvelous birds here. He had been
hearing about them since his Kenya days. He had offered to pay
the woman's way out and back, if she would act as his traveling
companion. It was too daunting a journey for him to make on his
own, he pointed out. She had agreed, and they had got here fine
and set up in the country, living for a few months in a tiny house
with her large family. Then things had started to break down. The
woman, her family, all the neighborhood, expected him to pay for
everything. With his money running out, he had objected to the
arrangement, and his companion and her family had abandoned
him, kicked him out. And so here he sat, without enough money
for a hotel and unable to change his flight home. He had not seen
the paradise flycatcher or the black parrot, he said. He had loved
the islands, however, especially Praslin and the Vallée de Mai.
"The wonderful skies here!" he said. "You just want to look and
look and look, don't you!"

Later that afternoon, at the airport, waiting for the slightly
delayed flight back to Djibouti, then to Paris and home, I struck up
a conversation with a prosperous and intelligent-looking gentleman
of late middle age. British, it turned out. He was a prospector for
an oil company that, in spite of his gregariousness, his eagerness to
announce that serious drilling would be under way in less than two
years, he would not name. Oh, yes, there was definitely oil here, he
said. Of course, once the oil came in, there was no way the country
would survive the way it was now.

"They never do," he said.

We sat in the lounge, waiting to leave paradise. He talked

about eating bats in Borneo, the rigors of prospecting for oil in Venezuela, the intricacies of Middle Eastern politics.

I listened but didn't hear much. My thoughts were still with the elderly British bird-watcher who had been hoodwinked and abandoned by his Seychelloise lady friend. His stepdaughter was wiring him enough to pay for his flight home, he said. She was rather vexed with him, he added.

"At least you'll soon be home," I said.

"Yes, but it's Sunday in England," he pointed out, "and the banks will be closed until Monday, by which time it will be late Monday evening here, long after banking hours." He would not be able to access the money for at least two more days.

He didn't ask me for help, not directly, but I offered him a hundred dollars anyhow, enough to pay for a few nights in a cheap hotel, which he declined. When I assured him that it was a loan, he relented. We exchanged addresses, and he promised to repay me as soon as he returned to England.

I never heard from the old fellow, of course. Months later, I calculated the time difference between London and Seychelles and realized that it was a mere four hours and Seychelles was ahead of London, not behind. Our meeting in Victoria had taken place at midafternoon on a Monday, when the banks in London had been open for business for at least two hours already, and the Barclays in Victoria wouldn't close for another two. The stepdaughter must not have existed. The Seychelloise housekeeper turned girlfriend probably didn't exist, either. Nothing was as it seemed. No one was who he seemed. Not even I.

INNOCENTS ABROAD

A dark and cold and old north European city like Edinburgh as a site for high connubial romance? As a place for chasing the erotic sublime? Not likely. As Boswell's Samuel Johnson said of Edinburgh Castle, the city's most famous sight, "It would make a good prison in London." Even Calvin preferred Geneva, and most of the Stuarts opted for France.

Well, yes, true enough. And, yes, when Chase and I were younger and more innocent (I should say, *differently* innocent), it never would have occurred to us to elope to this place. But now, entering middle age—with our imagery for romance somewhat less restricted than back when tropical sunsets and moonlit beaches or even Paris in the springtime when it drizzles were still capable of signifying blissful escape from the quotidian—now, we decided, Edinburgh might be just right. In middle age, after all, there are more complex, perhaps less clichéd, shades of meaning and desire connected to romance, and the imagery of love tends to shift in a corresponding way. It happens: one grows older, and different images and atmospheres and cities turn one on. One can only be grateful.

So why *not* elope to Edinburgh? we thought. Why not slip away from friends and family, job, phone, don't tell anyone what we're up to, just go—two consenting, unmarried, middle-aged adults eager to marry—and let the force of our affection for each other and the rich complexities of our romantically aroused sensibilities color this stony old city with the rosy innocent light of late love. Why not indeed? Besides, Chase's parents, after long, sometimes acrimonious negotiations, were in the middle of divorcing, and my four daughters from my first two marriages were not eager to be present at the commencement of their father's fourth. They weren't so much against the *idea* as reluctant to witness and implicitly endorse the ceremony personally. Eloping seemed the kindest thing we could do for everyone.

So that when, on our arrival at the airport, the sun was shining brightly in a soft blue sky straight out of Constable, we took it as our due, as merely natural and appropriate, rather than the near miracle that our taxi driver called it. There was even a rainbow in the northeast sweeping across the pewter-colored Firth of Forth to the steepled town of Kirkcaldy. And when, a few moments later, halfway into the city from the airport, the clouds pulled in from the North Sea and filled the sky with gray crumpled sheets against the treeless heights of Arthur's Seat, and a fine cold mist started to fall, we were not disappointed. We were entranced.

As we entered Edinburgh, the rain silvered the city, hardening the edges and soldering its seams and planes, giving to the cobbled streets and stone buildings the cool clarity of a high-resolution black-and-white photograph. This was midsummer northern light, dropping from the sky in planes as straight as the rain. Before leaving home, I had checked the atlas and learned that Edinburgh was located at fifty-six degrees north latitude, which put it on a line with Moscow, northern Saskatchewan, and Labrador. It was north of the Sakhalin Peninsula, north of most of the Aleutian Islands. Summertime daylight here fell like a hard-loving stare that wants everything revealed.

Historically, the city first appeared shrouded in Celtic mist, a place called Dineiden, "fortress of the hill slope," in a sixth-century poem. This I knew because Chase is a poet and had read the poem to me. In the seventh century, the Angles marched up from Northumberland and conquered the region and replaced the Celtic prefix *din* with the Old English suffix *burgh*. Then as now, the center of Edinburgh was Castle Rock, which we could see even from the outskirts—the high black escarpment where Edinburgh Castle is situated and where Malcolm III (1058–93) built his royal hunting lodge and, at the request of his sainted wife, Margaret, constructed the simple chapel that stands today, open to the public, the oldest building in the city. In 1128, David I, pious son of Malcolm and Margaret, established the Abbey of Holyrood along the sloping ridge a short ways east. The mile-long road connecting the two sites soon became the famous Royal Mile, the central spine of the city for the next six hundred years. You can stroll it today, the guidebooks assured us. We had every intention of doing so. We were here for a full five days.

Our hotel was the Howard on Great King Street, recommended by the woman who was about to become my mother-in-law, whose taste for simplicity and bourgeois comfort exceeded ours. There were plenty of large, stately, first-class hotels in Edinburgh—the Caledonian, the Carlton Highland, the George—but the intimate, European-style Howard seemed more appropriate, more . . . romantic. It was small—twenty-five bright, high-ceilinged rooms furnished on the frumpy side (heavy on the pink-fringed lampshades), but comfortable and attractive, with marble mantels and elaborately carved woodwork. There was a lounge where you'd expect to find Miss Marple taking tea and a dark, masculine cocktail bar and a twelve-table restaurant where no one spoke above a whisper. Unpretentious, homey, with a warm and helpful staff, the Howard seemed to attract mostly British and Canadian guests along with a few American regulars.

The hotel was located in a pair of renovated Georgian town houses in the middle of the district called New Town—which of course is not "new" at all, at least not to a North American. In 1767,

after a public competition won by the twenty-three-year-old archi-
tect James Craig, the district was laid out in true Enlightenment
fashion—broad, cobbled, tree-lined boulevards in grids and elegantly symmetrical parks and row after row of tall, cut-stone town
houses with bay windows and bow fronts and domed stairwells and
enclosed gardens in back.

This was when the city was the "Athens of the North," the time
of *The Edinburgh Review* and *Blackwood's* and David Hume and Adam
Smith and Boswell and his eminent guest Dr. Johnson and Burns,
Hogg, and Sir Walter Scott, and when we had unpacked and were
headed out in search of an early dinner (early by New York time,
late by Edinburgh: we were jet-lagging), we half expected to pass
one of these gentlemen on the stairs or outside on the sidewalk. It
rarely happens that a city you've envisioned wholly through literature matches your image of it. Balzac's Paris, even Hemingway's,
is long gone, and so is most of Dickens's London. But there was so
much of eighteenth- and nineteenth-century Edinburgh remaining
in its architecture and parks and streets that I could almost ignore
the purple-haired punks and the Japanese cars and German trucks
and the chic boutiques with branches in Beverly Hills and Tokyo.
As a novelist and university teacher, I'm supposed to be especially
susceptible to literary versions of a city. And I am. I had prepared for
my elopement by rereading Boswell's account of his Scottish tour
with Dr. Johnson, James Hogg's *Private Memoirs and Confessions of a
Justified Sinner*, Daniel Defoe's *Tour thro' the Whole Island of Britain,
Vol. III*, and Robert Louis Stevenson's *Edinburgh, Picturesque Notes*.
That first evening I walked the streets of Edinburgh's New Town
the way Elvis fans walk the streets of Memphis.

Actually, we walked everywhere in Edinburgh—no rental car
necessary, no hired driver, not even taxis or buses, although taxis
did not seem particularly expensive and the bus service was excellent and easy to use. No one place seemed more than an hour's stroll
from any other, and if one designed a set of daily tours for oneself, as
we did, one could see the entire city in four or five days. And really

see it, not cruise it. We got to talk to people and not just pass them by. One could study the buildings and browse in shops and have a decent lunch and afterward sit on a park bench and watch the children play and old men read.

Our first morning over breakfast at the Howard and every morning afterward, we spread out our street maps and plotted a walk. We had already checked in at the Register's Office, conveniently located only four blocks from the hotel, to make sure that our documents had arrived safely from the U.S. (marriage notice forms, our birth certificates, my divorce decrees), assuring ourselves that there would be no last-minute surprises, and now we had a few days to wait for our witnesses—old friends from the States, the poet Mark Jarman and his wife, Amy Kane Jarman, and their two children, Zoë and Claire, aged six and nine, who had volunteered to be our flower girls. They were driving up from Leeds, where Mark was a visiting professor on leave from Vanderbilt.

The truth is, getting married in Scotland is not much more difficult than arranging an elaborate dinner party in Manhattan, but to us it seemed like setting up the SALT talks. We checked and rechecked every detail, made lists, briefed and debriefed each other constantly. We were nervous and grateful that the natives spoke fluent English and seemed to have an efficiently run bureaucracy.

For generations, English teenagers have run north to get married in Gretna Green, just over the border, where no parental consent or residency was required. It's just as easy if you're American and no longer a teenager. One writes to the General Register Office for Scotland, New Register House, Edinburgh EH1 3YT, and requests two marriage notice forms (one for each party), a fees list, and the leaflet explaining the legal preliminaries to marriage in Scotland. One mails to the district office where the marriage is to take place the completed marriage notice forms and fees and several documents—birth certificates and, if one has been previously married, a certificate of divorce or annulment, or if one is a widow or widower, the death certificate of one's former spouse. These have to be in the registrar's hands four weeks before the marriage is scheduled to take place (six weeks, if one or both parties have been married before). For a civil service, one makes arrangements with the registrar; for a religious ceremony, one arranges it with the clergyman before completing the notice of marriage. One needs two witnesses over the age of sixteen, whether it's a religious or civil ceremony. The registrar prefers to meet with the parties two or three days before the marriage to discuss, among other things, the question of the two witnesses and to return your documents. And that's how one gets married in Scotland. Simple.

A walking tour of Edinburgh, we instantly learned, required proper clothing—sensible shoes, of course, but sweater, cloth cap, scarf, raincoat, and umbrella as well. Even in summer. If, for some bizarre reason, it turned sunny and warm, we could always peel layers off, but a minute later we'd find ourselves pushing against a cold wind, and then a biting rain would start to fall, and if Chase or I didn't have a sweater, we'd duck into one of the shops on Princes Street and buy one.

Our first full day's walk was probably the walk most tourists take—the Royal Mile, starting at the Castle and ending at the Palace of Holyrood. We made the usual stop at the Esplanade for the famous Military Tattoo, which I know thrills just about everyone who sees it, but the beauty of military march and drill has always been lost on me, even when the soldiers wear kilts and step to the squeal of bagpipes. We visited Outlook Tower and were properly impressed by its Camera Obscura and wandered between the high old houses of Lawnmarket. It's along this stretch of road that the city proper first emerged, with narrow "wynds" and "closes" (alleys, actually) snaking between six- and seven-story wood-framed houses and shops. Marshes to the south, beyond Flodden Wall, and the North Loch, where Waverley Railroad Station and Princes Street Gardens are now, kept the city long and narrow and high, which meant crowded and smelly and dark, until the eighteenth century, when the marshes were drained and the New Town was built.

From the Castle to Holyrood was only a mile, but we made it last the day. We toured Parliament Square and the High Kirk of St. Giles and made our way down High Street past the John Knox House to Canongate all the way to the palace and Holyrood Park, with the bald moorland heights of Salisbury Craigs and Arthur's Seat sprawled beyond. The people we passed on the streets, those we decided were not tourists (which is to say, those we took not to be German, Japanese, or North American), looked strangely like *us,* like my fiancée and me. Which is not that odd, since she's a Campbell on her mother's side and I'm a Gordon on my father's, and neither of our New England families had done much mucking about with the gene pool. The Edinburghers who looked like Chase were the dark Scots, slender with pale eyes and light skin and straight dark brown hair. Those who resembled me were the thick-bodied red Scots with florid complexions and round wide faces and sandy or red curly hair. The dark Scots looked Norwegian to us, and the red Scots looked Celtic, and probably were, at least on their mother's side or their father's. It was strangely familial, almost ghostly, seeing so many faces and bodies that resembled our own, and at times we felt we had wandered into a dream of family. I thought I saw my father and mother and their parents everywhere, and my aunts and cousins, too. And Chase saw her grandmother's face on the woman who served us tea one day, her uncle's on the man who sold us a silver pin. Were they here to help us marry, the afterimages of the families we had left behind? Without knowing it, was *this* why we had chosen to elope in Edinburgh?

We spent the second day in the city without leaving the New Town district, which is where most of the best museums are located. We lingered over the Reynoldses and Gainsboroughs at the National Portrait Gallery and admired the Titians, Goyas, Rubenses, and El Grecos at the National Gallery and the neolithic axes and bowls, Roman statuary, and medieval weaponry at the National Museum of Antiquities. Late in the day we visited the Scott Monument, which is indeed monumental, the largest memorial to a writer I have ever seen. A piece of High Victorian kitsch, it's a neo-Gothic spire and canopy over a neoclassical statue of Sir Walter and his loyal dog. How the Scots love their dogs. Taking the long way back to the hotel, we stopped for a reflective moment at David Hume's grave in Calton Old Burial Ground and honored Robert Burns at his memorial farther up on the hill. It was a day spent with the spirits of painters and writers.

We were taking in the sights like typical American tourists, cruising the abundant historical buildings and monuments, museums, parks, and public gardens, following our maps and guidebooks with energy and a single-minded determination not to miss anything worth seeing. But we were also lovers who had eloped to a foreign city, gone to a place that neither of us had ever visited before, a deliberate step out of time, a shared, lyrical solitude. And so we lingered in parks and dawdled along the avenues and squares, shopping in a leisurely fashion and trying out restaurants and pubs, strolling hand in hand in and out of galleries and bookshops and antique shops as if we had all the time in the world.

One day, our third, we wandered south of the Royal Mile and prowled the narrow streets and lanes around the Old College of the University of Edinburgh, toured the Royal Scottish Museum, Candlemaker Row, and Greyfriars Church, where we came upon the grave and statue of Greyfriars Bobby, a Skye terrier who in 1858 began a fourteen-year-long vigil over his master's grave, until the dog himself died. The Scots memorialize not just their writers. Earlier in the week we had spent a sweetly cheering hour inside the Castle grounds reading the names and dates of the pooches buried in the cemetery established there solely for the soldiers' dogs. A year before we had done the same thing in Aruba, in the Caribbean, where we discovered a large, well-kept pet cemetery near the old Exxon refinery.

We timed our walks so that in every neighborhood we were

able to sample another recommended restaurant—after London, Edinburgh probably has the best restaurants in the British Isles—or one of the fine old brass-and-oak-paneled pubs that seemed to appear on every block. A favorite lunch stop on the Royal Mile, which we returned to several times, was L'Auberge on St. Mary's Street, a charming, bistro-style restaurant on a narrow side street where we practiced our French. Chase's excellent pronunciation and my eccentric vocabulary made us a single speaker of pidgin French. Alone, neither of us would have dared to speak; together we talked on many subjects, which pleased us and seemed to amuse the waiters.

A fourth day was spent north of New Town, at the Leith waterfront among the medieval warehouses, with an extraordinary morning walking in a silvery mist through the Royal Botanic Garden, which is among the largest, greenest, and best maintained in the world. Founded in 1670 by the first professor of medicine at Edinburgh University, it is the second-oldest botanic garden in Britain, after that at Oxford, covering seventy-two acres, with eleven exhibition halls and a one-hundred-thousand-volume library and a woodland garden with four hundred species of rhododendron and even a heath garden, where we strolled among some thirty varieties of heather, while the mist walled out the world that surrounded us.

A ways beyond the garden, up in Leith and in sight of the Firth of Forth, we stopped for a late lunch at the Vintners Rooms on Giles Street, a wine bar and restaurant located in the refurbished cellars of a stone warehouse built in the twelfth century by the Holyrood monks for storing their claret. There, under vaulted stone ceilings, we lingered over a three-course French Provincial meal and drank an exquisite '85 Chassagne Montrachet and talked of how in years to come we would return here on our anniversary, to this very restaurant, this very table. And why not? During those few days and nights of wandering through the city of Edinburgh, in that brief interlude before we actually got married, we were transported magically out of all our familiar, crowded times and places, replacing them with a time and city that we shared only with each other. Over the years our memory of those few days and the city would become as much a part of our marriage as the wedding ceremony itself.

Then, at last, but just as planned, our friends the Jarmans arrived from Leeds and checked into the Howard in a pair of rooms adjacent to ours. Perhaps it was a conversation in the hotel lounge between Mark and me and overheard by the waiter, or maybe it was something said by one of the girls, who couldn't contain their pleasure—in the lobby Zoë, aged six, had announced to all, "I've been to many *public* weddings before, but never to a *private* one!"—or maybe it was because of the cables and calls that had started coming in from the States, as family and friends one by one figured out what we were up to, but suddenly the entire staff of the Howard seemed to be in on the secret, acknowledging it with winks and smiles and whispered congratulations.

That night, with the four Jarmans, we had a long, late prenuptial supper at Martins on Rose Street, which had become our favorite restaurant. It was a tiny, hard-to-find place tucked away in an alley off a lane off Hanover Street between Princes and George, where chef David Macrae specialized in exquisitely prepared Scottish fish and game and wildfowl, with cheerful, knowledgeable service and advice from the proprietors themselves, Martin and Gay Irons. The wines were fine, especially the '83 Rolly Gassman Auxerrois Moenchreben, and the crayfish nage and poached escalope of salmon perfect. After a round of desserts, the Jarmans, who were weary from their long drive, took their slumbering daughters back to the hotel, while Chase and I enjoyed a final glass of port and another wedge of cheese. Then we, too, took our leave and walked arm in arm back along George Street toward the hotel.

At Number 60A, a modest Georgian building that houses the Yorkshire Building Society Regional Executive Office, we stopped for a moment and read a plaque bolted to the wall. Here in 1811 the poet Percy Bysshe Shelley and his bride, Harriet, spent their honeymoon. Perfect. That Shelley had chosen Edinburgh for his honeymoon seemed wonderfully appropriate—never mind that Shelley's and poor Harriet's marriage ended badly. On that August night the whole world was an emblem for our love, and a bronze plaque honoring an adolescent poet's marriage nearly two centuries earlier posted on the stone face of a shut building was an omen, a blissful promise, and we walked joyously back through the starry nighttime to our hotel.

The sun shone brightly on the appointed day and continued shining all morning long. The deed was quickly and sweetly done. We were married in a pleasant, parlorlike room at the General Register's Office on Queen Street, next door to the house where in 1847 Sir James Young Simpson discovered the anesthetic capacity of chloroform. The nuptials were performed by Registrar Katrina Hoy, an intelligent, cheerful, red-haired woman who proudly informed us that she was the only woman in all of Scotland empowered to conduct a civil marriage. Zoë and Claire held the rings, while Chase and I held hands, and Amy held the flowers and Mark the camera, and when the vows were exchanged it's possible that we all wept a little. I saw no one's eyes but my bride's, so cannot say who else wept and who else did not.

LAST DAYS
FEEDING FRENZY

Five minutes out of Anchorage, past the karaoke joints and stripper bars, the fast-food outlets and flag-flapping car dealers, suddenly there was scree, glacial ice, and endless sky above, serrated cliffs and crashing waves below, and I was in the Alaskan wilderness. Snow-crested mountains tumbled through fir trees and sedimented rock into the cold zinc-gray sea, and the sight of it took my breath away, literally—my chest tightened as I drove—and I thought, I'm not worthy of this much beauty, no human is. But I'll sure as hell take it. And I did—I drank it in, ate it up, gobbled it down while I could, because I knew that it was not going to last. I was on the Seward Highway headed south through the Chugach State Park and National Forest, looping along the sawtooth edge of a long, narrow fjord off Cook Inlet called Turnagain Arm. It was the summer solstice, June 21, 1993, the longest day of the year, and a good thing, too: I was driving the length of the Kenai Peninsula today, from Anchorage to Homer, 225 miles, and had left Anchorage around 4 P.M., so wouldn't make Homer till nine or later and didn't want to arrive in the dark at the backwoods cabin I'd borrowed but not yet seen, where there would be no electricity, no running water, no company.

The only other vehicles on the highway this afternoon were elephantine RVs, pickups, and SUVs, all of which appeared to be registered in the Lower 48, most of them driven by late-blooming baby boomers taking early retirement. As they lumbered toward me or when, on the occasional straight stretch of road, I overtook and passed them, the drivers and passengers grinned and pumped fists or cheerfully flashed Vs-for-victory and two thumbs up, like we were all pals up here in Alaska. Their easy bonding bugged me. Then I remembered what kind of car I was driving along this long, lonesome, wilderness highway. I was at the helm of a brand-new, bright red ("sunset orange metallic") Hummer, test-driving for a slick New York–based men's magazine the about-to-be-released H2 model with the full-bore luxury package. It had all the bells and whistles: Bose six-disc CD changer and heated slate-gray leather seats and sunroof and OnStar system—all that and, as they say, more, more, more. It had wraparound brush guards and running lights and off-road lights and seventeen-inch off-road tires on cast aluminum wheels and the same Vortec 6000 6.0-liter, fuel-injected V-8 engine that powered the 1993 Corvette. It had a self-leveling rear air suspension system with an onboard air compressor. It had a thirty-two-gallon fuel tank. And needed it, especially out here in the wilderness, where filling stations were separated from one another by very long walks.

This was a vehicle that for sheer bulk and brawn couldn't be equaled by any other so-called passenger car on the highway. It might have been a guzzler, but there wasn't an RV or an SUV any-where that the Hummer couldn't knock from the sidewalk into the gutter with a simple dip and shrug of one broad shoulder. It was six-foot-six in height, close to seven feet wide, and just under sixteen feet long. It was built like a bank vault on wheels, thick all over and squared. Cut. Not an ounce of body fat. Driving it was like riding on the shoulders of Mike Tyson in his prime. It wasn't sexy, how-ever, unless you think Mike Tyson is sexy. People, especially guys, grinned, flashed the victory sign, and stepped aside. "Hey, champ, how's it goin'?"

I knew I wasn't supposed to like this car. It was the most politically incorrect automobile in America. Maybe in the world. I considered who had purchased the cruder, more forthrightly militaristic H1 model that preceded it, and who therefore would likely be first in line for the H2: Arnold Schwarzenegger, yes, I knew that, and Bruce Willis; but also Don King, Coolio, Karl Malone, Dennis Rodman, Al Unser Sr. and Jr. Ted Turner owned an H1, not surprisingly. And Roseanne Barr. And, of course, Mike Tyson, who'd bought a brace of Hummer H1s for himself and a few more for his friends. As party favors, I guessed. By and large, except for Ted Turner, maybe, this was not the green crowd.

I considered its heritage, its DNA. Its closest modern-day relative was the scruffy, friendly-looking Jeep, which had evolved out of the original, mud-spattered World War II jeep and still summoned the spirits of Ernie Pyle, Bill Mauldin, and a generation of unshaven, exhausted foot soldiers bumming a ride back to the base. The Hummer, however, was the direct descendant of the post–Vietnam War era's Humvee, which was to the old WWII jeep as Sly Stallone was to Audie Murphy. The Humvee was a jeep on steroids, built to handle anything from Afghan road rage to a good Gulf War. Its newest, civilian incarnation, the H2, was dressed out with enough leather and polished walnut dashboard trim and high-tech add-ons to pass for chic in the Hamptons or fly on Rodeo Drive, and enough tinted glass, CD speakers, and sheer size to become the official hip-hoppers' posse car. It was a gigantic steel jock strap. The vehicle went straight to the testosterone-drenched fantasy life of the adolescent American male, no matter how old he was, and butch-slapped it into shape. Driving down the Kenai Peninsula in my Hummer, I kept remembering how I felt when I was a kid in New Hampshire cruising around town in winter in a dump truck loaded with sand and a snowplow attached to the front, feeling larger and stronger and taller and wider and harder than anyone else on the road. It was a good feeling then, and, I had to confess, it was a good feeling now.

Along the Russian River, a short ways south of Resurrection Pass, I saw where all those RVs, pickups, and SUVs from the Lower 48 had been headed. The salmon were running, and the people in those vehicles were like hungry bears trundling to the riverbank to pack their bellies with fish and roe. The glacial river was cold and wide and fast and mineral rich, a strange, almost tropical shade of aqua, and thousands of fishermen and -women, but mostly -men, were lined up shoulder to shoulder for miles along both banks, mindlessly, recklessly, hurling their hooks into the rushing water and one after the other yanking them immediately back with a glittering, twisting salmon snagged at the end. It was the warm-up to an annual potlatch, an ancient midsummer harvest rite, and the native people had followed the example of the bears for thousands of years. But somehow, as I drove slowly past them, these people—in their greed and desperation to take from the river as many of the salmon that survived last year's rite as they could—seemed oddly postmodern. Postapocalyptic, actually. For soon there would be no more salmon returning here to spawn. We all knew that. Never mind the catastrophic effect of dams and oil spills and nuclear leakage, we knew that the millions of adult salmon being hooked, bagged, and tossed into coolers and freezers from California's Klamath River north to Alaska were likely to be the last of these magnificent creatures we'd ever see. And none of these folks flipping fish into tubs and coolers looked especially hungry. They were mostly on the overfed side of fitness. So why were they pigging out like this? I wondered. This was more like a feeding frenzy than a ritual, and it sure was not a sport, I decided, and drove on in my Hummer.

Halfway to Homer, I checked the onboard dashboard computer and noted that I was averaging just over ten miles a gallon. And did I connect that fact with the feeding frenzy I'd just observed along the banks of the Russian River? Of course, I did. These were the Last Days. The planet was running out of everything except human beings. Clean water, boreal forests, wild animals, birds, and fish—soon all of it would be forever gone. Fossil fuels, too. Gone. Yet we Americans, especially, were consuming fossil fuels at an accelerating rate, and to aid and abet our consumption, we were building and buying with each year more and more ten-miles-per-gallon vehicles—Suburbans and Expeditions and Navigators and Land Cruisers and $100,000 Hummers painted sunset-orange metallic. It was a different sort of Last Days feeding frenzy than the one along the Russian River, but related, and the planet, as if preparing to explode, was heating up. The paradox was that here in Alaska, with fewer people per square mile and more square miles of protected wilderness than any other state in the union, the calamitous effects of global warming were more obvious than anywhere on earth. Since the 1970s, mean summer temperatures in Alaska had risen five degrees, and winter temperatures had risen ten. The permafrost had gone bog soft, glaciers were shriveling, the ice pack was dissolving into the sea like sugar cubes, and on the vast Kenai Peninsula nearly four million acres of white spruce, thirty-eight million trees, had been killed by the spruce bark beetle, a quarter-inch-long, six-legged flying insect that, because of the increased number of frost-free days, reproduced now at twice its normal rate, enabling it to overwhelm the trees' natural defense mechanisms.

I wasn't puzzled as to why GM, Ford, and Toyota built and sold vehicles like the Hummer, the Expedition, and the Land Cruiser, and couldn't condemn them for it; they were in the automobile business, and these behemoths were big sellers. What puzzled me was why so many Americans were jostling for a place in line to buy one. It would not have surprised me if there were something deep in the human psyche, the vestigial male chimp-brain, maybe, that makes us rush to the trough as soon as we sense it's nearly empty and snarf down as much of what's left as we can. It isn't greed. It's an atavistic fear mechanism kicking in, the sort of move made by our lower primate cousins, chimpanzees, gorillas, and orangutans, whenever they notice that the troop's population has outgrown its food supply and they are going to have to move to a new forest, one controlled by an unfriendly, possibly tougher troop, or else stop having sex. In a paroxysm of anxiety, the big males instantly start gobbling up every banana in sight.

Such were my melancholy thoughts as I made the long, gradual descent on the Sterling Highway from the town of Soldotna to the old Russian settlement in Ninilchik. On my right was Cook Inlet and on the far side of the bay, profiled in purple by an evening sun still high in the cloudless sky, were the volcanic cones of the Aleutian Range. On my left, as far as I could see, was the ancient spruce forest, devastated by the work of that little yellow bark beetle. The trees were withered and gray, all of them dead or dying, miles and miles of tall, ghostly specters of trees that looked like they'd been hit by radioactive poisoning, as if the Kenai Peninsula were downwind from Chernobyl. I was doing eighty along the wilderness highway in my Hummer, cruising through a vast forest destroyed by the gas-gulping culture of which there was no purer expression than this vehicle, and I was feeling bad. Not that it wasn't fun to drive this damn thing. It was just that I'd have to be a cynic not to feel a wrench of conscience driving it here. These drooping gray trees were like accusatory ghosts.

The Russian settlement was from another century, however— a cluster of small, white, wooden houses with tiny windows and a graveyard and an Orthodox church atop a grassy hump overlooking the sea far below. It was a Chekhov story waiting to be told. I turned off the main road and found my way along a twisting lane down to the narrow beach at the base of a set of high, sandy cliffs shot through with runnels and caves. A magnificent pair of bald eagles flew back and forth along the cliffs, switchbacking their way toward the top, looking for an easy-picking supper of seagull and plover eggs. At the top, they crossed over me, gained altitude with a half-dozen powerful beats of their enormous wings, and headed out to sea, floating on rising currents toward the distant mountains. I wanted to follow them, and actually did try it for a while, driving the Hummer a short ways into the water and south along the beach, testing the manufacturer's claim that it could drive in twenty inches of water. It more than passed the test. For several miles I guided the vehicle over rock slabs and through shifting, wet sandbars, until the beach gradually narrowed, and soon I had no choice but to drive in the water now, for the tide was coming in, and I couldn't go back. I could only go forward and hope that I'd come to a break in the cliffs and a road leading away from the beach before I had to abandon the Hummer to the sea.

At the last possible minute, the beach suddenly widened, and the cliffs receded, and I came upon a caravan of a dozen or more RVs parked where Fall Creek entered the sea at Clam Gulch. A herd of bearded, big-bellied beer drinkers in duckbill caps and flannel shirts leaned on the hoods and fenders of their vehicles, smoking cigarettes and talking about fishing. These were the guys known in their hometowns as "hot shits." Their wives and girlfriends lounged in beach chairs close to a big driftwood fire on the beach and watched their kids chase their dogs.

The men spotted the Hummer first and reacted as if a mastodon were stomping up the beach toward them. Their mouths dropped; they grinned and pointed and called to their wives and kids to come look, look, it's a goddamned Hummer! A brand-new, bright red Hummer, its huge tires thickened with clinging sand, had come dripping wet from the bottom of the sea. They waved me to a stop and crowded around the vehicle, firing questions as to its engine, its weight, its cost, and when I had answered, they and their wives and children all stepped back for a long, admiring look as I dropped it into gear and pulled away in what I hoped was an appropriately cool manner.

The Hummer did that to me—made me feel watched, observed, admired for no deserved reason. I felt the way Madonna must whenever she leaves her apartment. Every time I stopped for gas, waited at one of the three stoplights on the 225-mile drive from Anchorage, or pulled over for a minute to photograph a spectacular view of moun-

tains and glaciers and sea, people came up to the vehicle and stared
at it as if waiting for an autograph. They stared in an appropriating
way—I felt myself enter their fantasy life. Mostly it was a guy thing,
especially young guys, teenagers, and preadolescent boys, whose
faces brightened with lust when they saw the Hummer. They
were clearly getting off on its sudden, overall impression of brute,
squared-away power. The women's gaze had a somewhat different
quality, however. To them, the profile and face of the Hummer were
grotesque, weird, almost comical looking, and they'd laugh, I felt,
if the vehicle didn't also signify the presence of a man with money,
which made it somehow socially acceptable. Everybody seemed to
have a fairly accurate idea of the Hummer's price tag.

When I drove it onto the long, narrow spit that was downtown Homer, slowed to a crawl by the sudden presence of Saturday
night, bar-hopping traffic, a crowd gathered around the vehicle and
kept pace with it, waving to me and hollering hey. You're never
lonely when you're the only boy in Homer with a Hummer. I rolled
slowly through the traffic, trying to ignore the gaping drivers and
pedestrians and not wrap the vehicle around a pole or kill somebody with it.

Suddenly among the crowd a dark-haired woman in a nurse's
uniform caught my attention. She was less than four feet tall—a
dwarf with a characteristically large, square face and head and
short, blocky body and muscular arms and legs. She had spotted
the Hummer, not me, for I was invisible to her, and a warm, utterly
delighted smile spread over her face, as if by accident she'd run into
a long-lost, dear old friend. I waved at her, and she waved happily
back, the recipient of an unexpected gift from a stranger.

Most of the town of Homer—described by a local bumper
sticker as A QUIET DRINKING VILLAGE WITH A FISHING PROBLEM—was
situated on the long spit of land extending several miles into the
Kachemak Bay and was made up of restaurants, bars, stores, and
motels catering mainly to the crowds of people who'd driven here
to fish for salmon and halibut. The parking lots were crammed with

RVs and pickups towing camper-trailers and boats, and every few yards was another charter fishing outfit. Halfway along the spit I came to a nearly landlocked bight, clearly man-made, about the size of a football field. A sign told me it was called the Fishing Hole. Curious, I pulled in and parked.

There was a narrow inlet from the sea and a gently sloped embankment surrounding the shallow saltwater pond, for that's all it was, a pond. People with fishing rods stood side by side and two and three deep around the Fishing Hole, while below them the water churned with trapped king salmon, and the people along the embankment hauled them in, snagging them without bait or lures. It was a pitiful sight. I asked around and learned that salmon eggs raised in hatcheries were transferred here as smolts, held captive in floating pens in the Fishing Hole until they were large enough to be released into the ocean. Later, when they were grown and the ancient impulse to spawn kicked in, the salmon returned to the Fishing Hole, their birthplace, in actuality a gigantic, carefully designed weir, and on a midsummer night like this, huge crowds of people scooped them up as fast as they could. The people stumbled against one another, stepped in each other's buckets, swore and shoved and cast again. "It's called combat fishing," a grizzled fellow in an NYPD cap told me. "It's wheelchair accessible," he added.

I climbed back into the Hummer and headed out to reconnoiter with the friend who'd loaned me her wilderness cabin for a few days. I knew only that it was a dozen miles from town and had no water or electricity and was located on the bay. Two hours later, my friend's directions in hand, I drove the Hummer off-road. It was after 10 P.M., but the sky was milky white. It felt like midafternoon, and the difference between what my watch said and what the absence of darkness said was disorienting and made me feel uncomfortably high.

The Hummer shoved its burly way through chest-high brush and ferns, over washes and gullies, and then up along a tilted ridge to a clearing, where the lane stopped in front of a small, slab-sided cabin with a short deck. I shut off the motor, stepped down as if walking ashore from a large boat, and stood in the middle of the ferny clearing for a few moments, savoring the silence and the view. Below the cabin was the bay, and across the bay was the Kenai National Wildlife Refuge, a vast, mountainous wilderness area split by three glistening white glaciers, a world where no Hummers roamed, where most of the salmon fishing was done by bears and the native people, where there was nothing like the Homer Fishing Hole and the white spruce trees had not yet begun to die.

After a long while, I went inside and made a fire in the woodstove and uncorked the bottle of red wine I'd picked up earlier in town. Out the window I saw the Hummer sitting in the brush, looking like an alien vehicle sent to earth in advance of a party of explorers scheduled to arrive later. I sipped wine and wondered what the space people, when they finally get here, will make of our planet. All those dead trees! All that flooded land and the dead villages that once prospered alongside the bay! And the dead and dying rivers and seas! The space people will shake their large, bald heads and say, "If the humans had stopped devouring their planet, they might have saved themselves. Those Last Days must have made them mad."

THE WRONG STUFF

Two days and three nights in Quito adjusting my sea-level cardiovascular and respiratory systems to the ninety-three-hundred-foot altitude, and I was out of there. Enough already. Enough hanging around the crowded, noisy New City cafés on Amazonas; enough window-shopping and strolling the jammed, narrow streets of the Old City; enough of tourist hotel life and of gloomy Spanish colonial churches and bleeding, thorny icons; and enough already of the international cadre of mountain climbers—those slender, tanned, super-conditioned young men and women in hiking shorts and T-shirts, those jaded connoisseurs-of-climb loung-ing around the patios of the hostels and outfitters on Juan León Mera like Aussie surfers waiting for the perfect wave. It was all very charming, even exotic, but not what I had come to Ecuador to see or do. So I was out of there, headed finally from the city into the mountains. And traveling the way I like best—alone, and by public transport—riding the packed Latacunga bus south from Terminal Tereste to El Chaupi.

It was a bone-dry morning, cool and clear, with an endlessly high sky above the mountains that ringed the city like Inca ruins. I gaped at the otherworldly scenery from the open window of the bus, while the rest of the passengers—men, women, children, and

babies alike—stared up at the dubbed *Star Trek* rerun on the TV
screen at the front. In minutes, the top-heavy bus had chugged its
way up and out of the congested bowl of downtown Quito onto
an arid ridge where it lumbered southward along the potholed
Pan-American Highway. Goats with eyes that flattened sunlight
like coins and an occasional melancholy cow foraged on the trash-
strewn shoulders of the highway. Scrawny blond dogs trotted
purposefully along the median strip as if late for an appointment
while huge, smoke-belching trucks and rattling old cars and overloaded commuter buses fought one another for the right-of-way in a
mad, mechanized, sixty-mile-an-hour rugby scrum. At the edge of
the road, thousand-foot cliffs dropped through scrub and eroded,
bloodred arroyos to the vast, tin-topped barrio spreading like an
effluent along the broad valley south of Quito.

It was scary up there. But exhilarating, especially after the
relative confinement of the last few days, and no one else on the
bus seemed scared, not with Spock and Captain Kirk and the crew
of the starship *Enterprise* watching over us. So I let it go and rocked
happily along with the others—black-haired, dark-eyed natives,
small, calm, cinnamon-colored people who smiled politely at the
oversized, gray-haired *yanqui* with the backpack and squeezed over
to make room for him.

I had come to Ecuador to climb in the Andes, like those elegantly tanned athletes back in Quito—although they all appeared
to be twenty-five to thirty years younger than I and gave every
indication of being in much better shape than I have ever been.
They had the body fat of ten-speed bicycles. Even the ponytails on
the men looked functional. The women in their nylon short-shorts
and mesh T-shirts and running shoes looked like they were built
to rescue men like me from ice crevasses and had been taught by
counselors how to do it in a nonthreatening way. I was in my mid-
fifties, and for more than six months had trained in pain for this, and
it did not comfort or reassure me to see people who seemed genet-
ically programmed to climb these twenty-thousand-foot peaks

between workouts. So I was glad to be away from them, at least for the day.

Most of the year, I lived in the Adirondack Mountains in upstate New York, where for exercise I took occasional day hikes and played a little tennis—aging boomer guy-stuff, nothing strenuous. It was my good friends and neighbors back home, Laurie and George Daniels, who had first signed on for this trek with Rock and River Guide Service and talked me into joining them. They are wonderful, intelligent people, owners of a small independent bookstore and health food store in Keene Valley, but they, too, were twenty or more years younger than I, built like gazelles, and they were experienced climbers. Laurie did triathlons and was a rock-climbing guide. George had a ponytail. I was, therefore, secretly relieved that on this first climb, my test run at altitude, they had decided to stay in Quito with the other members of our expedition and help Alex, our guide and wagon master, buy supplies. If I had made a serious mistake and had wasted six months of nonsmoking, lung-bursting, muscle-developing daily exercise, not to mention several thousand dollars in transportation and equipment costs, I preferred to find out alone.

An hour out of Quito, the bus shuddered to a stop and dropped me and my backpack off at the side of the road, then rumbled on to Latacunga. I was suddenly the only human being in sight, and except for the steady rush of the wind, it was absolutely silent. The sun was shining brilliantly, and the air was desert dry but cool, barely fifty degrees Fahrenheit. Across the highway was the entrance to Cotopaxi National Park. A dusty, rutted track led through eucalyptus trees and over humpbacked ridges, where it wound across the plain toward Mount Cotopaxi in the distance—the highest active volcano in the world, and the object of all our desires on this trek. In nine days, after several preliminary conditioning climbs of somewhat lower mountains and a day of "snow school," learning how to climb a glacier, we were scheduled, Laurie and George and I, our guide Alex Van Steen, and the four other *yanquis* in our group, to climb to its 19,400-foot snow-covered summit.

Not today, however. Despite the blue sky overhead, I couldn't even *see* Cotopaxi today. It was shrouded in clouds, a vast, white, shapeless mass that rose like a storm from the *alto plano* in the east and blotted out the horizon. For some reason, I had started thinking of the mountain as She, as the mother of all volcanoes in Ecuador's fabled Avenue of the Volcanoes. Chimborazo, in the north, at 20,561 feet, was the slightly taller father, an extinct volcano nicknamed El Viudo, the widower, and no longer smoldering. Cotopaxi, La Viuda, boiled beneath her snowy cap, and long plumes of steam rose regularly from the crater. The last time she erupted was 1928, and the slopes and plains that surround the mountain are covered for miles with ash and room-sized ejecta from that eruption.

Today, though, I was after smaller game—the three twelve-thousand-foot peaks of El Chaupi. *Lomas,* they're called, "hills"— towering behind me in the west and tied together by a scalloped, narrow twelve-kilometer ridge. I turned, grabbed up my day pack, and started walking. A mile or so ahead of me, the land rose abruptly from the valley to the first of the *lomas*. Soon, I feared, my body will tell me that I am a vain, deluded, late-middle-aged fool and should have stayed home. But, on the other hand, I thought, if I am lucky, perhaps my body will call me master and will say, Where to next? Rumiñahui? Only 14,436 feet. Or how about Sincholagua? Great views of Cotopaxi, and only 16,500 feet! And in nine days, master, the great Cotopaxi herself!

It was not so much the climbing that had made me anxious, because I knew I'd put myself into pretty good shape and had climbed alongside George and Laurie back home over the summer, and God knows, *they* were in shape. It was the altitude. Over the years, I'd hiked long chunks of the Appalachian Trail and climbed most of the higher Adirondacks and White Mountains in New Hampshire, but this was the first time I'd ventured this high. I'd heard and read too many stories of perfectly fit climbers of all ages getting to twelve and fourteen thousand feet and succumbing suddenly to altitude sickness—nausea, blinding headaches, disorientation, hallucinations, even unconsciousness and permanent brain damage. It's like seasickness, only a lot more dangerous: some people get it, some don't, and regardless of how much climbing you've done in the past, you can't tell in advance which you'll be this time out. Back in Quito, on first arriving from the States, I was noticeably short-winded, but only for a day, and by the second day was able to walk the city, uphill and down, with relative ease. I was cheered to learn that George and Laurie, on their first few days in Ecuador, had suffered somewhat more than I. Still, this was three thousand feet higher than Quito, and at two hundred pounds, I was hoofing a lot more body weight than either George or Laurie, and it was all steadily, steeply uphill.

Another hour of climbing, first through cultivated slopes and terraced hillsides, then out along a treeless, fast-rising ridge with spectacular views of the valley below, and I was halfway up the first, the smallest, of the three peaks, Loma Sal Grande. I was breathing heavily, but without much difficulty, feeling strong and competent and very relieved. No light-headedness, no nausea, no headache. No noticeable brain damage. Surprisingly, it wasn't much more difficult than climbing in the Adirondacks, and in a way easier: these Andean mountain paths—old winding goat and donkey trails—were smoother by far than the rocky, root-tangled trails at home.

But I didn't want to get overconfident—this was the first real test of my training program, begun halfheartedly eight months earlier, during my annual winter residence in Princeton, New Jersey. A half-pack-a-day man, the first thing I did was quit smoking. Then, to the boom-box throb of alternative rock, I began lifting free weights in my suburban basement three afternoons a week, and on the other days rode my bicycle along the old canal towpaths from Kingston to Lawrenceville. Although at the time I wore a fifteen- to twenty-pound spare tire around my waist, I wasn't terribly out of shape—your typical moderately aging exercised ex-athlete, I guess. But I hadn't tried to put myself into condition for serious, sustained athletic activity in decades, not since the days when little more than a slight swerve in my daily routines got me fit again. Now, however, it was taking a complete, wrenching reversal of direction, and I hated it.

In May, when I returned to upstate New York, I got serious. Five mornings a week, I climbed one hour steeply uphill and one down on a two-mile path into the state forest adjacent to my land, gradually reducing my total time over that course to an hour and forty-five minutes, then an hour and a quarter, until I was able to make the circuit in less than an hour, practically running the whole way. Once a week, sometimes twice, I took a daylong hike up one of the higher mountains in the region, Algonguin, Giant, or Marcy. Also, three afternoons a week, I bicycled for two hours up and down the Adirondack back roads, logging more and more miles each time out, taking on higher and longer hills, until, by late August, when I made the long, steep, five-mile ascent through Cascade Notch to Lake Placid, I was drawing incredulous stares from passing motorists—Who *is* that gray-haired idiot? By mid-October, it was dark from 5 P.M. till 8 A.M., and the snow had started to fly, so I had to switch from hiking shoes to snowshoes and put my bike away, but no matter—I was as ready for the Andes as I would ever be. As ready, at least, as I was *willing* to be.

All the way up the winding trail to the summit of Loma Sal Grande, I'd been unavoidably faced away from mother Cotopaxi; my view had been mainly of the three linked peaks ahead. The path through shiny tussocks of *ichu* grass was smooth enough, thanks to generations of donkeys, milch cows, goats, and their keepers, but the trail was narrow and vaguely defined, and several times I wandered off it onto a dwindling tributary and had to clamber over tipped, hummocky fields of the tough, knee-high grasses to get back on route. The solitude was splendid. I met no other climbers—no humans at all since the three native women I had spoken to back at the highway, who had given me directions to the path and giggled shyly at my broken Spanish.

It had gotten much cooler as I ascended from the valley floor, but I was still in T-shirt and hiking shorts, kept plenty warm by exertion. The humidity was extremely low, and the steady wind blew my skin and clothing dry. I knew that I was losing a lot of moisture and was glad that the heaviest item in my day pack was water—two full liters bought this morning at the *bodega* next to my hotel in Quito. I was also carrying rain gear and a fleece jacket, in case the weather changed, and extra socks, an emergency medical kit, a spicy Argentine chorizo and chunk of hard cheese for lunch, and, for snacks, several Reese's peanut butter cups, from the carton in my luggage hauled all the way down from the States.

Finally, I crossed a pocked, stony collar and scrambled to the summit of Loma Sal Grande, a narrow, bony fist of volcanic rock, where I stopped to rest and take in the astonishing scenery. An oval bowl three thousand feet deep opened below the three humped *lomas* like a pale green fjord. To the north, I could make out the black rooster-comb caldera of Pasachoa, and slightly to the right, the rusty crown of Rumiñahui. Then, suddenly, as I turned farther to the east, there she was—Mount Cotopaxi, looming over my shoulder as if she'd been following me all along, so much taller and broader and more magisterial than the other mountains and sparkling white against the deep blue sky, shocking in her immensity and apparent nearness. A nearly perfect cone rising from a vast umber plain, Cotopaxi dwarfed the *lomas* of El Chaupi, so that, from my little peak, after my first modest Andes ascent, I found myself looking, not down at the world in triumph, as I had expected, but up, in awe.

For the rest of the afternoon, except for lunch at the summit of Santa Cruz, the third and highest of the three *lomas,* I was ridgewalking and keeping a wary eye on a long, low bank of dark clouds rolling across the northern valley from west to east, coming in from the Pacific. Gradually, the clouds blocked my view of Pasachoa, then Rumiñahui, and finally they swallowed even Cotopaxi. By the time I started down from Santa Cruz and made my way across its broad, grassy shoulder, descending in the general direction of the Pan-American Highway, it had begun to rain. I pulled on my poncho and rain pants and plodded steadily downhill, chilled and drawn swiftly into my hooded thoughts, for there was little I could see now that was not ten feet in front of me—the next turning in the narrow footpath, a low, slick boulder beside it, the drooping branch of a eucalyptus tree.

This is how it is when you climb, and I have never gotten used to it: first you expand out of yourself and enter the vast world that surrounds you, and then, just as quickly, you are forced by weather or fatigue back to your secret interior life, and you lose awareness of the outside world altogether. It's a rhythmic, alternating expansion and contraction of consciousness that feels like the creation of mind. More than anything else, this is what has drawn me back to the mountains all my adult life. Not the scenery alone, those grand vistas of sky and rock and colliding planes of light; not even the rejuvenating, but increasingly difficult to find, solitude of the mountains; and certainly not the "conquest" of a particular summit, marking another notch on my walking stick, another patch for my backpack, like a bumper sticker on a car that's been driven up Pikes Peak. No, for me, it's the feeling of the creation of mind that occurs during the ascent and descent of mountains, an experience that is available to me almost nowhere else and at no other time.

Another hour of trudging downhill on the switchbacking trail in the cold rain, immersed in freely associating thoughts and random memories, then, gradually, almost reluctantly, as if waking from an interesting dream, I noticed that the rain had let up. I stopped to pull off my poncho and rain pants and knocked back another peanut butter cup. A few hundred yards farther down the trail, I clambered up and out of a narrow gully and unexpectedly found myself once again face-to-face with mother Cotopaxi glistening white in the dazzling late-afternoon sunlight. And there was a lovely omen, a double rainbow arching across her snowy breast, and for a long time I stood there, until the rainbow had nearly faded from sight, before continuing my descent in the lengthening shadows to the broad valley below.

Down on the highway, I waited barely fifteen minutes before one of the overloaded Quito-bound buses hissed to a stop, and I scrambled aboard. It was jammed with people, no seats available, and I was forced to stand all the way back to the city—a tall, smiling, strangely elated *yanqui* bent almost double by the low roof of the bus. The seated, tired natives, returning home from a long day's work in the fields and shops of the hinterlands, studied me with dignified, mild curiosity, as if I had been beamed up to the bus from the surface of a newly discovered planet. Which seemed only appropriate, for that is exactly how I felt, all the way back to Quito.

The night before, at the Alameda Real Hotel, I had met my fellow trekkers and our guide for the first time. To give myself a few extra days of adjusting to altitude, I had flown into Quito before the rest of the group—except for my friends George and Laurie, who had come down two whole weeks earlier to travel and hike on their own in the small Indian villages north of Quito. Tanned and tested and ready for the more difficult climbs ahead, George and Laurie had met up with me two days before, and we'd spent a cheerful, companionable weekend wandering the streets and parks of the city, waiting for the arrival of our guide and our as-yet-unknown fellow trekkers from the States. To my delight, the hotel—filled with intrepid travelers, mostly young diesel-powered German tourists and American Elderhostelers—had overbooked and had put me into a large, luxurious suite at the $75 U.S. price of the single I had reserved months earlier. Also, the hotel had a satellite dish with the same feed as at home, and I'd been enjoying CNN, C-Span, and MTV. I had just finished watching Evander Holyfield knock out Mike Tyson in the eleventh and had crawled

sleepily into my king-sized bed when there came a sharp knock
on my door.

In my underwear, I stumbled in darkness over my scattered
gear, opened the door a crack, and saw a large, drooping, walrus-
style mustache. Then I made out the tall, big-faced man wearing it.
He was clearly tired and irritated, as was the woman behind him. I
noticed huge, overstuffed backpacks and two enormous duffels on
the floor beside them. Americans, I surmised, when he said their
names, which I didn't quite catch. I was in their room, he informed
me, and would have to move. Coming down the hallway were two
more people looking for their rooms—a young, bearded man and
an even younger woman, both of them wearing loaded backpacks
and dragging duffels the size of body bags. Behind them, pushing a
cart loaded with at least four more body bags, came a man I recognized, our guide, Alex Van Steen, whom I had briefly met nearly a
year before at the Rock and River Lodge in the Adirondacks when I
first signed on for this trip.

There had been a screw-up. I was supposed to be sharing a double room with the young bearded fellow—whose name was Mark,
I soon learned, an FBI agent from Westchester, New York—and my
pleasantly large suite with the king-sized bed was supposed to have
been held for the mustachioed man, Fred, and his wife, Beth. Fred, I
later discovered, was an ex-headmaster of a private school near Syr-
acuse and was now a househusband caring for his and Beth's new
baby. Beth was a pediatrician. They were both Seventh-Day Adven-
tists. The young woman struggling with her duffel and backpack
behind Mark was named Michelle, a pretty, twitchy physical therapist from Arizona. The one solo woman in our group, she'd been
assigned a single room—no problem there—while Alex, our guide,
was supposed to share a single room with the expedition gear. Laurie and George, of course, had settled properly into a double and no
doubt were deep in sleep by now, where I wanted to be.

It took a while, after introductions were made, to straighten
out the rooms and rumpled feelings. Fred and Beth grumpily

agreed to take Alex's single, which turned out to have a queen-sized bed, so that I wouldn't have to pack up and move all my gear at midnight, a task I expressed a sharp distaste for, and Alex and I and the expedition gear would share "my" suite, Alex insisting on sleeping on the pullout couch, graciously leaving me the king-sized bed. Not an auspicious beginning, I thought, as later I settled back into bed. The simplest, most logistically and socially uncomplicated aspect of our trip should have been these few first days in a large, modern hotel in Quito, and somehow we had made it complicated and then had dealt with the complications rather gracelessly. Or at least I had.

Alex was in the other room, anxiously going over his checklists and spreading gear across the furniture—ice axes and rope and tents and medical kits and cookstoves and fuel and pots and pans, plus all his personal gear, sleeping bag and ground pad, crampons, climbing harness, parka, rain gear, snacks, cold-weather clothing, double-lined plastic boots—all the stuff that we each had been told to bring ourselves and had filled our backpacks and duffels with. Then, just as I was dropping into sleep, Alex called out, "We meet for instructions in the lobby tomorrow morning at eight!"

"Well, I'll be heading out right after," I answered. "Alone." I am not a happy camper, thought I. And we haven't even started camping yet.

By the next evening, however, following my triumphant climb of the three *lomas* of El Chaupi, I was confident and anxiety-free, ready for more difficult climbs, maybe even ready for mother Cotopaxi herself. Feeling more sociable than at Alex's morning meeting in the lobby, and a little guilty, perhaps, for my lack of consanguinity in the hallway the previous night, I joined my fellow trekkers for dinner at a cavernous Italian restaurant a few blocks from the hotel. Ecuadoreans dine late, so we had the restaurant to ourselves. Alex sat at the center of our long table, and over dinner, just as at the morning meeting, whenever Alex spoke, which he did often and long, the members of the expedition went on high alert. In particular, Mark, the FBI agent, and Michelle, the physical therapist, who sometimes yanked out their pocket notebooks and wrote down his advice, observations, instructions, and detailed memories of other, more arduous and dangerous climbs—McKinley, the Himalayas, even Everest. Fred, who wanted to climb McKinley next year and viewed this trip as mere preparation, hung on to our guide's every word and asked many questions. His sober wife, Beth, who seemed not to want Fred to try McKinley, listened attentively, but perhaps for her own reasons. My friend Laurie, who had learned ice climbing back in the Adirondacks from Alex and had worked alongside him at the Rock and River Lodge, viewed him as a personal friend, admired his guiding skills, and was gently amused by his garrulousness. George followed her example, usually.

Bright-eyed and tanned, with a movie star's chin and cheekbones and a professional mountain climber's taut, muscular build, Alex was eager to instruct neophyte and expert alike. As the evening wore on, however, I began to think that perhaps he did not have total confidence in this group's ability to climb the mountains that lay before us along the Valley of Volcanoes—first Pasachoa, then Rumiñahui and Sincholagua, and finally Cotopaxi—for he had a tendency to overinstruct, even to overarticulate, as if we were hard of hearing or English were our second language. Consequently, I, too, began to lose confidence in our ability—especially mine—to complete our mission. After all, these folks were at least as experienced climbers as I (or more so, certainly in Laurie's and George's case) and they were all decades younger than I and looked to be in great condition, even Fred, who was an unusually large man and seemed slightly awkward for it, but appeared nonetheless to be very strong and brimming with great good health. They had all taken mountaineering classes of one type or another, and Fred and Beth had let it drop that they were Forty-Sixers, which meant that they had climbed all forty-six of the Adirondack Mountains over four thousand feet, a club I didn't ever expect to belong to. Half of them were serious vegetarians, even. If Alex was sufficiently worried about them that he was giving them breathing lessons, what must he think of me, at my advanced age, with my lack of experience and all my bad habits and years of sloth?

Early the next morning, we loaded our small hired bus with our duffels and backpacks and all the equipment and food we'd need for the next nine days, and eagerly, if a little nervously, set out from Quito for the mountains. As we left the city and rode up into the green hills and south toward Pasachoa, described in the itinerary as a 12,500-foot "acclimatizing hike," Alex pointed out the various other mountains hoving into view, right, left, and ahead, chattered in Spanish with the driver, drilled his charges from time to time on how to conserve energy and oxygen at altitude, and answered the occasional question put by Fred, Beth, Mark, or Michelle—while George, Laurie, and I gazed out the windows at the passing scenery like excited school kids on an outing who could hardly wait till we reached our destination and could get out and run around in reckless circles.

Eventually, about thirty kilometers from Quito, we turned off the main road onto a cobbled, winding track that crossed over rocky streams and passed through the carefully cultivated land and paddocks of a large *finca,* the Hacienda San Miguel, until at last we reached the sloping base of Pasachoa, where there was an empty parking lot and a small, deserted cinder-block building that housed a rudimentary environmental education center. We disembarked, slung on our day packs, checked our water supplies, rubbed on sunblock, and began to walk through a large forest preserve where the narrow trail wound like a dimly lit tunnel through bamboo groves and dense shrubbery and dripping eucalyptus trees. It was very hot and humid, and as the trail shifted slowly uphill and walking turned into work, I began to sweat and wonder, Where are the mountains? Where are the *views?* Why am I *here?*

Soon, however, the forest thinned, and the trail broke free of it and led out onto cleared, grassy shoulders, and I could now see—with the broad fields and hillocks spreading out below, and the great peaks of the Valley of Volcanoes gleaming in the distance—how high we were and how far we'd come; and up ahead—with the black, spiky caldera of Pasachoa beckoning at the end of a long, narrow, fast-rising ridge—how far we had yet to climb.

As we walked, there was a great deal of energetic, almost obsessive talk about training regimens and equipment, which I'd begun to regard as coded talk about bodies—one's own. Were my companions, without admitting or even knowing it, talking about themselves? It was as if, behind an apparently earnest desire to describe one's backpack, hiking shoes, gaiters, and crampons, there lurked an almost narcissistic self-absorption. It struck me that I was learning something useful about the younger generation and the true meaning of sports consumerism. On the other hand, I thought, maybe I just don't have the right stuff.

Periodically, Alex would stop the party and bid us sit, while he instructed us on walking, breathing, and resting techniques. They seemed to be the same little tricks that, without knowing it, I'd been using my whole life. Consequently, I let my attention wander from the lecture and instead contemplated the surreal beauty of the Andean landforms, so that when, at the next stop, he quizzed us on these techniques, I ended up the bad student again. Perhaps the lectures were useful to the others, and we might need to remember them later, when out on the glacier-covered breast of Cotopaxi, but, for me, when I think too much about walking and breathing and resting, I tend to do them badly, so I tuned out: I was feeling strong as a donkey today, even stronger than on the *lomas* of El Chaupi yesterday, and didn't want to screw it up. Risking the role of rogue mountaineer, then, and the loneliness of the *isolato,* I started separating myself from the group emotionally, and physically, too, and found myself more and more often walking alone, either at the front of the pack or way at the back, as we wound our way slowly up and over the grass-covered humps below Pasachoa and out along the narrowing ridge toward the high dark edge of the caldera.

It took more than five hours, and, strangely, the higher and steeper it got, the easier seemed the climb. Was this a symptom of hypoxia—altitude sickness? I wondered. Brain damage already? More likely it was the simple, clean thrill of getting out onto the crisp lip of the caldera of an ancient Andean volcano, 12,500 feet up, and the sight of the terraced valley thousands of feet below, the forest crumpled at the base like a dark green blanket, and the conifers spiking the higher slopes opposite like the pikes of an advancing army of knights under the cloudless, taut blue canopy overhead— and in the distance, majestic and serene in the soft afternoon sunlight, the beautiful white cone of Cotopaxi.

Laurie and I were the first to make the top—as close as we could get to it, at least, without technical rock-climbing equipment, as there was a vertical twenty-foot headwall between us and the true summit—and stood dazed with delight on the small ledge, as one by one the others joined us there, red-faced, puffing, and genuinely thrilled. And for the first time, I was happy to see my fellow trekkers and to be able to share with them this hard-won pleasure.

Soon, however, even there, the talk turned again to training regimens and equipment and other mountains climbed in the past, and I pulled away and, with George and Laurie, began the descent. We arrived at the bus an hour before the others, just as the afternoon rain began. When all had returned, we rode on to the town of Machachi, several miles south—tired and wet, but cheerful, all in all, for no one in the group seemed to have suffered symptoms of altitude sickness, other than unusual fatigue (Fred and Michelle), and headache (Laurie and Beth), and nausea (Mark).

At Machachi, we put up for the night at a comfortable old mission-style bed-and-breakfast located next to a railroad station and named, appropriately, La Estación. We were the only guests, and after an ample four-course dinner, the group sprawled around the living room fireplace and listened in dim light to Alex's account of climbing the north face of Everest. It was a tough story to tell, tough to listen to, for the attempt had ended in tragedy for two men he had been close to, and it had nearly taken his own life as well. As he talked on, his voice dropping almost to a whisper, I found myself surprisingly moved, as much by Alex's grief and pain as by the story itself. Finally, I was starting to get it, the climber's mentality—one in which mountains were not a metaphor for life, but were life itself. And climbing mountains, for a man like Alex, was not an allegory for the difficulty of life, but was the difficulty itself. So that an account of failing to reach a summit or of falling and injuring oneself or of a friend's dying in the attempt was the actual story of one's actual life. This was the story that Alex, who spends more than three hundred days and nights a year at altitude, was really telling, and as he talked on, I felt guilty for not having listened well enough earlier. I saw that, for Alex, and maybe even for some of my fellow trekkers, the apparently obsessive concern with equipment and fitness and the techniques of breathing and walking and resting was like a Puritan's concern with his conscience, a Buddhist's with his koan, or a warrior's with his weaponry—it's what gets him through his life.

The next day found us in the middle of the vast Cotopaxi National Park, at the end of a rutted, almost invisible track ten miles out on the desolate, pampaslike plateau that surrounds Mount Cotopaxi. We unloaded our duffels and backpacks from the bus and watched the vehicle lumber off for Quito, and then we were alone on the enormous, darkening, henna-colored plateau—ten of us, including Alex and two Ecuadorians, Colón, a taciturn, wry, young man who would help guide the party for the remainder of our trek, and Elias, a sweet-smiling native man who would stay in camp and guard our equipment while we climbed the days away. Surrounded by our duffels and packs, we all stood glumly in the cold rain at the steep bank of a narrow, fast-running stream, the Hualpaloma. For the next four days, this 12,500-foot-high treeless piece of the *paramo* by the Hualpaloma would be our campsite, before we moved on to the Jose Ribas Refugio, the base camp at 16,500 feet, located just below the glacier on the rounded north-facing shoulder of Cotopaxi. There were low, bald, rolling hills in the near distance, pitted and cluttered by volcanic rocks like a lunar landscape, and to the north, beyond the hills, the three cloud-shrouded peaks of Rumiñahui, which we were scheduled to climb tomorrow. Off to the right of Rumiñahui, also lost in the mists, was Sincholagua, scheduled for two days later. And behind us, with only her rocky, broad skirts visible, was Cotopaxi, our final goal, the reason we were here in the first place.

Alex quickly divided us into pairs—George and Laurie, Fred and Beth, himself and Michelle, and Agent Mark and me—and passed out the tents, and we commenced to struggle in the raw wind to get them pitched. We were all very cold, and the rain didn't help. Also, we had gotten a late start from Machachi, and it was close to dark. It took a while, but finally we had the small, two-man tents up and our gear stowed inside them. The two married couples were bunked in their own tents, and Mark and I would share one. Colón and Elias shared a tent, and Alex planned to sleep in the floorless cook tent, unless it got too wet. Barring serious rain, Michelle had her single again. While Alex cranked up the gas stoves and prepared our Spartan evening meal of instant soup, powdered potatoes, and boiled carrots, the rest of us retreated to our respective shelters to unroll sleeping bags and change into warmer, dry clothing and hide awhile from the elements.

This was when I discovered two things that would have a decidedly negative impact on my Andes camping experience. In my hurry to leave home, I'd grabbed a nylon stuff bag from several in the hall closet, thinking it contained my almost-new downfilled sleeping bag, only to discover now that it contained instead an ancient, torn bag that I'd long meant to toss out. It was halfemptied of its down filler, a flattened, moldy sack of loose feathers with a ripped seam at the foot and no zipper at the side to close it around me. Also, I'd somehow left my new inflatable ground pad behind in the hotel in Quito. Consequently, not only would I be sleeping in the sorriest imaginable excuse for a sleeping bag, I would have to lie in the thing with nothing between it and the cold, damp ground.

Mark, whose duffel was twice the size of mine and whose expedition pack had more compartments, zippers, straps, bells, and whistles than a sport utility vehicle, blew up a ground pad the size of an inflatable doll and spread his shiny, nearly weightless, elegantly expanding, waterproof, cocoonlike bag over it. I gazed at my tent-mate in envy. When he finished, he glanced at my sad sack, politely looked away, and said nothing. I had clearly failed him. Sheepishly, I offered him a Reese's peanut butter cup, but he declined it, opting instead for one of his high-nutrient Power Bars.

Later, half a roll of duct tape from Alex's emergency pack helped patch my sleeping bag, but only temporarily. All night long, my stockinged feet kept breaking through, and whenever I turned in my sleep and yanked my chilled feet back inside, I tore the tape from the side of the bag, opening it to a wave of cold air that inevitably woke me. Fresh feathers spilled onto the cold ground and floated idly in the dark above my face, while Mark snored peacefully from the warm comfort of his cocoon. It was a long, miserable, freezing night, and I was deeply grateful when, shortly after five, I heard Alex walk from tent to tent, waking his charges for breakfast like a drill sergeant.

Soon I heard the low chortle of the gas stoves heating water for tea and hot chocolate. I quickly dressed, pulled on my climbing boots, grabbed my insulated mug and plastic bowl and spoon, toothbrush, toothpaste, and soap, and stepped outside. The *ichu* grass, silver-soldered by frost in the predawn light, crunched underfoot as I walked to a spot a hundred yards downstream from the tents, where I performed my ablutions in the dark. My breath made clouds before my face, and the surface of the stream steamed in the cold air. In the east, behind the sharply silhouetted horizon, the night sky was fading to peach. Pale swaths of stars fluttered overhead where the sky was still blue-black, and a chalky three-quarter moon hovered in the west. It was a splendid, affirming moment, and once again, despite my terrible, sleepless night, I was glad that I had come here. The sun struck the entire eastern side of Cotopaxi, setting it ablaze, as if ice could burn, and her cloudless summit rose imperiously into the sky, taking fresh command of the vast, still-darkened plain below.

One by one, my companions emerged from their tents, and we gathered before the cook tent for breakfast—cold Pop-Tarts, apples, hard rye bread smeared with peanut butter. Another Spartan meal. I filled my plastic insulated McDonald's mug with hot water and made tea. Then I looked around and noted that my fellow trekkers were all drinking from steaming, high-tech stainless steel personal Thermoses. These were serious people; I, obviously, was not.

No time to dwell on real or imagined inadequacies, however. Today we were to climb three-pronged Rumiñahui, all the way to the rosy, sunlit summit of the middle prong. It towered in the northwest quadrant, 14,436 feet high, with its broad base at Lake Limpiopungo, a four-mile walk from our camp across the rolling plateau. We filled our packs with the clothing and food we'd need for the ten-hour climb and the changes in weather we'd likely encounter up there, and headed out, the plateau still dark in the shadows cast by the berms and *lomas* in the near distance and, behind them, Mount Cotopaxi—she-who-blocks-the-very-sun.

We hadn't walked more than a quarter mile in the frosty dawn when, as we rounded a long, morainelike ridge, we interrupted a meditating coyote that darted into the darkness as we approached, startling us as much as we had startled it. Then in the distance we began to see horses grazing, semiwild and unbroken, alone, in pairs, and in small herds, lifting their long, angular heads warily to watch us pass slowly by. They were beautiful, small, thick-bodied animals, the same stock as the horses the Spanish rode in on half a millennium ago. Rumiñahui, in Quechua, means "face of stone" and is named for one of the Inca generals who fought the invaders. Now, like equine ghosts guarding and honoring the old native general's spirit, hundreds of the sturdy descendants of the conquistadors' horses roamed the *paramo* at the foot of his mountain. In shape and color, they looked like the horses painted on the walls of Iberian caves forty thousand years ago, and I wondered if the painted horses had performed the same service as these living animals. Perhaps they, too, had been protectors of the spirits of nameless warriors slain by foreign invaders.

By the time we reached the sprawling, shallow lake, more a marsh than a lake at this time of year, the sun had fully risen in a nearly cloudless sky. We marched single-file around the northern edge of the lake, hopping from dry spot to dry spot, then circled uphill from the lake alongside a narrow, fast-running feeder creek. Alex was in the lead, I was at the rear, and one by one the troop crossed the creek fairly easily. Until it was Fred's turn. Wearing a Capilene turtleneck jersey, black tights, hiking shorts, and Gore-Tex gaiters, Fred had come out this morning carrying two adjustable aluminum hiking poles with nylon wrist straps attached, and with his long, slightly off-balance stride, he looked more like a man cross-country skiing for the first time than one walking for the millionth. He was the least well-conditioned member of the group, I was discovering, and tended to drop back from the others, puffing and red-faced, and if you got behind him—which I sometimes did, lagging back at the rear to catch some silence and solitude—you had to watch out or you'd get hit in the eye with one of his flailing poles.

Now, as he rock-walked his way across the stream, he suddenly slipped, and in he went. He was quickly out, embarrassed but hearty and hale nonetheless, striding in wet boots and gaiters uphill in a manly fashion, as if nothing untoward had happened. But it had scared me, and I think scared the others, Alex in particular. It was suddenly clear—from the steep ash and soft-rock slope looming ahead of us and the arroyos that tumbled away on either side—that a simple misstep like that could be deadly.

I decided to keep some distance between me and Fred's poles and moved up to the front of the group as we ascended the long, broad ridge that came off the central summit. Around midmorning, clouds moved in, obscuring our views of the terrain above. Before long, we were socked in entirely and had lost sight of the terrain below as well. The temperature was dropping steadily as we climbed, and around noon it began to rain. We stopped and changed into rain gear, hats, and gloves, and plodded on. After a while, the rain changed to sleet. Then hail. Then snow—until we couldn't see more than a few feet of the trail ahead. Close by, the crumbly black rock took on an otherworldly look, strangely detailed and in sharp focus, as in a high-gloss silver-plate photograph, and the high-altitude flowers at the side of the trail and out along the slopes looked like they'd been candied—*chocho de paramour,* Colón called it, a tender lavender-blue bud on a tough low bush, and another named, in Quechua, *chuguiragua,* glowed green, blue, and red through the thin skin of ice and the padding of wet, sticky snow.

The narrow, winding trail was very slick. Also, the pitch of the slope had increased considerably in the last hour, and we were moving as if in slow motion. Breathing was difficult and came in short, shallow, rapid puffs, and my legs felt like iron ingots. This was hard going. But when I looked back, I saw that everyone in the group was making it—even Fred, whose decision to wear gaiters and lug his sticks along seemed prescient now. No one looked happy, however, and for the first time, everyone was silent.

We were slogging across a reddish, sandy rise, our boots sunk to the ankles in powdery ash, and might have been climbing the sifting side of a Sahara dune, except that we were at nearly fourteen thousand feet—when, suddenly, powerful beams of sunlight broke through the snow, and the clouds swirled and parted and drew away. We could see! We were above the storm in bright sunlight with a huge blue sky overhead and a long, steep, rock-strewn ridge ahead of us that led straight to the knife-blade summit. This section of the ascent was a hand-to-rock scramble and probably the toughest part of the climb. Yet it seemed almost easy, thanks to the shocking beauty of sky and cliff hovering above and—as the clouds behind us broke and flowed off to the south—the sight of the long, bony ridges and knuckled arêtes and the deep, pale green arroyos thousands of feet below, where the *paramo* spread out beyond like a particolored map. Halfway between us and the *paramo,* two of Ecuador's seventy-five remaining condors, like black-winged hang gliders, rode the sun-warmed air currents in wide, spiraling loops.

The last few hundred yards to the summit were a hard pull over crumbling plate-sized rocks. Fred, Mark, and Michelle had slowed considerably, evidently suffering from the altitude, but they kept climbing, even if with tiny, numbingly slow steps. They were not to be stopped, not this close to the summit. Alex fell back and watched them closely, checking for signs of AMS, acute mountain sickness. It's a common enough syndrome, and its mild form causes nausea, headache, breathlessness, and lassitude. Its severe form, however, is characterized by ataxia—loss of balance, loss of muscular coordination, and mental confusion—and can lead quickly to life-threatening pulmonary and cerebral edema. Rapid diagnosis and treatment is essential, and according to Peter Hackett, renowned author of the bible on the subject, *Mountain Sickness: Prevention, Recognition, and Treatment,* there are three cures for AMS: "Descent, descent, descent!"

It's the guide's decision, not the climber's, when to descend, and evidently Alex felt that Fred, Mark, and Michelle were not yet in danger, for they kept coming and finally joined the rest of the group, where we had gathered on a narrow, protected shelf fifteen feet below the table-sized summit. Then, one at a time, in the order we had arrived at the shelf, we each climbed up to the summit itself and stood there alone. Laurie went up first, and after a few moments came down looking stunned with pleasure, as if she'd interviewed a deity.

Then it was my turn. I reached the top crawling on hands and knees and stood unsteadily up. Despite the cold wind and sunlight basting my body and face, I opened my eyes wide, and in a rapture that was in every way new to me, gazed away like a blissed-out anchorite. When I could think again, I thought, For the rest of my life, I will be trying to regain this feeling! I don't know how long I stood there bedazzled like that, staring out at the universe—in memory an hour or more, but in fact probably only two minutes. Eventually, I made my way back down to the protected shelf, and when each of the others had taken his turn at the top, we began the descent.

We got back to the main supporting ridge fairly fast and, at Colón's suggestion, followed an alternate route down to the *paramo,* bypassing the lake, a path that turned out to be easier but longer than our route up, so that by the time we reached the plateau, the sun was heading toward the horizon behind us. We were by now exhausted, and camp was still four miles away. Also, to complicate things, a dense fog was creeping in, and before long we couldn't see more than fifty feet in front of us.

Cold and wet and bone-tired, we plodded in a southeasterly direction, trusting our guides, Colón and Alex, to bring us through the fog to our campsite. An hour went by, then nearly two. The fog grew thicker. Once in a while huge volcanic rocks like dark gray icebergs appeared out of the mists. But we might as well have been crossing the Arctic in a blizzard—everywhere we looked, it was the same. By now, everyone had a different idea of how far the camp was and in what direction it lay. Even our guides seemed unsure. We were almost too tired to care—in retrospect, a dangerous state of mind—when, suddenly, as we came around the front of a low berm, a coyote loped out of a nearby gully and trotted to the top of the berm, where it stopped and looked back at us. Was it the same coyote we'd seen at dawn? We peered around at the landscape, which seemed newly familiar. Twice, then, we had accidentally come upon the same coyote's den, and it hadn't fled until we were almost upon it, possibly because it had pups there. But we knew where we were now, and where the camp was. In silence, each of us thanked the coyote for pointing the way and passed on.

After our long trudge back to camp, we were almost too exhausted to complain of a cold supper (malfunctioning stoves) eaten standing around in the dark. And at the end of another freezing, bumpy night in my pathetic sleeping bag, while Mark snored comfortably beside me, I woke at six thirty determined to enjoy in my own way the one free day of our expedition. Luckily, the weather cooperated. It was a splendid day, warm and sunny, and after breakfast George, Laurie, and I lit out together—a four-hour hike across the *paramo* to a distant set of grass-topped hills, where we picnicked and basked in the reflected light of gleaming Cotopaxi. Later, we followed the meandering Rio Hualpaloma out onto the rolling plain, where brown rabbits bounded across our path and disappeared into the high silver-tipped grass. In the distance we saw bands of wild horses being rounded up by gauchos and moved to fresh grazing land. We passed several small herds of llamas—whose pursed lips and long-lashed, soulful eyes reminded me of Uma Thurman—tended by lone native shepherds who nodded solemnly at us.

On our way back to camp, we looped out toward the center of the broad plain and visited an Inca ruin, a long, rectangular mound fifty feet high. We climbed to the top, where the cut-stone remains of a mostly unexcavated fortress gave a commanding view of the entire valley, and for a long while stood there with the fresh southerly breeze in our faces and traveled backward in time to when these lovely mountains and the wide valley between them were new.

Later, back at the camp, where only Elias, the watchman, had stayed the day, we went upstream a ways and bathed under a heavy, cold waterfall and dried in the sun like contemplative turtles. Afterward, we changed into clean clothing, aired out tents and sleeping bags, tended to our gear, and packed for tomorrow's trek to the top of Sincholagua. It had been a much-needed, rejuvenating interlude. We three felt pleased with ourselves, for we had grown stronger and more confident with each new day's test. And we were beginning to learn how to look at this landscape, so unlike anything we had seen before, to understand its logic and scale and to anticipate its forms, and consequently it did not seem as intimidating as it had. Also, more personally, we had needed, in a sense, to renew our friendship, to get away from the others for a while and talk about people and places and notions that only we were familiar with.

Roused at 5 A.M. by Alex—after another long night of having my back pummeled by the lumpy ground and my blood curdled by my cold-pack sleeping bag—I was ready and eager to climb Sincholagua. We had prepared our packs the day before. They were heavier than on Rumiñahui—this time we were carrying serious cold-weather clothing and gear, as well as rain gear. On the IGM 1:50,000 map, Sincholagua is shown with a permanent, mile-long ice cap, but in recent years the snow line has receded and there is no longer any glaciation at the top. Still, the fog and rain on the plain down here turned into snow and ice up there, and at 16,400 feet, the temperature would be much lower than on Rumiñahui.

We left camp and crossed the darkened plain at a brisk pace, set purposely by Alex, who explained that this was going to be a longer, tougher climb than any we'd yet attempted, so we'd have to move fast to make it out and back by nightfall. Which was fine by me, Laurie, and George—we were feeling like Sherpas this morning. Gradually, the dawn light spread silver and gold wedges across the *paramo* and slowly gilded the mountains from the top down. Behind us, Cotopaxi filled the sky, dominating the landscape, and every now and then I peered back at her and tried to pick out the route that we would follow, tracing how, three days hence, at midnight, we'd leave the *refugio,* its tin roof a tiny, shining dot situated just below the bottom edge of the glacier at 16,500 feet, and from there follow a spiraling route over the snow, pass to the right along the lower lid of a large, shaded, eye-shaped break in the glacier, where we'd turn back and cross up and over the brow of the eye, then slowly switchback across the ice in the fading dark, until at dawn, just as the sun cracked the eastern horizon, we would reach the top.

For days, every time I looked at Cotopaxi, I had traced out that path, and each time it had seemed inhumanly high and steep, impossible for any but a professional climber like Alex to follow. But this morning, finally, I believed that I could do it. We crossed the Rio Hualpaloma, and when the trail started to rise from the plain toward the base of Sincholagua, I realized that our pace had slowed considerably. We passed over an ancient Inca stone wall, then crossed a bridge, and after negotiating a shortcut through a large, walled paddock of llamas guarded by a pair of native shepherds, we hit the first real hill since leaving camp. No longer worried about my own chances—or George's or Laurie's, either—of completing this or any other climb, I had started worrying some about the others, especially Fred, whose rapid heart rate was alarming his wife, Doctor Beth, who took his pulse at every rest stop and wrinkled her brow with concern, and Michelle, who was clearly suffering from the altitude. Her pretty, heart-shaped face was taut with strain, and she was walking at a much slower pace than on Rumiñahui. Mark, too, showed symptoms of altitude sickness; he was moving very slowly today and seemed dispirited.

Soon the group was undergoing fission. Alex walked ahead with me, Laurie, and George, climbing the grassy hills and ridges at what felt to us a useful, enjoyable pace, while Colón, our second guide, fell back with the others. Whenever we reached the top of a long slope or came to an arroyo or cliff that marked a transition between ascending zones of difficulty, we would stop and wait for the others to join us. Then, in a discreet way, Alex would check them for altitude sickness and decide anew whether to push on.

We had gathered on a rocky shelf where the trail dropped down a vertical twelve-foot embankment to a narrow arroyo and led across a dry streambed to the main ridge up Sincholagua. For the last half hour, Alex and I had been chatting optimistically about my joining him next year, perhaps with George and Laurie, and climbing Rainier. Just like the others, I, too, was now yakking obsessively about equipment and training regimens and other mountains than the one we were on—a result, I suppose, of my growing confidence and pleasure in my ability to meet this challenge, and perhaps the vanity of a middle-aged man surprised to find himself keeping pace with people in their twenties and thirties. It was a pleasant discovery, and I was savoring it.

First Alex went over the embankment and swung down to the rock-strewn bottom. Mark followed, making it to the bottom safely, but with difficulty. Handholds and footholds were hard to locate without help—he had to descend with his balance tipped by the weight of the pack, his belly facing the rock, his hands clamped on to slippery rotten-rock outcroppings, and his feet hidden from sight, except to the person below. Michelle went over next, with Mark and Alex spotting, and made it safely down. Then it was my turn. I proceeded exactly as the others had. I got halfway down the wall, so that my head was at the level of the shelf, with my weight held solely by my grasp on the crumbly rock there, while my feet groped blindly somewhere below for a hold. Finally, my left foot managed to find a cleft in the wall. Then, just as I transferred my weight—off balance, due to the pack—onto that foot, the cleft gave way, and I was falling. I remember turning in my fall, watching the

rocks at the bottom speed toward me, and I remember rolling in
midair to avoid hitting my head and spine, hoping instead to land
on my shoulder, and then I remember a sound that I recognized as
the snap of bone. I was flat on my back, looking at sky. A second
later, Alex's face, dark with fear, hove into view, and I knew at once
that my trek to Cotopaxi was over.

E P I L O G U E

My right collarbone was broken in two places. Up there on the
sloped shoulder of Sincholagua, Doctor Beth and Alex fixed me up
with a homemade clavicle splint, and I walked slowly back down
to the camp, four hours below, lugging my pack on my left shoulder while the others continued on. Depressed and slightly disoriented from the fall and the pain, it was hard to grasp what had
happened and, maybe more important, what wouldn't happen. I
might just as easily have fallen and broken my collarbone while
stepping from the shower at home—my accident was in no way
a consequence of the difficulty of the climb or of my being out of
shape or ill equipped. Right stuff or wrong stuff had nothing to do
with it. Bad luck was all. Okay, maybe overconfidence had made
me slightly less cautious for a few seconds than I should have been,
but still, that's the sort of mental state I deal with every day of my
life. It could have happened to anyone, especially me, anywhere,
even at sea level.

Given what I'd set out to do—climb at high altitude in the
Andes—I'd succeeded. I'd made myself fit enough to keep pace and
sometimes even to exceed the pace and endurance of serious climbers still in the bloom of youth, and getting myself into that condition hadn't required a significant sacrifice of time or energy. In the
last few days, my fellow trekkers, affectionately and without irony,
had taken to calling me "The Beast"—no small compliment for an
aging boomer.

The greatest disappointment, of course, was that I would not make it to the summit of Cotopaxi, which since my first arrival in Ecuador had become my heart's desire. But the distinction between failure and disappointment is important. I had not failed; I was disappointed. I'd learned, certainly, that I was more than capable of doing this extremely difficult thing, but I had not been able to do it. A strange mix of melancholy and elation, then, accompanied me as I made my slow way back down the side of Sincholagua and plodded across the plain toward our tents. At the camp, I rested awhile, eventually setting myself the task of gathering firewood, so that when my companions returned cold and exhausted, they'd be greeted by a blazing fire.

They were back by nightfall, a thoroughly dispirited bunch, even George and Laurie, after having been forced to turn back well below the summit. My fall had left the group depressed and discouraged, and several of them were still struggling with altitude sickness. Despite my campfire, everyone retired to his tent early in a funk. I was in considerable pain and had to lie on my back all night long, as cold as I have ever been and as uncomfortable, and slept only intermittently and for a few minutes at a time.

The next day we broke camp—although I could but stand and watch while the others did the work—and, when the bus arrived, loaded it with our gear and rode across the *paramo* and up the long, winding track to the parking area at the foot of mother Cotopaxi. From there, it was a steep 2,000-foot hike up to the hut, the *refugio,* which was located at 16,500 feet, where the glacier began. Determined to make it at least that far up the side of a mountain that I had come to love, I walked ahead of the others, whose climb was slowed by the weight of their backpacks. It was a sad, lonely walk for me. Regardless of how strong I felt, regardless of my ability to deny the pain of a busted collarbone, there was no way I could join the others now—no way I could swing an ice ax, haul a heavy backpack, cling to a rope, and make my slow way up to the windblown summit and see the sunrise from above the earth. Still, I wanted to climb as far up the side of the mountain as I could, to get at least as far as the *refugio,* and I trudged stubbornly ahead until I made it.

Afterward, I descended alone to the bus and rode back to Quito, where I spent the night at the Alameda Real Hotel. The next day I hired a car and traveled for three days—waiting for my scheduled departure for home—in the Indian villages of the north, day-hiking through the twelve-thousand-foot-high *lomas* up there and spending my nights in small hotels. It was interesting travel, and solitary, the way I usually prefer it, but anticlimactic and lonely. I missed my fellow trekkers—the bumptious Fred and his walking sticks; my tentmate, Special Agent Mark, whose love of equipment was exceeded only by his surprising love of seventies quasi-metal music by groups like Rush and Pink Floyd; Doctor Beth, calm and disciplined and thinking constantly of her new baby at home; Michelle, anxious and fatigued and suffering from altitude illness, but courageously keeping on nonetheless, as if her whole sense of self-worth depended on having climbed these mountains; and, of course, my old Adirondack chums, George and Laurie, who, on returning home, would tell me everything I missed; and finally, our garrulous guide, the incomparable Alex, whom, if he learned to cook, or hired someone who could, I would follow anywhere. But most of all, I missed the mountain, Cotopaxi, looming over my shoulder, blocking the sun, inviting me, like a grand seductress, to come back, come back and try again.

FOX AND WHALE,
PRIEST AND ANGEL

Three years after my attempt to climb Cotopaxi in 1997, I returned to the Andes for an even more difficult climb, Aconcagua, at 22,834 feet the highest mountain in the world outside the Himalayas. On the tenth day, at 16,170 feet, the wind rose and the temperature dropped and light snow began to fall. Two days before, under a cobalt-blue sky, we'd hauled ourselves and our gear over slurry talus and scree from the base camp at Plaza Argentina across the rock-scabbed skin of the Glaciar de Relinchos to Camp One. On a broad ledge where the glacier squeezed between one of Aconcagua's uplifted, sedimentary skirts and rubble tumbled from the side of her slightly lower sister peak, Ameghino, we pitched our tents.

We double-poled them and lashed them to large rocks with nylon rope, then hauled ice from an exposed slab of the glacier to melt for drinking, cooking, and cleaning, and got the stoves fired up.

We were nine men, six moderately experienced climbers and three guides. With more than six thousand feet still to go, we were exhausted, and one of us, Chris Zanger, the youngest and possibly the fittest, was showing early signs of altitude sickness: a viselike headache and nausea and disorientation. It had been our toughest day so far. The trail had switchbacked over moraines and alongside deep crevasses where glacier melt splashed over room-sized boulders to the broad Valle de los Vacas thousands of feet below, the slowly ascending valley we'd hiked a week earlier, twenty-seven miles in from the road that runs between Mendoza, Argentina, and the Chile-Argentina border.

Early in the day, I had glanced off to my left and had spotted, trotting along the edge of the crevasse between us, a large red fox. For a long time, the fox over on its side of the crevasse kept wary pace with us on ours while we slogged along, the weight of our packs steadily increasing, it seemed. With each turn in the zigzag trail our breathing became more labored. One breath per step. Then, after a while, two. Then, as the day wore on, three. I stopped and studied the fox. It sat and looked across at me. In this extreme Andean glacial world the sight of a red fox trotting watchfully across a page of a large-print geological history of the planet was like a hallucination. The fox is an animal I have long honored—a personal totem, practically. It's situated at the etymological base of my first name; its image is tattooed on my left arm. It was as if I had spotted across the crevasse a cousin or a neighbor from home. What the hell are *you* doing here? I almost said. Then it darted behind a boulder and was gone—an omen or a charm, I couldn't tell which. I asked the man next to me, my Toronto friend David Young, if he had seen the fox.

"Missed it," he said and kept climbing.

By the time we'd finished supper and cleaned up, the wind was gusting at fifty miles per hour. Snow was falling in tiny pellets. We retreated, three men to a tent. David and I shared a tent with Michael Zanger, one of head guide Alex Van Steen's two assistants and father of Chris Zanger, the young man suffering from altitude sickness. The eldest members of the group—I was about to turn sixty, Michael was right behind me, and David was in his early fifties—we'd taken to calling our tent the Assisted Living Facility. Nights we read poetry, mostly from Rilke's *Duino Elegies,* and listed favorite bebop musicians.

None of us wanted to hang around outside, as we had every evening so far, and watch the sky transform itself into the celestial universe of the Incas, a darkened theater of the old sky god's birth and death and resurrection. We were too tired, and it was too cold, even with parkas on, and the wind was howling now, up to seventy miles per hour and sustained, making it difficult to talk normally. We'd begun to shout to one another. Mostly it was Alex shouting, making sure that we were prepared for a tough night—he'd attempted Everest twice and knew what to expect. Check the ropes again! Make sure your packs are weighted down with rocks on top! For Alex, this was a military-style expedition, and his role was that of the war-weary lieutenant, whose first responsibility was to get his men, not safely up the mountain, but safely down. We did as told, then withdrew to the darkness of our tents and curled up inside our sleeping bags and waited for sleep.

The sound of a sustained seventy-mile-an-hour wind is like no other, especially when a thin nylon skin is all that separates you from it. It howls like a stampeding herd of prehistoric animals for ten or fifteen minutes straight, long enough for you to start thinking that you've grown used to the roaring and can sleep in spite of it, because it's steady and the volume does not vary. So you close your eyes and unclench your hands and drift toward a dream of home. Then suddenly it stops. Black silence. No one in the tent speaks. You can hear the others breathing rapidly in the thin air. You blink your eyes open and wait and count off the seconds, ten, eleven, twelve . . . and then the howl returns at full volume. The tent fabric slaps against itself like the sails of a galleon in a hurricane, and you pray that the ropes and the double poles hold, because if the tent starts to tear anywhere, the whole thing will be shredded in minutes, and you will die of exposure. The trap you're in protects you, but barely. It can also kill you.

We'd gone through three consecutive nights and two days like this. We melted snow, cooked, ate, pissed, and washed in our tents, leaving only when absolutely necessary to shit behind a rock. Day and night merged. Time stopped. We feared wasting our headlamp batteries, so we rationed our reading and sought a semihibernated state of consciousness. Sleep we treated with suspicion. At this altitude, when you fall asleep, you neglect to breathe rapidly enough to compensate for the thin air, and periodically you lurch awake, gasping and light-headed and disoriented, as if you're suffocating. You *are* suffocating. You may even be suffering from cerebral edema, which can be cured only by descending the mountain, a thing we could not do because of the storm. In the middle of the second night, David, who slept next to me, sat up suddenly, moaned, and mumbled incoherently. Talking in his sleep or altitude sickness? I shook him and gave him the only diagnostic test I could think of: "Say something witty, David."

After a few seconds, he said, "When we landed at the Lima airport, the money changers and taxi drivers outside were like grizzlies at a salmon run." Then added, "Don't worry, man, it's just a panic attack."

The wind took on a personality. It became a monstrous god with a malignant will, like Melville's whale, and it was difficult not to take its punishing power personally. I ran down the list of my recent and ancient sins of omission and commission, hoping that if I could find a crime that warranted my execution, I could somehow claim extenuating circumstances, and the wind would stop. For the first time since beginning this climb, I saw that I had put my life at risk. And, unexpectedly, I was ashamed. I thought of my wife and my children and my grandchild: If I die here, once again they will have every right to remember me only with anger.

On the morning of the third day, the whale swam away and the wind stopped, leaving behind a wake of playful gusts, as if to remind us that it was merely absent, not weakened, and might well return soon. The sky cleared, and the temperature rose into the twenties. We stumbled from our tents blinking and grinning like inmates granted last-minute pardons by the governor and proceeded to change out of our funky clothing and air out our stinking sleeping bags by draping them over rocks and tent lines. After breakfast, we began the climb to Camp Two, 18,900 feet, at the base of the Polish Glacier. The bearlike, affable Michael Zanger, David's and my personal guide, as we thought of him, would not be with us, however. His son, Chris, whose altitude sickness had worsened, needed to descend at once, and Michael would take him.

On an expedition climb like this, you ascend the mountain twice. You climb high and sleep low at each camp, dividing your supplies and gear into two hauls, so that you can carry the load you don't need immediately to the next higher camp, stash it, and return to the lower camp for a second night. Three days earlier, on our first ascent from Camp One to Two, before the windstorm hit, as we chugged steadily uphill, the highest peaks of the Andes—gigantic, snow-covered, serrated blades of uplifted rock—had unfolded all the way to the horizon, a literally breathtaking sight, and I had caught the first glimmers of a fantasy evolving into a hallucination, and it had eased my climb considerably. Now, on our second ascent, it returned unbidden, a full-blown hallucination, no longer a fantasy. I was a coca-chewing Inca priest in vicuña cloth vestments, and instead of hauling a fifty-pound pack on my back, I was carrying a young girl, perhaps ten years old. She was drugged against the cold and the effects of altitude, and I had been entrusted by her family and the people of her village with the responsibility and honor of carrying her to the top of the Inca world, to Aconcagua, the Quechuan Sentinel of Stone, to give her over to the god of the Incas, who, in gratitude, would bless the coming year's crops and keep the village from famine. She was not heavy, though she wore gold amulets on her wrists and ankles and a brilliantly colored dress woven of wool spun from the hair of baby llamas. It was as if her body were made of feathers or as if she were inhabited by a bird, a condor, pumping its huge wings and half lifting me from the tilted ground as I climbed up and up and the mountains slipped from above to below me.

At one point, while we were slumped on the ground taking one of our hourly rest breaks, I leaned in to David and in a low voice told him who I was and what I was doing here. He would understand, I knew.

He nodded. "Do you know her name?" he asked.

"She has no name," I said. "She left it in the village for another to use."

"You're very lucky," he said as he stood unsteadily and, grunting from the effort, wrestled his pack onto his back.

There was for me and David a dense, complex context for this trek, one created inadvertently by the week we had spent earlier in Peru, hiking the grassy ridges and pre-Columbian terraces outside Cuzco, gazing on the remnants of the Inca walls in the ancient city, and wandering awestruck across the plazas and through the magnificent stone temples of Machu Picchu. David is a playwright and screenwriter and a longtime friend. Our fevered imaginations tend to fuel each other, and in Peru, we had given ourselves over to wild speculations and intellectually reckless intuitions regarding the history and sensibility of the ancient Incas. In our minds, this landscape was connected seamlessly to the Inca ruins and their sacred art. For us, climbing Aconcagua was a pilgrimage, not merely an assault on one of the so-called Seven Summits.

On the sixteenth day, we made it from Camp Two to High Camp, 19,350 feet, the last stop before the summit attempt. Our two backup summit days had been used up when we got socked in below by the windstorm: either we made the top tomorrow or we'd have to try again another year.

The plan was to wake at 3:30 A.M. and, weather permitting, get to the top by 3:00 P.M. and return to High Camp by dark. The wind was steady but not gale force, and the sky was dark, and hard flecks of snow pecked our cheeks. It did not look good.

We were up and more or less ready to leave camp in the pre-dawn dark as scheduled, but Alex was worried about the wind and held us back until, finally—as the sky in the east turned milky white and the stars overhead blinked out one by one—he gave the word, and we bucked into the wind and headed uphill. The craggy top of Aconcagua glowered in the rising sun thirty-five hundred vertical feet above us. The trail switchbacked and curled partly over open scree and partly over snow, passing through fields of *neve penitentes,* or "snow nuns," as they're called, head-high columns of white ice left as residue by the melting glacier, and along narrow, windswept ridges with thousand-foot drops on both sides. We were using crampons and ice axes, moving carefully because of the tricky surface and slowly because of the altitude. Barely a month before, four young Argentinean climbers had fallen to their deaths here.

David was working hard, too hard, it seemed. His face was gray and pinched, and his usual running repartee and sly jokes were noticeably absent. I was struggling, too, fighting exhaustion and the cold and the treacherous footing and the altitude. The Inca child was still on my back, but she had grown heavy, as if she had wakened from her drugged sleep and was now afraid of her fate and wanted to go down from the mountain, back to her mother and father in the village far, far below. The condor had released her. She struggled against the straps that held her to my back and tossed her head from side to side, throwing me off balance several times, causing me to trip and nearly fall.

Around 2:30 P.M., less than an hour before our turnaround time, we were climbing the Canaleta, the maddeningly loose, rock-studded collar of the summit, when David stopped, all but collapsing in Alex's arms, and sat down heavily in the snow and quietly said, "Fuck it. I'm sick." He couldn't go on. "Now I know," he gasped, "what it's like . . . when the tank is empty." His head felt stuck with needles, his stomach and bowels were roiling, and his mind was wobbling on its axis. He said that he was afraid he was going to shit his pants.

Alex told us to go on; he would stay below with David. "Turn around at three thirty, no matter how close you are to the top," he said.

"You going to be okay?" I asked David.

"Yeah, sure. You go on." His breathing was labored and shallow.

With grave reluctance I put him out of my mind and joined the others making their slow, arduous way up the narrow path toward the top, looming barely two stone's throws above our heads. I think I'm going to be able to do this, I said to myself. But then two things happened. About three hundred feet from the summit, Ed Chiasson, a cardiologist and the largest man in our group, walking just in front of me, stumbled from exhaustion. He swung around off balance to face me, and the gleaming blade of his ice ax slashed the air between us, grazing my chest as it passed.

"Jesus, Ed! Watch it!"

A house call from Doctor Death, I thought, and felt the blood drain from my face. Ed's face was expressionless, blank. He hadn't heard me. I doubt he even saw me. He turned and resumed walking: one step, three breaths; another step, three breaths more; and on, nearer and nearer to the top.

I followed for a few feet, and then—this is the second thing that happened—I pictured David below us, sick and maybe getting sicker by the minute, while he waited with Alex for our triumphant return from the summit. I had utter faith in Alex's judgment and knew that he would take David down at once if he got worse. But what if that happens while I go on ahead without him? What if David's brain starts to swell and bleed, what if his lungs fill with water, what if he has begun to die, while I stagger on with the others just to tag the summit? And what if the next time Ed stumbles, his ice ax tears through my parka into my chest? And, yes, what if I stop climbing now, here, a few hundred feet from the top, while I still seem to have the strength to get there but might not have enough left to get down? If I stop now, what will happen? What will it mean?

It was a Zen decision, which is to say, not a decision. I simply stopped in my tracks and turned and descended to where David and Alex huddled, waiting on the trail, and joined them there, relieved to find that David was okay—still sick but not worse—and sure to improve as soon as we started down.

I didn't regret turning back so close to the summit, but I didn't quite understand it, either. An hour later, the others rejoined us, exultant, grinning—except for Ed, who clearly had emptied his tank and had kept going nonetheless. Alex roped us together in a line, with Ed, utterly depleted, in the middle, so that if he fell as we traversed the windblown Cresta del Viento, the treacherously narrow, snow-covered ridge from the Canaleta to the Independencia *refugio* with the darkened Gran Acarreo yawning below, we'd be able to stop his fall with our ice axes.

When we made Independencia, a wind-blocking knob with a small, one-man plywood A-frame beside it, we collapsed in a scattered heap in the lee of the knob to gather strength for the rest of the descent to High Camp. We were slightly behind schedule, and light was fading fast. I lay on the ground a short ways apart from the others and sank into myself, wondering morosely if I had failed to accomplish what I had set out to do—a thing that I had trained to do for a full year and on which I had spent thousands of dollars. I wanted to know, at bottom, how to regard myself. For in the end, wasn't that the point of a venture like this, to learn better how to regard oneself? One does not climb a mountain because it is there; one doesn't climb a mountain to conquer it. Perhaps, I thought, one climbs a mountain for the same reason one enters a monastery: to pray.

My thoughts were broken by the appearance of a stranger next to me, a climber with a backpack and parka, crampons and ice ax, just like us, but a young woman and, most strange, alone. She seemed to have come up the mountain rather than down—but why would someone be ascending at this time of day? She sat down beside me and unwrapped a fruit bar and shared it with me. She was a lovely, dark-haired woman in her mid-thirties, perhaps, with an easy smile. I asked her why she was here, and in a soft Balkan or Eastern European accent she answered that she was meeting a friend.

"Are you alone, then?"

"Yes, I've been here for several days," she said. "Waiting for my friend."

I asked her where she was from, and she said Slovenia. Slovenia? I checked my companions a few feet away: They were gazing wonderstruck in her direction. She was evidently not a hallucination—unless we were all having the same vision.

"Did you make it to the top of the mountain?" she asked me.

I shook my head sadly, no.

She smiled. "That doesn't matter. Beyond the mountains there are more mountains. And the journey is always more important than the arrival."

I smiled back, comforted by these familiar bits of ancient wisdom. For the first time in my life, I actually believed them. She asked if she could take my picture with her camera. I said certainly. She stood and snapped off a photo with a disposable drugstore camera and calmly turned and left the way she had come.

I felt then an inexpressible peacefulness and remembered Rilke's line "Every angel is terrifying." Yes, but to a conflicted mind a true angel is a balm. They're terrifying only if we don't believe in them, I thought. A few moments later, my companions and I, without mentioning the mysterious Slovenian visitor—or visitation, as I thought of her—continued our descent to High Camp.

Over the next few days, as we made our way down the side

of the mountain to the Plaza de Mulas and out along the Valle de los Horcones, I spoke with David of the woman I'd met up there at twenty-two thousand feet, and with the others, too. Yes, they had all seen her and had been as startled by her appearance as I. But they had not heard her speak, and no one, other than David, seemed to know that she belonged solely and wholly to the mountain and that she was still up there, waiting at the *refugio* for her friend.

OLD GOAT

The stomach-churning Tata Air flight from Kathmandu deep into the eastern Himalaya dropped suddenly between terraced green ridges outside Lukla. Minutes later the Twin Otter DHC-6 skidded to a stop at the Tenzing-Hillary Airport, a landing strip the size of a meadow with a steep, rock-cluttered hill at one end and a thousand-foot drop-off at the other. We quickly gathered our packs and gear and hit the trail north, headed toward the distant, snow-covered peaks.

Though not exactly a walk in the park, the first two days from Lukla were easy—a gradual three-thousand-foot ascent followed by two nights and a day at 11,300 feet in a bare-bones hostel in the cross-roads trading town of Namche Bazaar, where we studied our maps and acclimatized slowly to altitude. In our free time we climbed nearby summits, growing new oxygen-heavy red blood cells by climbing higher in the daytime than where we slept at night. It was cold, the nights especially, but clear, and in both moonlight and sunlight the sky-high jagged mountains were sharply detailed, as if my bespectacled eyes had magically regained their perfect youthful sight. The ridges and peaks were igneous wedges out there, not sedimented ledges, and I could almost see the tectonic plates moving, the Indo-Australian Plate plunging under the Eurasian, driving the mountains up into the sky.

It's said that if the mountains are high enough, you're likely to meet your feared true self up there, the self that evades you down below. It's probably one of the several reasons why we do it, climb mountains. And indeed, I came face-to-face with my doppelgänger, my nemesis, in the Himalaya. But not in the thin air of a snow-covered summit. I met him early, on one of the lower slopes, a day out of Namche Bazaar barely halfway to Renjo-La, the first of the three high passes of the Sagarmatha National Park. I must have been looking for him even before I arrived in Nepal. Maybe as far back as a year ago, when I signed on for this monthlong trek and then talked two friends into joining me.

Besides our Sherpa guide, Dambar, and his assistant guide, Gaushal, and two porters, Yam and Prim, who seemed to have been named by Samuel Beckett, there were three of us: Gregorio Franchetti, a twenty-four-year-old film student; Tom Healy, a fifty-year-old poet; and me, the seventy-two-year-old scribbler who'd instigated this trek. Like son, father, and grandfather, Gregorio, Tom, and I are men of three different generations, and we're close friends. We have climbed in the Adirondacks together, and two years ago we climbed Kilimanjaro more or less to commemorate my seventieth birthday. This, however, was a climb at a whole different level of physical and mental difficulty and risk. And I was two years older. For men the age of Gregorio and Tom, if you're well made to begin with, and they are, a couple of years' aging usually improves you. At my age, however, in two years your body can unexpectedly maderize, like an old-vine chardonnay stored at too warm a temperature. All of a sudden, gone. Undrinkable.

On the fourth day of the trek, we were ascending a narrow winding trail, making our way up a long valley gouged into the moraine by an ivory-colored river of ice melt off the Bhote Koshi Glacier. We passed packs of resigned yaks descending from Tibet top-heavy with goods, mostly Chinese knockoffs of high-end climb-

ing gear and clothing to sell in the stalls of Namche Bazaar and Lukla
to inexperienced trekkers surprised by and unprepared for the cold
and the effects of altitude. We were headed for a high-meadow farm
settlement called Thame. From there, for the next three weeks, we
would steadily make our way deep into the Himalaya, to within
three kilometers of Tibet. We would climb half a dozen mountains,
three of them above eighteen thousand feet; cross the famed Three
Passes, Renjo-La, Cho-La, and Kongma-La, also near and above
eighteen thousand feet; visit Everest Base Camp; then trek back
down to Lukla and in triumph catch our Air Tata return flight to
Kathmandu. That was the plan, anyhow. The hope.

Crossing the Dudh Koshi River on a narrow suspension bridge
strung between two cliffs, I meant not to look down at the milky
river crashing against rocks five hundred feet below, but then suddenly remembered Thornton Wilder's scary novel *The Bridge of San
Luis Rey* and looked down anyhow. If the swaying bridge, as in the
novel, were to inexplicably give way, I wanted to see where I'd be
hurled. What I saw down there was a small herd of mountain goats,
the brown Himalayan tahr, grazing on the far bank like suburban
deer, six or seven females and kids and a large male with a shaggy
mane watching over them. The tahr looks like a cross between a
goat and an antelope; it's rare to see them in a herd, especially with
the male present.

An old goat, I thought. Like me.

The trail, where we left the bridge, cut sharply uphill, away
from the river. Coming down toward us was an elderly man, European or North American, picking his labored, careful way over
rocks and roots with climbing poles. Poor guy, I thought. Definitely
too old for this. Balance clearly shot, legs trembling, shrunken lungs
sucking air even on the descent. Too much vascular hardening,
too much lost muscle and bone mass to handle this tough a climb.
There comes a point when an old man ought to stay home by the
fire, I thought.

But then behind the man appeared a slim, very attractive blond woman in her early thirties. The old guy drew near and looked me squarely in the face. I looked him back and realized that I was probably the same age as he—a fellow septuagenarian. Neither of us smiled or acknowledged the other. Though we stood and stared at each other for several long seconds, neither of us wanted to see or be seen by the other. We were the same, he and I, and neither of us appreciated the fact. I knew he was hoping that I'd think the young woman was his mistress, not his granddaughter or niece, and that I'd think him an old goat, like the bearded brown alpha-male tahr, and not an old fool. And indeed, I did hope that the young woman was his mistress, not his granddaughter or niece. But I still was not sure he wasn't an old fool trying and failing to do what's done best by much younger men. Even—perhaps especially—as regards the young woman coming along behind him. For the first time I saw the problem. Barely four days into the trek and at a relatively low altitude, I'd met my feared true self: a man who could as easily be an old fool as an old goat.

But wasn't that one of the reasons, maybe the main reason, why I'd decided to make this trek in the first place, to figure out which of the two I really am? I hadn't considered it back then. I was just working my way down my bucket list, which was growing shorter by the year. Not because I was checking things off the list, so much as I was running out of time—the lion-in-winter syndrome. Climbing in the Himalaya had been on my list for a decade. But at seventy-two I could remember sixty-two like it was yesterday. Which made eighty-two look a lot like tomorrow. And no matter how you cut it, eighty-two is elderly. It's not the new sixty-two. It's not the new anything. I'd reached the age where it was pretty certain that if I didn't go to the Himalaya now, I'd never get there.

To pull it off successfully I'd have to lift my level of fitness higher than it had been since my thirties. I'm not healthy because I exercise regularly; I exercise regularly because, thanks to my genes, I happen to be healthy. For years I've worked out mainly to counter the effects of sarcopenia, the loss of 1 percent per annum of our bodies' bone and muscle mass after the age of forty, even while we sleep. Back in November, six months before the Himalaya spring climbing season, I swapped that old, easygoing, three-days-a-week, maintenance-level routine for a more strenuous daily training regimen, alternating aerobic and weight-lifting workouts in the gym with long, thigh-punishing bike rides. I took my body, like an old Volvo, its warranty long since expired, to the shop for a thorough drive-train check and tune—blood work, EKG, echo-cardiogram, even a colonoscopy—and got prescriptions filled for Cipro (against dysentery) and Diamox (against altitude sickness). Also Viagra—my doctor explained that Viagra was rumored to have been originally developed to deal with pulmonary and cere-bral edema associated with altitude sickness. In an emergency, he said, if the Diamox is too slow to act, pop a couple of Viagra and quickly descend. So Viagra's a multipurpose drug, I thought. Good to know.

By April my weight was down from 215 to 190, and I was feeling stronger than at any time in the last twenty or twenty-five years. Yet one never knows, as I'd learned in the Andes and on Kilimanjaro, until one is actually on the mountain. My two climbing pals, Gregorio and Tom, had signed up early in the year. Gregorio, who planned to make a film of the trek, said he had cut back on his smoking and was doing some jogging and yoga. Tom, in his role as chair of the Fulbright Foreign Scholarship Board, had spent the year traveling and worried that he'd laid on a few extra pounds at embassy dinners. I wasn't concerned about their fitness level, however. Only my own. Two years earlier, climbing Kilimanjaro for the third time, I'd discovered that in the five years since my previous ascent my sense of balance had gone into seri-ous decline, and though I was still plenty strong enough for the climb, I was working much harder than Tom and Gregorio, tak-ing great care not to fall—like that old guy with his poles—while my pals hopped from rock to rock like teenagers. I'd worked since then on recovering my sense of balance by means of a specified set of exercises, but worried about what new physical or neurological or psychological diminishment I'd discover while trying to climb in the Himalaya.

Tom, who was in Indonesia on a Fulbright mission, planned to meet us in Kathmandu. Gregorio and I convened in New York to complete our packing and fly out of Newark together. Gregorio was already filming. Making a visual record. It would be hard to lie about this one, I thought, even in print. On my way to a meeting with my publisher, I popped into a Barnes & Noble to pick up a long novel to carry to the mountains in my backpack and chose for its combined portability and length a pocket edition of *Great Expectations*. I'd somehow managed to reach the edge of old age without having read what was, to judge by the cover, John Irving's favorite novel. Another, if minor, item on the bucket list to check off.

A little later, I was in my editor's East Fifty-Third Street corner office with him and his boss, both men of a certain age—which is to say, baby boomers, men not quite my age yet, but close—and we ended up talking about how all our male near-contemporaries, ourselves excepted, of course, were suddenly getting old. We mentioned mutual friends' hip and knee replacements, prostate cancers, stents, retirement parties. I observed that nowadays when we wake up in the morning the only thing that's stiff is our back and heard nervous laughter of recognition.

Gregorio, struggling with tripod and camera and mike and lights and batteries and cables and laptop, in addition to backpack and duffel stuffed with clothing and climbing gear, filmed our taxi ride to Newark airport. It was amusing and endearing to watch him, a young man obsessed with his self-selected, open-ended task, working alone without financing or a contract—the sort of task, as an aging professional writer, I no longer seemed capable of taking on. He filmed our departure on United's fifteen-hour flight to Delhi and filmed our overnight wait in Indira Gandhi International Airport for the connecting flight to Kathmandu and filmed our bleary-eyed arrival early the next morning, where we checked into the Dwarika's Hotel.

In the sixties, Kathmandu was the first stop out of San Francisco on the hippie trail, and a lot of my college friends had passed through the city back then. I'd missed it in my own youthful wanderings. And Gregorio's parents weren't even born then. While waiting for Tom to come in from Indonesia via Singapore, we hit the chaotic, congested streets of the district called Thamel and pushed through crowds of panhandling European and American dreadlocked kids with clustered tattoos and piercings searching for the long-gone ghosts of Allen Ginsberg and Jack Kerouac. We visited, and Gregorio filmed, the famous Hindu temple Pashupatinath, where we inhaled human ashes blown from the open-air cremations smoldering on platforms above the Bagmati River and watched stoned sadhus, for small change from tourists, lift rocks tied to their penises. We stopped at the round Buddhist stupa Boudhanath, placed like a gigantic white navel at the center of the Tibetan exile community, where during a sudden rain shower we drank beers in the Tibet Kitchen Boudha Stupa rooftop café and agreed that the Hindu shrine and rites were medieval and obsessed with death and rebirth, while the Buddhist shrine and rites, where pilgrims of all ages happily circumambulated the temple even in the rain, were good-natured, almost clownish, an Asian parallel to preclassical Greece, more life-affirming than the Hindu, we decided. Another good reason to climb high mountains: it gets you out of the house. We weren't just trekkers, mountain climbers. We were travelers, too.

That afternoon Tom arrived, and later we met for a briefing with Samden Sherpa, who, with his energetic mother, Yankila Sherpa, ran Snow Leopard, the outfitter we'd hired for the trek. Back in the early 1970s, before the era of "adventure tourism" hit the Himalaya region, the American writer Peter Matthiessen came to Nepal to search for the elusive, endangered, near-mythical snow leopard, a quest that became, as these things often do, a search for his own soul. With the help of Yankila Sherpa and her late husband, Matthiessen pulled together a group of local guides and porters and trekked all over northwestern Nepal. After Matthiessen returned to the States to write his prizewinning book *The Snow Leopard,* the Sherpas kept the group together as one of the first outfitters in the country and named it after the book.

Samden Sherpa also brought to the meeting Dambar Magar, the man who would guide us into the Himalaya, and a second guide, Gaushal Magar, Tibetan-descended Nepalese cousins, both broadfaced, short, stocky men in their early forties. Dambar spoke excellent colloquial English, obviously a man with a gift and affection for language. Gaushal, who seemed not to speak any English at all, smiled benignly throughout the meeting. Dambar had a brightly lit, charismatic flair and intensity that seemed consciously designed to attract and hold our attention. He talked rather steadily throughout the meeting and listened not at all. Evidently narcissism is not culturally specific, I thought, and wondered if in the upcoming weeks we'd be able to meet his need for attention.

Now, five days later, as we decamped from the high-meadow settlement of Thame and headed up the Bhote Koshi Valley to a lodge at Lungden, my question was being answered. Since landing at Lukla, Dambar had been bugging us endlessly with jokes and song-and-dance routines. He was a knowledgeable guide, experienced and more than merely competent. But his need to entertain everyone in hearing range was starting to irritate us. Perhaps me especially, the Old Goat. At times it was like climbing with Robin Williams or Liza Minnelli. Or both.

The plan was to acclimatize at Lungden, at 14,370 feet, for a day and two nights before attempting Renjo-La, the first of the three high passes. We were many miles west of the more popular routes into the Himalaya now, so there were very few fellow trekkers and no more yak trains coming across from Tibet or down from Everest Base Camp in the east. We were in high tundra, crossing the arid, wind-scoured zone between the tree line and the snow line, scrambling uphill across scree and waist-high boulders. I could see that if I was going to get over the upcoming passes, climb the mountains ahead, and cross the dangerously melting glaciers beyond, I'd have to focus all my attention on the task at hand. I couldn't keep nodding and smiling in approval to keep my loquacious guide happy. I decided to confront Dambar and try to explain my difficulty.

After we dropped our packs on our narrow bunks, I took Dambar aside and said, "Look, I'm an old man, and this is hard for me. To do it successfully, I need to concentrate. To concentrate, I need you to be quiet," I told him.

Dambar misread me, however. He said he was confident that I could complete the climb successfully. And not to worry about being such an old man, he said. Plenty of old men who were even older men than I had completed this same trek with total success.

I doubted that, having been reliably informed by a friend back home that, regardless of age, most of the trekkers who sign on for the Three Passes route don't complete it. She herself is a mountaineer and guide who had recently returned from the Annapurna region and knew whereof she spoke. "Just pay close attention to your body," she advised me. "No matter how fit you are, don't go all macho and push it till you collapse or fall. That's how these mountains kill people."

The cut-stone lodge at Lungden was rough and cold. The common toilet was an overflowing latrine, and the entire building stank of it. There was only one other climber at the lodge with us, an enormous, middle-aged Australian who called himself Rocket. He liked to drive fast, he explained. "Like a fookin' rocket!" Traveling alone without guide or porter, he'd been at the lodge in Thame the night before and limped into Lungden a few hours behind us, a delightfully eccentric man who told us he was a ladies' hairdresser in Perth. He had a substantial belly, spindly legs, claimed to smoke six cigarettes a day and carried several, maybe many, pints of whiskey in his huge backpack, which he now and then pulled out and sipped from as he climbed. This was the fourth time he'd gone trekking in the Himalaya, he said. "Me wife says I'm a loner, and I s'pose I am."

Something about him reminded us of Elton John, his affable, unflappable weirdness, maybe, so we called him Rocket Man, which he liked, and soon he began referring to himself as Rocket Man. His knees were in pain, and he wasn't sure he could make it over the passes and on to Everest Base Camp, but unlike the other climbers we'd met so far, all of whom were intent on summiting, as if cutting notches in their belts, Rocket Man, with an equanimity I envied but couldn't match, didn't seem to care. "Nah, if it gets too fookin' tough, I'll just head back to Namche Bazaar."

He was going straight up Renjo-La the next morning without taking the extra day and night of acclimatization, which seemed at the time like a good idea. None of us liked the lodge at Lungden—it was filthy and dark and cold—so we proposed to Dambar that we skip the extra day like Rocket Man and go up Renjo-La and on to Gokyo Camp tomorrow instead.

Dambar said he was concerned that without more acclimatization and rest it would be too tough for me. I assured him that I was feeling strong and so far the altitude hadn't bothered me at all. It seemed clear that, despite what he'd said earlier, Dambar was indeed concerned about my age. In the end we prevailed, and he agreed to depart the next morning at five thirty. It would be a long day, he said and then broke into a Bollywood song cycle and danced away.

Later, after a supper of *dal bhat* and *momos,* Tom, Gregorio, and I, in hats and parkas and gloves, huddled in the common room as close to the fire as possible. With each stop the meals had gotten more and more fundamental, with fewer and fewer fresh components. Between the tree line and the snow line is the protein line, above which no meat other than nearly inedible reconstituted dried yak steak is available. Otherwise it was mostly combinations of rice and noodles and cabbage and turnips and carrots and the steamed clumplike dumplings called *momos*. The lodges are called teahouses (probably because when you arrive they serve hot tea from a Thermos), but now that we were at the very end of the inhabited world, they weren't much more than minimalist barracks. No electricity, no running water, no heat, except in the common room from a metal stove for burning yak chips. Beds were a thin slice of foam rubber on a piece of plywood. Toilets were a shared hole in the ground, or floor, at the end of the hall. Forget washing.

Tom, who at fifty could imagine being sixty, but not seventy, asked me what was the difference between how I felt about my body ten years ago, when I was in my early sixties, and now. Tough question. Especially since I was in better shape now than I was back then. I said the main difference was fear—fear of being in denial as to my inescapably diminished powers. Which could result in over-confidence and absurd and embarrassing moments of public exposure of weakness and vanity: i.e., exposure as an old fool.

Back in November, when I had the self-confidence, the chutz-pah, to sell Tom and Gregorio on the idea of making this trek, it was on the assumption that I myself could successfully climb these passes and mountains. But if I couldn't actually do it, I'd be exposed as an old fool. And there's nothing worse than being an old fool. Climbing Renjo-La tomorrow would be a crucial, self-defining test for me. And unless I passed it, my pride and our friendship, among other things, would be impaired. We three might travel together again, but we'd probably not go climbing together again.

We headed out the next morning in darkness and cold, guided by headlamps, locked inside our individual thoughts. It wasn't long before the sun cracked the horizon and revealed Renjo-La above, a V-shaped notch in a jagged line of three snow-covered twenty-one-thousand-foot peaks, Makalu, Cho Oyo, and Lhotse. I chugged steadily onward and upward at my chosen slow pace, while Gregorio lugged his camera and tripod ahead and set up to film us as we ascended toward him; then, when we passed by, moved ahead again and set up at a farther, higher point. Tom seemed to withdraw inside himself and climbed in front of me a ways, more or less alone. Our porters, Yam and Prim, carrying two duffels each, had left the lodge at Lungden even earlier than we and were now well out of sight. Gaushal stuck close to Gregorio and helped carry his film equipment. Dambar stayed by me. I couldn't tell if it was because he thought of me as the old goat, the alpha male and leader of our group, or the pathetic old man who could screw up the entire climb if he fell and broke his leg or back and had to be helicoptered out. The old man might well not make it over the pass at all—too weak, too old—and would have to go down to Lungden by nightfall and return to Namche Bazaar the next day and wait alone for fifteen or sixteen days while the others completed the trek without him.

Dambar continued to natter incessantly on, until again I asked him, somewhat grumpily, to be silent so I could concentrate. He got it this time. He said, "Sorry, sorry, sorry!" and put on a surly sulk, as if to punish me for having hurt his feelings—suggesting that passive-aggressiveness is no more culturally specific than narcissism.

By midmorning Rocket Man was far behind and way below us, a slow-moving ant in the distance. I avoided looking ahead of me and up—it discouraged and depressed me to see how far and high the pass was and how far ahead of me Tom and Gregorio were. After six hours of climbing, my lungs were burning and my thigh muscles were threatening to go into spasm. Also, I was woozy—my brain was oxygen deprived from the altitude—and the switchbacking trail crossed treacherous, icy slabs of shale and slag. The temperature was dropping fast now, and a sharp wind shaved the rubbled face of the mountain. Patches of ice and snow crumbled underfoot. The slabs of shale and slag gave way to large, slippery, bronze-colored boulders. To keep from falling I fastened my gaze to my feet and ignored whatever might be above and ahead of me and how far up the mountain I had yet to climb. I lowered my head and kept climbing, wrapped in profound solitude, as alone as a human being can be. My world was my body, and my body was suffering. Hour after hour, short step by short step, a hitch up and over one suitcase-sized boulder onto another, where I grabbed a catch of diluted breath, lungs rasping, blood pounding in my ears like a locomotive piston at full bore, and then another boulder to negotiate, my steps slowing and getting shorter, and between each step a deep inhalation, a gasp for air nearly emptied of oxygen, until it seemed I was closer to suffocating than to breathing and was barely moving at all.

I was almost startled by my sudden arrival at the pass. Strings of brightly colored prayer flags snapped, crackled, and popped in the freezing wind. Gregorio was filming, Tom was resting off to one side, and Gaushal, Yam, and Prim were grinning and waving, happy to see the old man reach the pass, while Dambar, his sulk now dissolved, celebrated with dance and uninhibited song, and this time I didn't mind it at all.

In fact, I barely heard or saw him there. I stood with my back to the way I had come and looked out from the high, wind-pummeled pass. Before me the cloudless blue sky opened above a vast snowfield and the Machherma Glacier. Three thousand feet below, a north-running chain of turquoise lakes led to a broad, fawn-colored valley, and beyond the valley the Ngozumba Glacier sprawled from north to south for fifty miles. At the far horizon, carving out great chunks of sky, loomed half of the ten highest mountains on the planet: Lhotse, Lhotse Shar, Makalu, Cho Oyu, and the highest of them all, dark and glowering, the only peak covered in clouds, Sagarmatha, Mount Everest.

It was as if I had emerged from a fallen world far behind and below me and had entered another, purer world from above, from the sky. One climbs a mountain, not to conquer it, but to be lifted like this away from the earth up into the sky. This is what the ancient Buddhists and Incas knew, perhaps what all ancient peoples knew. Climbing a mountain is how one clutches the sky and enters it with one's body still intact, still connected to the earth, flying through the air with one's feet on the ground and one's head and hands in the sky. It's a way of practicing, not for dying, but for death itself—a way to greet the gods on their own terms.

I had climbed to 17,677 feet and had crossed over Renjo-La, the first of the three high passes and the first real test of our trek. Feeling no ill effects of altitude, I was confident now that—barring an accidental slip and fall, which of course could happen anywhere along the way, and if it did, would not make me an old fool—I would complete the rest of the trek. My spirits were high, I was even a little giddy, and for the first time found Dambar's comic routines entertaining, as we traversed the snowfield and rounded the gray, rubble-filled skirt of Ngozumba Glacier and stopped for a moment before beginning our descent to Gokyo, a clutch of low, cut-stone trekker huts and lodges beside the distant lake.

It might get harder and higher over the next sixteen days, but I knew now that as we ascended and descended those upcoming passes and peaks I was going to be made stronger by it, not weaker. I knew that I would make it successfully to the end. Standing here at the eastern edge of Renjo-La Pass with the wind off the high Himalayas in my face and a broad glacial valley sprawling thousands of feet below, I was no longer the anxious, perplexed man who wasn't sure if he was an old goat or an old fool, and it made me capable of finding poor needy Dambar's quirky narcissism amusing and culturally interesting. I was able to accept him simply for who he was.

By the time we got down to the hut in Gokyo Tom was suffering the beginnings of altitude sickness: lethargy, headache, chills. Not seriously enough yet to go to a lower altitude, but cause for concern. Gregorio seemed okay, but said he felt drugged and was thinking and moving slowly, as if underwater. I felt fine, a little leg-heavy, but otherwise ready to climb another mountain.

Rocket Man would pull in by dark, four hours after us, his bad knees about to give out, and the next morning, after his first cigarette, announced that he was through and was heading back down to Namche Bazaar. After he departed, Dambar led us on a scheduled six-hour hike from Gokyo up along the Ngozumba Glacier to view a string of glacial lakes, and that afternoon we climbed Gokyo-Ri, an eighteen-thousand-foot mountain with a twenty-five-hundred-foot vertical approach from the hut. But Dambar may have been right after all, and we shouldn't have left Lungden for the first pass without the extra day and night of acclimatization. After the long walk to the lakes and climbing Gokyo-Ri, Tom would become truly altitude sick, dangerously so, and would have to descend immediately with Gaushal to lower altitudes for two days and nights to reacclimatize.

He would rejoin us east of Cho-La, the second of the three passes, for the rest of the trek. We would make it to the Everest Base Camp, which was crowded and cluttered with refuse and old used-up climbing gear, as helicopters shuttled back and forth carrying out injured and altitude-sick climbers and the bodies of the ten climbers who had died on the mountain that week. The afternoon we came to visit, 150 climbers were strung along the dark bony shoulders of Everest. It would turn out to be the only depressing day of our climb. We would traverse melting glaciers with five-hundred-foot-deep sinkholes where a year ago there had been hard-packed trails. We would cross Kongma-La, the highest of the three passes at 18,159 feet, and summit 18,195-foot Chhukung Ri, the tallest of the mountains on our itinerary. Gregorio would make his movie, or at least shoot it so that it could be edited later in New York. Inspired by the extremity of the climb and the world that surrounded us there, Tom would draft most of a book of new poems. And I would finish reading *Great Expectations,* but only because I had nothing else to read up there.

The image of that sturdy septuagenarian with the climbing poles whom I'd come face-to-face with on our first day out of Namche Bazaar—the original old goat, as I now thought of him—stayed with me till the end of our climb and beyond. He had been my nemesis in the beginning, my doppelgänger, my feared self, a man too old to be out there climbing in the Himalaya in the company of a much younger person, a beautiful young woman, for God's sake.

Now, however, I admired that old guy and hoped I was a little bit like him. All he was doing was taking the measure of his absolute physical limitations, marking the nearness of the end of everything, getting as close to that leap into the void as he could while still standing on the planet. He was no old fool. And if he wasn't, then I was no old fool, either.

AUTHOR'S NOTE

The names of some of the individuals in these essays have been changed to protect their identities.

I would like to thank my assistant, Nancy Wilson, for her help with research and in preparing the manuscript for publication. And as always, I am grateful to my agent, Ellen Levine, and my friend and editor, Dan Halpern, for their patient support of this project.